The men that tanned the hide of us,
Our daily foes and friends,
They shall not lose their pride of us,
However the journey ends.
Their voice to us who sing of it,
No more its message bears,
But the round world shall ring of it,
And all we are be theirs.

To speak of fame a venture is,
There's little here can bide,
But we may face the centuries,
And dare the deepening tide;
For though the dust that's part of us,
To dust again be gone,
Yet here shall beat the heart of us,
The school we handed on!

We'll honour yet the school we knew
The best school of all
We'll honour yet the rule we knew
Till the last bell call
For working days or holidays
And glad or melancholy days
They were great days and jolly days
At the best school of all.

'The Best School of All'

150 Years of Clifton College

'The Best School of All'

150 Years of Clifton College

Edited by
CHERYL TRAFFORD

FOR CHARLIE COLQUHOUN (1953–2008)

OC Society Secretary, schoolmaster par excellence,
sportsman, historian and, above all, gentleman.

'The Best School of All': **150 Years of Clifton College**
© Clifton College and Third Millennium Publishing Limited

First published in 2009 by
Third Millennium Publishing Limited,
a subsidiary of Third Millennium Information Limited.

2–5 Benjamin Street, London
United Kingdom, EC1M 5QL
www.tmiltd.com

ISBN: 978 1 906507 03 9

Illustrations reproduced by permission of the sources listed on page 200.

British Library Cataloguing in Publication Data
A CIP catalogue record for this book is available from the British Library.

Edited by Cheryl Trafford
Designed by Matthew Wilson
Production by Bonnie Murray

Reprographics by Studio Fasoli
Printed in Slovenia by Gorenjski-tisk

Contents

Foreword

Founded somewhat late among Victorian public schools, Clifton could just have been another one of those schools. In fact, however, it has, for most of its history, been unusual: it is in a city; it has always had a large minority of day pupils; and for more than 125 years it had a Jewish House. The city of Bristol has always had a strong mercantile and entrepreneurial tradition. Clifton's first Headmaster was a liberal thinker of great vision and strength of character. Between 1925 and 1962 all four Headmasters were, unusually, Oxbridge dons. For these and other reasons the Clifton ethos is not conformist: it is liberal, tolerant, welcoming and inventive. The same is reflected in Clifton life. Exceptional scholarship exists alongside a wide range of academic ability. Most pupils take part in team and sports activities and in art, music and drama, which enriches their education. Nor should we overlook the Chapel. This remarkable building, unique among public schools in its size, creates a Christian awareness that persists long after pupils leave.

On behalf of the Council, I thank all those who have contributed to the building of this ethos – teachers, governors, pupils and staff. May it flourish for another 150 years. Lastly, may I thank our editor, Cheryl Trafford, tireless in her work in the Pre and now in this book, which I very much hope you will enjoy.

A.R. Thornhill
Chairman of Council

Introduction

The Best School of All aims to draw together the strands of a remarkable 150 years. This is not a history, nor is it the story of individual Houses; rather it is a celebration of various aspects of a great school.

Undoubtedly our days at school influence our future and the kind of people we become. Many Cliftonians were in both The Pre and The Upper School, which means that all their schooldays were spent in one institution. These experiences have not always been seen through rose-tinted spectacles, but many individual contributions in the pages that follow tell of a fondness and a recognition of having been somewhere special, and of a feeling of belonging to a vibrant community full of great characters.

The Close, Big School and the Chapel remain deeply etched on Cliftonian memories, and it is hoped that readers will enjoy familiar scenes and perhaps even learn something new about their alma mater. Sadly there is not room to include everyone and every aspect, but my deepest gratitude goes to all the contributors who have described a school full of learning and discovery, adventure and fun and friendship and very little 'side'. Thanks also go to the publisher, Third Millennium, whose founder and Chairman Julian Platt is an Old Cliftonian, for their support and guidance. Part of the School Song reminds us of the generations that have been at the school and, in celebrating a milestone, they must feel sure that the heart of Clifton College continues to beat as it is handed on.

Cheryl Trafford
Editor

A Brief Chronology

1862	Clifton opened (30 September)		1912	Golden Jubilee
1865	Poole's House opened		1912	Scout troop formed (February)
1867	Chapel and physics and chemistry laboratories opened		1927	Science School added
1868	First Guthrie Commemoration held (22 May)		1941	Move to Bude
1870	Percival Library built		1942	US troops in Clifton (November)
1875	School Rifle Corps established and attached to the Bristol Engineer Corps (December)		1943	Clifton became HQ of US First Army (October)
1876	Junior School opened for boys under 11		1945	Return from Bude (March)
1878	Jewish (later Polack's) House opened		1962	Tribe Building added
1882	North aisle extension to Chapel built		1968	Redgrave Theatre opened
1886	Dedication of Church of St Agnes		1980	Coulson Centre opened (March)
1897	Old Cliftonian Society founded		1982	Sports Centre opened (June)
1908–10	Beggar's Bush purchased		1987	First girls in the Pre (January)
1909–12	Chapel further extended		1987	Clifton became fully co-educational (September)
			1992	Butcombe opened as Pre-Preparatory School
			1999	Clifton College Services Ltd (CCSL) established

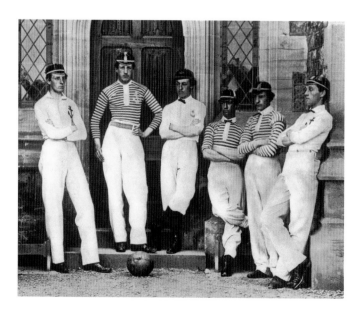

List of Headmasters

Headmasters of Clifton

Rev. John Percival	1862–79
Rev. James M. Wilson	1879–91
Rev. Michael G. Glazebrook	1891–1905
Rev. Albert E. David	1905–10
John E. King	1910–23
Norman Whatley	1923–39
Bertrand L. Hallward	1939–48
H. Desmond P. Lee	1948–54
Nicholas G.L. Hammond	1954–63
Stephen J. McWatters	1963–75
Stuart M. Andrews	1975–90
A. Hugh Monro	1990–2000
Dr M. Stephen Spurr	2000–05
Mark J. Moore	2005–

Headmasters of the Preparatory School

E.G. Sharp	1930–46
L.H.A. Hankey	1946–67
J.W. Hornby	1967–83
R.S. Trafford	1983–93
Dr R.A. Acheson	1993–2008
J.E. Milne	2008–

Headmistress of Butcombe

Dr W.E. Bowring	1995–

Building

1

Opposite: *Aerial view of the School, the Zoo, the Downs and the Avon Gorge.*

BEGINNINGS

Clifton College was created by Bristol businessmen for the sons of Bristol businessmen, following a legal ruling that the city's grammar school could not turn itself into a boarding school on the model of Dr Arnold's Rugby. Yet Clifton's founders believed that their new school could

First foundations

Today's famous panoramic view from College Road across The Close was almost complete by 1890, a mere 30 years after the school was first conceived. The Chapel, already extended in 1882 by the addition of the north aisle, would be enlarged more spectacularly in 1912, but not until 1927 would the Gothic Science School be added, while the starkly functional extension to School House belongs to the opening years of the twenty-first century. When the school first opened in 1862 only School House and Big School had been built. Benches had to be borrowed from Bristol's Victoria Rooms for the opening ceremony, attended by a mere 60 pupils, and of the 76 boys listed in the Register for that first term, only 26 came from outside the city. The image above shows Charles Hansom's original design for the School buildings showing Big School and a matching hall linked by a two-storey section.

soon become a national school, as Bristol stood 'at the confluence of three great railroad systems'. The railways would, indeed, transform the educational map of Britain, though John Percival's vision of using the rail network for a team of peripatetic masters for subjects in which there was a shortage of teachers did not materialize. Within 20 years Clifton's roll would reach 600 pupils. Like the railways, the new school was launched as a limited company, with shareholders having the right to nominate entrants.

The prospectus displayed a drawing of Charles Hansom's original design for the School buildings. It showed not only Big School but also a matching hall linked by a two-storey section fronting The Close, with an imposing central tower. The architect's first design was soon modified. The second hall was replaced by the Chapel (moved from its projected site in Guthrie Road), and the linking section was set back to its present alignment, with a central tower similar to the later Wilson Tower.

That so little of the grand design was built by the time the first boys arrived is a reminder of the speculative nature of the whole project. It is perhaps not surprising that the Headmaster appointed in 1861 – an assistant master from Rugby – got cold feet, withdrawing his acceptance in favour of the safer prospect of the headship of King Edward's Birmingham, his old school.

Having been left in the lurch by the Rev. Charles Evans only a few weeks before Clifton College was due to open and with Evans's name appearing in the prospectus, the College Council had to move fast. They went back to Frederick Temple at Rugby, the man who had recommended Evans. Temple could suggest only the 27-year-old John Percival.

Thomas Woolner's Bust of Percival

A founder member of the Pre-Raphaelite Brotherhood, the sculptor Thomas Woolner RA (1825–92) was commissioned by Clifton to complete a bust of John Percival in 1880. Early in his career Woolner despaired of his prospects in Britain, emigrating to Australia in 1852. Returning two years later, he achieved success with his busts of Alfred and Emily Tennyson, and a series of important commissions followed, establishing him as a leading portrait sculptor. By 1880 he was a professor at the Royal Academy and responsible for the busts of W.E. Gladstone, Charles Darwin and Cardinal Newman. The bust of Percival (below), which is technically in the form of a classical herm, is executed with a dramatic naturalism. By eliminating all extraneous detail, such as a costume or pedestal, Woolner presents a penetrating image of the first Headmaster.

J. YARKER
PRE WAH, 1996–2004

John Percival (Headmaster 1862–78)

Born in Westmorland only seven weeks after his parents' marriage in 1834, Percival never lost the flat vowels of his native Cumbria. Sent to nearby Appleby Grammar School, he benefited from the tradition of classical scholarship that, a century earlier, had brought George Washington's uncle across the Atlantic for his schooling there. From the grammar school Percival went on a classics scholarship to Queen's College, Oxford, where he won a junior mathematics scholarship before taking a First in both classics and mathematics and (through illness) a pass degree in history. Elected to a college fellowship, he left after two years to fill a supposedly temporary teaching post at Rugby.

He had been there only another two years when the unexpected vacancy occurred at Clifton. During his interview Percival was reminded that he was not only young but also unmarried. He is said to have replied: 'A few years will correct the former and a few weeks the latter.' He was appointed, and in mid-October he brought his new bride, Louisa Holland, to School House after a two-day honeymoon at Clevedon. The Headmaster and his wife were met by Clifton boys, who unharnessed the horse from the carriage and dragged the couple home in triumph.

RELIGION AND SCIENCE

The opening ceremony on 30 September 1862 took place against the background of a national debate provoked by the publication of Charles Darwin's *Origin of Species* three years earlier. Percival prefaced his inaugural sermon with a prayer for God's blessing: 'O prosper Thou our handiwork, and be with us and watch over us in our daily work and our daily prayers.' Work and prayer – academic endeavour in a Christian context – were the objectives of all Victorian foundations, as they had

Below left: *The early laboratory.*

Below: *William Ashwell Shenstone FRS was appointed assistant science master at Clifton in 1874. He moved on to become science master at Taunton School (1875) and then Exeter School (1877) before returning to Clifton in 1880 as Head of the science department where he remained until his death in 1908. An accomplished glass-blower, he solved the problem of constructing chemical apparatus in silica and was an author of many scientific papers.*

Above: *Percival's Library and Museum.*

Inset: *Lionel Cohen, who agreed to help Clifton gain the grant of a Royal Charter.*

been at Henry VI's Eton 400 years before. What made Clifton distinctive was the equal weight given to scientific and religious study. The first 'natural philosophy' laboratory, designed by Charles Hansom, opened in 1867, the same year as the Chapel. By 1871 there were separate laboratories for physics and chemistry, in which pupils carried out individual practical work, while there were also special classes in zoology, physiology, botany, physical geography and civil engineering.

Percival showed his commitment to science teaching by his early provision of laboratories – thought to be the first school laboratories equipped for practical experiments by pupils – and by his staff appointments. Eight of the men he appointed to teach the sciences went on to university professorships, five of them later becoming Fellows of the Royal Society. As early as 1871 *Nature* could claim that Clifton was 'foremost, if not positively the first' among schools teaching science, and it praised Percival for 'the magnificent example he has set in science education'.

Even Percival's library had to rub shoulders with science. In 1870 the first stage of the library was built at the Headmaster's expense, and was named after him by a grateful College Council. At first the library shared the space with the school's natural history museum, but in 1875 the library and museum were partitioned, when a 'voluntary movement' by masters, boys and

friends funded the eastward extension, including classrooms beneath. The open cloister was added at the same time. The Wilson Tower, with the Council room and Sixth Form room, had to wait until the end of Wilson's headmastership in 1890. The tower fulfilled Hansom's grand design by linking the library range with the east cloister wing.

BOARDERS AND TOWN BOYS

The only boarding house to be built as part of the nucleus of early buildings was School House. Other boarding houses, owned by the respective Housemasters, were built either in College Road or in what is now Percival Road. T.E. Brown and H.G. Dakyns were the key boarding Housemasters of the first decade. Brown (1830–97), the Manx poet, remained in post for almost 30 years, while Dakyns, following C.H. Cay in 1869, was Housemaster until 1882. Dakyns, an Old Rugbeian, was Percival's first appointment. He was asked by Percival at interview when he could start. 'Oh, quite soon,' he replied. 'In two or three days at most.' That wasn't soon enough for Percival: 'There's a train in an hour's time; they are rather hard pressed down there. I think you had better take that.' The remaining boarding houses, which now carry the names of those who were Housemasters during Percival's last years – Oakeley's, Wiseman's and Watson's – all opened in the 1870s, and in 1878 Percival cemented his reputation for liberal innovativeness by opening a Jewish House that would enable Jewish boys to attend an English public school while living within a Jewish 'family'.

Lionel Cohen, a leading Tory and future MP who had met Percival on visits to Bristol, agreed to help secure Clifton's grant of a Royal Charter by speeding the passage of a private bill through Parliament. As a *quid pro quo*, Cohen suggested opening a House for Jewish boys at Clifton, promising to find sponsors to pay the fees of eight boys if the House failed to fill. The first Housemaster, appointed in 1878, was Bernard Heymann, the only non-member of the Polack family to become Housemaster for a hundred years. His successor, Joseph Polack, was the last of Wilson's staff appointments, but hardly the least significant. Wilson could not have guessed that his Parthian shot would establish a dynasty.

Schoolboys and Schoolmasters

The calibre of Clifton's early schoolmasters is attested by the distinction of their subsequent careers. Apart from the eight science staff who went on to university professorships, Clifton's physics laboratory assistant in the 1880s, Richard Gregory, would 60 years later become President of the British Association. One of Percival's early mathematics teachers, though briefly and on an informal basis, was Alfred Marshall, the future Cambridge economist. And the first Cliftonian to return to teach under Percival was H.S. Hall of School House, whose algebra textbooks would become bestsellers.

No fewer than 20 of the men appointed by Percival and Wilson during those first three decades – ten appointments apiece – became headmasters of British schools. Some of them were appointed to day schools: City of London School, Edinburgh Academy, St Dunstan's College. Twice during these early years Clifton supplied headmasters not only to King William's, Isle of Man (where Wilson's father had been the first principal and where Wilson himself was sent until he was 16), but more locally to Bath College. William Furneaux, though teaching for only two terms at Clifton, eventually became a reforming headmaster of Repton and Dean of Winchester. Old Cliftonian St John Gray, who had the distinction of being appointed to the Clifton staff twice, later became headmaster of Malvern. This was a remarkable tally for a school only a generation old.

These men were schoolmasters first and foremost. Clifton was never meant to be an academic hothouse.

Instead, it was a place where each boy was encouraged to be the best possible version of himself. Percival instructed his staff in the Masters' Memoranda that: 'It is of great importance to the life of the school that there should be as little as possible of a barrier between masters and boys; that our relations with them should be not so much professional as those of friends.' And in his sermon on the opening day he had tried to reassure the less academic: 'It is not given to everyone to be clever. The great majority amongst us will never be able to attain to any intellectual level, let them labour as they may.'

Yet there was no lack of academic success. Clifton's first university open scholarship – to Cambridge – was won in 1865. By the 1870s awards in mathematics and natural sciences appear among Clifton successes at both Oxford and Cambridge. In 1890 there were 13 Clifton awards at the two universities, six of them in mathematics and science. Similar successes would continue during the first few years of Wilson's successor.

Above: *Rev. T.E. Brown was described by O.F. Christie as a 'wit, a poet, a scholar, a man of genius'. He ran Brown's House from 1864 until 1892. He came from the Isle of Man and is recognized as one of their greatest poets in a stamp.*

Left: *Headmasters, staff and OC's on the occasion of the School's Jubilee. Note the dates on the roof for the night-time illuminations. Seated, at the front, from left to right, four of the five Headmasters: M.G. Glazebrook, J. Percival (Chairman of Clifton Council 1895–1917), J.E. King and J.M. Wilson.*

Above: *The Junior School, built in 1876 on the site of the present Science School.*

Top right: *Original share certificate signed by John Guthrie and Henry Wasbrough.*

Far right: *In 1865 the Rev. R.B. Poole opened the second house for junior boys and he was succeeded as Housemaster there by Rev. P.A. Phelps in 1877. In 1987 it was converted into the first girls' house in the Pre.*

The Jewish House was not the only pastoral innovation made by Percival. The School, launched as it was by Bristol businessmen, had a significant number of day boys from the outset. It took until 1874 for the 'Town Boys' to be divided for organizational purposes, but the following year North Town and South Town became independent Houses under their own Housemasters. This arrangement, initiated by Percival, gave day boys at Clifton a status far superior to the indignities they endured at other, older boarding schools. Initially housed in classrooms, the day Houses moved into newly built Town Rooms in Guthrie Road during Wilson's time.

JUNIOR BOYS, HIGH SCHOOL GIRLS

Percival had hoped to throw open the doors of Clifton to a total of 150 boys from less affluent Bristol homes, in the tradition of the endowed grammar schools that W.E. Gladstone's Endowed Schools Commission was now investigating. The Headmaster suggested that half the fees should be remitted by the School, and the other half funded by public subscription. Percival appears to have interested the commissioners in his proposal that Clifton College should become the 'first-grade' school that the commission wished to see established in Bristol, on the understanding that Clifton would admit at reduced fees 'boys of the class who now attend the Bristol Grammar School'.

The College Council rejected the Headmaster's proposed scheme, arguing that 'it was distinctly not as a Citizen School that Clifton College was established, but rather as a school of the class of Marlborough or Cheltenham, or even Rugby (if possible) or Harrow'. According to the Council minutes of 18 June 1870, Percival had to content himself with explaining why he thought it 'exceedingly inadvisable to refuse to negotiate with the commissioners'. A year later, a joint letter 'in favour of throwing open the College to boys of all classes without regard to their social position' was sent to the Council from all the assistant masters. It received a polite but non-committal reply. However, in the 1877 Royal Charter the School's purpose was

defined as the education of 'boys and young men' instead of the earlier 'sons of gentlemen'. If Percival had had his way, Clifton would have evolved as a very different school from the one we usually give him credit for. Not for another century would the Clothworkers' Company's 'primary-school scholarships' for entry to The Preparatory School – replaced in the 1980s by John James Scholarships and the government's assisted places scheme – realize a fragment of Percival's vision.

In the 1870s a co-educational school was unthinkable, but there was growing pressure for female education. In 1871 the National Union for Improving the Education of Women of all Classes had been formed. Three years earlier Percival had opened the Bristol branch of the Association for the Promotion of the Higher Education of Women – with his wife, Louisa, as secretary. Oxford dons came to lecture on history and literature, while masters from the grammar school gave lessons in physical science and languages. Percival also had a hand in starting Clifton High School (where his daughter Bessie was one of the first pupils) and in founding University College, Bristol (1876), which attracted a high proportion of female day students.

17

Redland High School, founded in 1882, had to wait until the opening of the railway from Temple Meads to Avonmouth. By then Percival had left Clifton for Trinity College, Oxford, but he agreed to become Redland High School's first president – on the condition that his role would be more than merely decorative. He had hardly arrived at Oxford before he played an important part in the founding of Somerville Hall (later Somerville College), and when the ancient universities refused to award degrees to women students he proposed marking the Queen's Diamond Jubilee by developing Royal Holloway College into a Queen Victoria University for Women.

MANLY SPORTS

Percival called one of his five sons Arthur, and another Launcelot Jefferson – a nice blend of Gothic chivalry and American Enlightenment. At Percival's Clifton nobility of character was to be fashioned not only in Chapel but on The Close, as Sir Henry Newbolt's poems 'Clifton Chapel' and 'Vitaï Lampada' demonstrate. *The Cliftonian* for December 1879 was censured by editors of other school magazines for 'being for the most part devoted to nothing but accounts of football matches'. Rugby football was played from the first term, with Henry William Wellesley (great-nephew of the Duke of Wellington) as captain and ex-Rugbeian Graham Dakyns as coach. As early as 1864 a friendly match was played at Marlborough, which had been founded 20 years before Clifton. One of the Clifton XV wrote that the match 'had more the appearance of a hostile encounter rather than a friendly football match'. But he added that 'all differences and grievances were forgotten during the jovial supper with which we ended the day'. Regular matches between the two schools began only in 1891, when the match was drawn.

School runs were also organized from the first term, again by Wellesley. For the first ten years they were paper-chases, but in 1873 the School was divided into two packs. The upper pack ran over the Long Penpole course, the lower pack over the Short Penpole. There were Rugby Fives courts from the beginning, and in 1863 prizes were already being awarded. From 1872 an open rackets court was in use, marking the first steps in a sport that would bring Clifton national distinction. Athletics sports were first held in 1863, and the first gymnastics competition was held five years later. By then the Gymnasium had been built on the site originally assigned to the Chapel. These were still

Left: *The Governor's Cup presented to the winners of the Clifton v. Marlborough match. Shown here is the victorious Clifton team in 2006.*

Below: Cricket on The Close, *1912. W.H.Y. Titcomb, pastel.*

Bottom left: *A.E.J. Collins (standing fourth from right) and the Clifton XI in 1902.*

Lieutenant Colonel Sir Francis Younghusband

Born in 1863, Francis Younghusband left School House in 1880 and entered Sandhurst, where he prospered, despite being less than 5 feet 5 inches (165cm) tall. Like many Cliftonians of his generation, he chose to pursue his army career in India, and in 1882 he joined an expedition to Manchuria. In 1887 he travelled alone with hired guides from Peking, through the Gobi desert and over the Himalayas to Kashmir, an exploit that gained him a medal from the Royal Geographical Society. After a few years as political agent in India, he became a correspondent for *The Times* in India, Rhodesia and the Transvaal, and he took part in the Jameson Raid in 1895. He married in 1897 and went out to India again where he impressed Lord Curzon, the viceroy, who in 1903 appointed him leader of a mission to Tibet, where both Britain and Russia wished to extend their spheres of influence. Commanding a force of about 10,000 men, he reached Lhasa and negotiated a treaty in 1904 that committed Britain to a strong interventionist role, in line with his imperial philosophy. 'The Empire must grow: we can't help it,' he had written in 1901 to Henry Newbolt, his school friend, who referred to his exploits in his poems. Although Younghusband was knighted for these achievements in 1904, his treaty was repudiated by Britain in 1906 as he was considered to have exceeded his

Lieutenant Colonel Sir Francis Younghusband.

authority. By then he had written three books recounting his experiences and been awarded honorary doctorates by Cambridge and Edinburgh universities.

After a spell as resident in Kashmir from 1906 to 1910, Younghusband returned to England, spending the rest of his life in a bewildering variety of activities. He wrote over 20 books in all, some of them about India but the majority about his ideas on religion, which were strongly influenced by mystical notions drawn from the East. In 1916 he founded the Fight for Right Society, for which Parry wrote the music to 'Jerusalem', and he was at various times vice-president or president of the Royal Geographical Society, the Royal Central Asian Society, the Royal India and Pakistan Society, the Sociological Society, the Society for the Study of Religions, the Religious Drama Society and the World Congress of Faiths, among many others. He also promoted mountaineering and was influential in the Alpine Club and Himalayan Club, encouraging attempts to conquer Mount Everest. He died in 1942, one of the most fascinating – and eccentric – of Old Cliftonians. A prize-winning biography, *Younghusband*, by Patrick French was published by HarperCollins in 1994 and is highly recommended.

D.O. WINTERBOTTOM
STAFF, 1967–94

---

chiefly internal sports, with no inter-school fixtures, though two Cliftonians took part in the public schools gymnastics competition at Aldershot in 1884.

In the 1880s the School shooting team, which had its first recorded match in 1877, won the coveted Ashburton Shield at Bisley no fewer than three times, in 1884, 1885 and 1888, although it did not win the shield again until 1926. A cadet corps was started at the end of 1875. As befitted the strength of science and mathematics in the School, it was an engineer corps attached to the Bristol Engineer Volunteers. The first Clifton Register records an initial strength of 100 cadets and describes the corps as 'by no means the least important or successful of our games'. Within a year the Head of School was appointed cadet captain. This

was Romer Younghusband, one of three day boy brothers from a distinguished military family.

Sir Henry Newbolt was later accused of glorifying war by presenting it as cricket on a grander scale, and his celebration of Clifton cricket does indeed make an easy transition from 'a breathless hush in the Close tonight' to 'the sand of the desert is sodden red'. But the School's cricketing fame is not due entirely to Newbolt's verse. In 1871 Clifton met the MCC at Lord's for the first time and won a convincing victory over a team containing several professionals, and the Clifton XI was judged the best school team the MCC had encountered that year. The earliest school match, against Sherborne in 1865, ended in a tie, but from 1873 to 1887 the Clifton XI won all its Sherborne matches except two. From 1872 there was an annual match against Cheltenham, while the first Tonbridge match was in 1899. The best indication of Clifton's cricketing prowess in the 1870s and 1880s is found in the university match. The *Daily News* remarked that 'the pick of the Eton and Uppingham elevens goes to Cambridge, while Oxford, through a year of good and evil fortune, has drawn on Clifton'. In 1878 all the Cambridge wickets were taken by Clifton bowlers.

Yet during Percival's and Wilson's years success was won while work and games were kept in a sensible balance. As an early Clifton Housemaster wrote:

Ever since the school began, the games have been regarded as an essential part of the education of the place, and it has always been part of our unwritten constitution to keep games and work so harmoniously combined as to avoid anything like a division into those that work and those that play; and on these lines the development of the games has always run.

It sounds a long way from John Cleese's later dismissive reference to 'Clifton Sports Academy'.

James Wilson (Headmaster 1879–90)

James Wilson's sermons did not assume that he was addressing prospective saints. He urged the pupils to recognize that their 'powers of mind grow with use', and told them that their past must not become a handicap: 'Each morning you start afresh with new powers and new capabilities.' Wilson told the boys that his duty was 'to build up the faith in your soul on the foundation of Jesus Christ,' but he warned leavers that Chapel certainties would seem less certain outside. Contemporary society was debating whether religion could be 'anything else but a delusion, and a superstition and a sham'. The attack came from all sides: 'Historical evidence, comparative religion, physical science, natural history, all will proclaim in your ears that they know no God.' How were Cliftonians to confront such adversaries? Wilson advised: 'Be modest, and do not suppose you can know all things at twenty-one.' It was excellent schoolmasterly advice, but Wilson had difficulty in finding a bishop to ordain him. At the last minute he was ordained by the

Serving the Community

Chapel collections went to charity from the beginning, but in 1869 a committee of masters urged that Clifton should assist the poorer families of Bristol. So a 'ragged school' was established in Sidney Alley, The Dings. This closed in 1875, when a new board school was provided under the 1870 Education Act. Clifton then adopted the growing parish of St Barnabas, which already had a population of 10,000.

The first curate appointed to support the hard-pressed vicar later described the 'muck-heaps and farm-refuse on which jerry-builders had set up rows of houses that periodically flooded'.

When Wilson became Headmaster in 1879 William Booth had just turned his own Christian mission in London's East End into the Salvation Army, while the Clifton mission had become 'a temperance coffee house that was run at a loss'. A new curate took over. A Mission Hall was built in 1882 to a design by Charles Hansom. In 1884 a working men's club was opened, and in 1885 the city council purchased for public use what was left of the old Newfoundland 'gardens', which Wilson now had laid out as a park.

The year 1886 saw the dedication of the Church of St Agnes, the first church built anywhere for a public school mission. The Headmaster of Eton preached the inaugural sermon, while in Lent the pulpit was filled by a succession of Wilson's fellow headmasters. Wilson himself was a different kind of clerical headmaster from Percival. Lacking his predecessor's white-hot intensity, Wilson's approach, whether to the literal truth of scripture or to human frailty, was more flexible. He reminded his staff of the French maxim: 'You have no right to make miserable those whom you cannot make good.'

Left: *The Clifton College Mission at St Agnes.*

Above: *Canon Wilson aged 90 in 1931.*

Top right: *St Agnes Parish Church, consecrated on 2 March 1886, when the whole of Clifton College – masters and boys – crowded into the church to hear a sermon by Dr Percival.*

Bishop of Exeter, Frederick Temple, who had once appointed him to teach science at Rugby.

Wilson's Christian faith took practical forms. In March 1889 news arrived at School House that Newfoundland Road and St Agnes were under water. He ordered candles and essential food, commandeered a boat from the harbour and moved it on an empty coal cart to the flooded area. For hours he and the boatman passed candles and loaves of bread through the upper windows, and when the floods receded the College fire brigade spent Sunday hosing out mud from all the affected dwellings. A fund was quickly set up, and the Mission Hall became a relief centre. Wilson later made the city council replace the damaged culvert that had caused the flooding.

In the summer after the floods some 250 visitors from St Agnes were entertained at Clifton 'to commemorate the successful close of our work in the parish of St Agnes, and to take leave of our friends there'. Clifton now began to support the Mission to Working Boys. In August 1890 the first camp for Bristol boys was held at Burnham, and *The Cliftonian* reported that although some of the boys preferred chasing rabbits, most took part in the inter-tent hockey, athletics and cricket matches in a competitive spirit 'that would almost compare with our own House matches'.

IMPERIAL SHADOWS

In December 1890 James Wilson preached his farewell sermon in Chapel, before leaving to take up his new duties as vicar of Rochdale and Archdeacon of Manchester. He reminded the school and the Old Cliftonians present that they could not relax their efforts: 'There is a great work yet to be done for England by the public schools. And your school, which sends out a stream of men strong in the faith, jovial through hope and rooted in charity, will deserve well of our country and our church.' Wilson is famous in Clifton's annals as its only Headmaster to face an assassination attempt by a pupil – thanks to his quick reflexes, the knife sank into his arm and not his chest – but 'the Jimmy', as he was affectionately known to the boys, was more than a folk legend. One biographer hails him as 'mathematician, classicist, astronomer, schoolmaster, social reformer, parish priest, archdeacon and, from 1905 to 1926, Canon Residentiary of Worcester'.

Wilson lived to be 95, and he claimed that he did his best work when he was in his eighties. Perhaps, after so Olympian a figure, Clifton now needed a more conventional Headmaster. Percival, at this time headmaster of Rugby, wanted Herbert Warren, OC, president of Magdalen, who politely declined the invitation. H.A. James, headmaster of Cheltenham, accepted but was persuaded to withdraw by his outraged pupils. So Michael Glazebrook was the third

choice. A former scholar of Balliol, he took a First in classics and a second in mathematics. He enjoyed the added distinction of being the second man to jump 5 feet 11 inches or, as *The Cliftonian* claimed, the first to jump 6 feet (1.52m).

Michael Glazebrook (Headmaster 1890–1905)
Manchester Grammar School, where Glazebrook had been High Master, was Clifton's chief competitor in winning Oxbridge entrance awards in mathematics and science, and he is usually given credit for maintaining Clifton's high academic standards. The 13 Oxbridge awards of Wilson's last year were matched in 1891 and 1892. Many of the 40 or so Oxbridge Firsts won by Cliftonians between 1891 and 1894 belonged to Wilson's boys, but Glazebrook can claim credit for the 14 Firsts in classical and mathematical Mods at Oxford in 1892–94. After 1893 the number of entrants to Woolwich and Sandhurst exceeded the number of university entrance awards in 1897–98 by a ratio of five to one. The following year brought 12 entrance awards, but it was not until Glazebrook's last year that the number of awards again reached double figures. Nevertheless, in 1895 the College Council regarded the list of honours gained at the universities and military academies as 'so remarkable' that, in commending the results to the governors, it took the opportunity of 'congratulating all concerned'.

The altered balance between university and military honours reflected the imperial expansion of the 1890s and a more imperialistic spirit among the middle classes. At the beginning of 1897, Victoria's Diamond Jubilee year, her speech at the opening of parliament (as printed in the press) devoted four and a half lines to Ireland, five to the West Indies, seven to Matabeleland and Mashonaland, nine to Egypt and 24 to India. In July the *Illustrated London News*, reporting on the review of the fleet at Spithead, saw Britain's unparalleled naval power as evidence of Britain's commitment to her subject peoples. In March of that year the College Council had gratefully accepted the Headmaster's offer of one or more scholarships of £25 for boys intending a naval career. Within two years Old Cliftonians would be involved in a land war in South Africa where 43 of them died. Newbolt's verse on the war memorial commemorates them:

> *Clifton, remember these thy sons who fell*
> *Fighting far over sea;*
> *For they in a dark hour remembered well*
> *Their warfare learned of thee.*

But as Clifton entered the Edwardian age numbers were in decline, falling from 664 in 1890 to 528 in 1905. School magazines are not always reliable historical evidence, but *The Cliftonian* carried complaints of 'a spirit of indifference' (1896), 'singular apathy' in support for school debates (1897), 'fatal self-complacency' (1901) and 'the decline in physique which has lately made itself manifest in our football' (1903). Letters to *The Cliftonian* complained about the state of the museum too. In 1897 a correspondent wrote of 'the faint odour of putrefaction' arising from the natural history collection, which had been destined for the Wilson Tower but was not transferred there until 1922. Meanwhile, the library continued to accommodate all the museum's exhibits,

simply absorbing the successive bequests of birds, insects and minerals. Only when the scientific exhibits were at last moved out could the partition be removed and the true dignity of the library be displayed.

Glazebrook twice tendered his resignation (in 1897 and 1898), but the Council, chaired by Percival (now Bishop of Hereford), persuaded him to stay on, and he finally resigned in 1905. With characteristic generosity, Wilson acknowledged that Glazebrook had taken over when 'the first creation of a new ideal was over', when there was 'no further visible expansion' and only 'the less inspiring work of details, of correction, of consolidation'. Glazebrook is remembered as an austere, allegedly humourless figure who insisted on high standards but did not inspire affection. His portrait reinforces that impression. Yet in a long section he contributed to the Masters' Memoranda he reminds the staff that the senior boys to whom are entrusted great responsibilities are still only boys: 'We, who give them the responsibility, which is often a heavy burden, ought to regard their stumbles with charity.' There was evidently humanity behind the stern demeanour.

SAFEGUARDING THE FUTURE
Augustus David (Headmaster 1905–09)
Glazebrook's successor, the Rev. Augustus David, was himself a grammar school boy, who went from Exeter School on a classical scholarship to Queen's College, Oxford, taking Firsts in Mods and Greats. After teaching at Bradfield, he was appointed by Percival to the Rugby staff, and he was to become the fourth of Rugby's assistant masters to be appointed Headmaster of Clifton. From Rugby he had returned to Queen's as fellow and dean, before arriving at School House while he was still in his thirties. David had the shortest tenure of any Clifton Headmaster (except the first abortive appointment of Evans), but in his four years in Bristol he showed the same energy and decisiveness that he would display in his first four full years as headmaster of Rugby before the outbreak of war. He left Rugby in 1921 to become Bishop of St Edmundsbury and Ipswich, having previously turned down the headmastership of Eton and three offers of a bishopric. He was too dedicated a schoolmaster to desert his school in wartime.

David's arrival at Clifton had an immediate impact on numbers, which rose from 528 in 1905 to 654 in 1909. Oxbridge awards quickly reached their former numbers, as the lull between two wars saw fewer Clifton

Music at Clifton

The Diamond Jubilee brought Glazebrook's greatest legacy. In 1896, after teaching music for 32 years, W.F. Trimnell retired, and Clifton's unmusical Headmaster appointed Arthur Peppin as organist and director of music, telling him that 'music had no footing in the school, and he must make a niche for it'. That was a little unfair. There had been Choral and Orchestral Societies since the 1860s, and in 1874 the Choral Society gave Big School the Father Willis organ on which a Housemaster, Oakeley, gave Sunday recitals, attracting voluntary audiences of 100. In 1873–74 Samuel Sebastian Wesley wrote two settings of 'Let us now Praise Famous Men', the simpler of which was regularly sung at Commem. Harry Plunket Greene, who made his Clifton debut in 1879 as a soprano (see Chapter 6), returned as an OC to sing at concerts in the 1890s and at intervals in later years until (remarkably) 1931. Hubert Parry's music for Newbolt's 'Best School of All' was dedicated to 'Harry Plunket Greene, Arthur Peppin and the Clifton boys'. At the Queen's Golden Jubilee in 1887, 300 Cliftonians went to Bristol Cathedral (where Trimnell was deputy organist) to hear choral works by Handel and Mendelssohn. Now, at the Diamond Jubilee, a Music School was built on the Headmaster's kitchen garden in Guthrie Road. By the time Peppin moved to Rugby in 1915, Clifton's musical tradition was well established. Douglas Fox would later write: 'The vast improvement in the status of music in nearly all the public schools was very largely initiated by Clifton.'

THIS MUSIC ROOM IS
THE GIFT OF PAST
AND PRESENT MEMBERS
OF THE HOUSE
IN MEMORY OF
HARRY PLUNKET GREENE
(O.H. 1877–1881)
1937

Above: *Plaque in Oakeley's House commemorating Harry Plunket Greene (inset).*

entrants to Sandhurst and Woolwich. When Edward VII and Queen Alexandra visited Avonmouth in 1908 the Headmaster and the Head of School presented a loyal address, and the King graciously described Clifton as 'famous for patriotism, scholarship and sport'. He was aware that many Old Cliftonians had served 'in my army, and have distinguished themselves in all parts of the world'. They were 'men of honour, and men of energy and intelligence'. The Headmaster had earlier decided that the physical fitness of current Cliftonians would be improved by Swedish drill and longer hours of sleep. David also introduced Civics, an early example of the kind of political education that would lead to Victor Gollancz being sacked from Repton. But David's two most important legacies were the enlargement of the Chapel and the acquisition of new playing fields.

In 1908 the OC Society decided to mark the School's Golden Jubilee by adopting the Headmaster's proposal for more outdoor space. Having examined three possible sites, the Society decided to bid for 48 acres of pasture and woodland on the far side of the Avon Gorge – 'Beggar's Bush piece' as it would come to be called – and in 1909, just before David moved to Rugby, work began on Sir Charles Nicholson's design for the enlargement of the Chapel. Bishop Percival, still chairman of the Council, envisaged 'a fine central lantern tower with suitable transepts – a tower that would have an uplifting effect and give the Chapel a nobler character'. Nicholson's interpretation turned a conventional, narrowly linear public school chapel into what was virtually a Greek cross, admirably suited to the new Anglican liturgy of half a century later. In the 1990s *The Times* printed a photograph of Clifton Chapel under the mistaken impression that it was Bristol Cathedral.

THE PASSING OF AN AGE
John Edward King (Headmaster 1910–23)

When David left Clifton for Rugby at Christmas 1909 *The Cliftonian* remarked sadly: 'We have not only lost our Headmaster, but the Marlborough match as well.' By the time Clifton's new Headmaster was installed, the Chapel extension was nearly finished. John Edward King, the first non-ordained Clifton Headmaster, had been a boy in the School under Percival. Winning a classical scholarship to Lincoln College, Oxford, he became a fellow and tutor after some teaching experience at St Paul's School. In 1891 he left Oxford to succeed Glazebrook as High Master of Manchester Grammar School, before moving

in 1903 to Bedford School. He was 52 years old when he took up the Clifton post, having been appointed in preference to Percival's 28-year-old godson, William Temple, who went instead to Repton, greeting the assembled school with the words: 'Here I am, the newest of newcomers. Pray for me.' Temple did not stay to see Repton through the war, making way for Geoffrey Fisher in 1914, so perhaps the Clifton Council was wise to value King's experience above Temple's charisma.

The year 1910 had brought Clifton a new Headmaster and the nation a new king. Edward VII died in May, and there was now a coronation to prepare for. The year also saw not only the completed Chapel extension, but also the final purchase of the land at Beggar's Bush. Much stone-picking by gangs of Cliftonians would be needed

Above: *Children of the Victoria League forming a Union Jack on New Field, 28 June 1912.*

Below: *Lord Roberts taking the salute at the march past, 19 July 1912.*

Lieutenant Colonel R.F. Truscott OBE

During his lifetime Roy Truscott compiled 13 books and eight boxes of information about the school. Each is meticulously indexed and contains cuttings and photographs of the day-to-day achievements of OCs and developments in the school. Truscott went to Poole's in September 1892 and then on to Brown's, leaving in 1899 to go to King's College, Cambridge. He was called to the Bar, and during the First World War he served with the Sherwood Foresters, reaching the rank of lieutenant colonel.

Above: *Roy Truscott and G.R. Pilkington with Colonel R. Pilkington MP, on a Sunday afternoon, 1897. Photographed at the Avon Gorge.*

After the war he worked for the family printing business, where he was regarded as a wonderful employer. *The Cliftonian* of June 1938 noted that 'he never relaxed his efforts on behalf of his old school'. For many years he was honorary assistant secretary of the Old Cliftonian Society, and he was made a life governor the year before he died.

Interestingly, one box contains an obituary written by a close friend who wanted to make sure that future readers knew something about this quiet and unassuming man who had such a great love of the school. Clifton owes him a great debt, because his collections form the basis of the school archives.

before games could be played there, but this was undoubtedly a far-sighted investment. Bristol's 1911 coronation festivities took place during the school holidays, but the College buildings were illuminated, giving the neighbourhood 'a festive and patriotic appearance'. The buildings were again illuminated in the School's jubilee year, when George V and Queen Mary visited the School. The cadet corps formed a guard of honour, while 2,500 local schoolchildren formed a 'living flag' on the New Field. In the South Quad the Headmaster and masters, members of the College Council and the Head of School greeted the arrival of the royal coach. Meanwhile The Preparatory School entertained veterans of the Crimean War.

But behind the glamour of coronation and jubilee lay threatening signs of national and international crisis. Since 1909 the Liberal government had been locked in confrontation with the House of Lords after peers had

defied 150 years of precedent by throwing out the budget. To one constitutional crisis were added renewed demands for Irish Home Rule. Winston Churchill even proposed a federal system for the United Kingdom, with Irish, Scottish and Welsh parliaments and English provincial assemblies. There was also widespread industrial unrest. In the coronation year, while Rupert Brooke at Grantchester was preparing his poems for publication, there was violence in the Welsh coalfields, the Riot Act had to be read in Liverpool and 2,000 troops were stationed on Merseyside. In Clifton's jubilee year 40 million working days were lost through industrial action compared with fewer than 3 million in 1909. Both the rise of the Parliamentary Labour Party and the suffragette campaign calling for votes for women signalled a changing world, what would come to be called 'the strange death of Liberal England'.

More ominous for the immediate future was the international situation. In July 1912 a cadet corps field day, held at Beggar's Bush with other school contingents, was inspected by Field Marshal Lord Roberts. At tea he told the Clifton cadets about the OCs with whom he had served in India and South Africa, including William Birdwood, the Younghusbands and Douglas Haig. Many of those who heard Lord Roberts speak would soon be caught up in warfare more horrendous than anything Newbolt could have imagined. The roll of names, which Eric Gill's assistant later engraved on Clifton's Memorial Arch, records 578 dead out of some 3,000 who served. It is impossible for us, a century later, to conceive what such casualty lists meant for the School, its staff and its Headmaster.

Yet at Commem in 1912 John Percival, then aged 78, spoke of the same ideals he had brought to Clifton half a century before: 'Free from all bondage to outworn traditions, we aimed at a life more humane, perhaps, and not less manly than those which prevailed in older places.' Canon Wilson, preaching to a Sunday afternoon jubilee congregation, claimed for Clifton a truly liberal tradition: 'The gates are open, wide open, in this school to thought of every kind – to the widest range of literature, science, philanthropy, that any one can bring.' The jubilee year saw decisive victories over both Rugby and Cheltenham XIs, while there was a service in Chapel on 30 September to celebrate those first beginnings in 1862.

S.M. Andrews
Headmaster, 1975–90

Soldiering

2

Opposite: The Memorial Arch. The gateway was unlocked by Earl Haig in a ceremony on 30 June 1922, and the names were then unveiled. The names of 578 Cliftonians who died in the First World War are carved on the two inner side walls, and those of the 275 Cliftonians who fell in the Second World War are carved on the inner walls above the side entrances and below the windows. The name of one, who died in the Korean War, has been added to the outside of the north wall.

Right: The shooting VIII, 1897, and (inset) the Ashburton Shield, won by Clifton in 1884, 1885, 1888 and 1926.

BOY SOLDIERS

After the Battle of Waterloo in 1815 the British army rested on its laurels until the Crimean War (1854–56) and the Indian Mutiny (1857) revealed gross inadequacies in both its organization and performance. Public opinion was outraged, and successive governments hastened to introduce a raft of reforms. In 1859 the Lord Lieutenants of the British counties drew attention to dangers ahead, including possible hostilities with France and the Fenian terrorists in Ireland. In response to this, Rossall School in Lancashire became in 1860 the first school to register a cadet force, consisting of some 70 pupils, who were enrolled as the Rossall Rifle Volunteers and attached to the 65th Lancashire Regiment. Other schools followed suit, and in December 1875 Clifton set up a School Rifle Corps, which was attached to the Bristol Engineer Corps. This made it the first Engineer Cadet Corps in Britain.

Although Clifton was only 13 years old in 1875 it had nearly 600 pupils, and many of them were not at first impressed with the idea of a cadet corps, which, it was thought, would detract from a proper regard for the most prestigious extra-curricular activity – cricket. However, several influential masters supported the corps and joined at the humble level of sapper. These included the second master, T.E. Brown, and two more Housemasters, T.W. Dunn and C.W.A. Tait, who were quite happy

(and probably amused) to be ordered around the parade ground by pupil NCOs. Rifle shooting was so effectively taught that the School team won the coveted Ashburton Shield at Bisley three times in the 1880s.

In the same year that the corps was founded Percival also established the military and engineering side at Clifton to complement the existing classical and modern sides, and he appointed H.S. Hall, an Old Cliftonian, to be in charge of it. Hall was a mathematics teacher whose *Elementary Algebra for Schools* eventually sold 1.5 million copies. By the time he retired in 1901, 150 Clifton boys had passed directly into the Royal Military Academy at Woolwich and a further 120 into

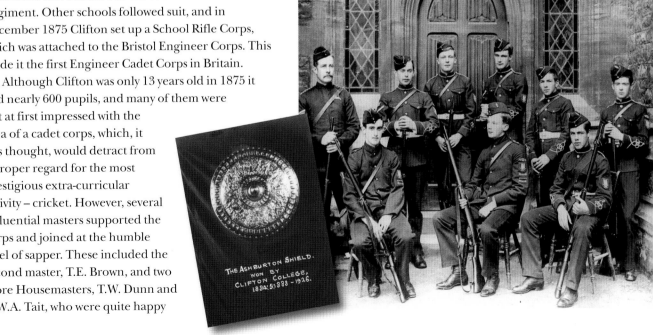

Sandhurst. By the turn of the century, therefore, Clifton had, in addition to its excellent record for classical scholarship, become well known as an army school. This reputation was no doubt enhanced by Newbolt's poems 'Vitaï Lampada' and 'Clifton Chapel', both of which became internationally famous for their compelling idealization of patriotic warfare.

Some 16 OCs fought in the Afghan and Zulu Wars, and the first OC to be killed in action was Captain J.W.W. Darley, who died at Abu Klea in 1885 when serving in the British force sent to rescue General Gordon in Khartoum. By 1893 there were 389 OCs in the Army List, and 347 served in the South African (or Boer) War, which ended in 1902. A total of 43 died, and their memorial at Clifton is one of the finest of Alfred Drury's sculptures, with the chivalric figure of St George clad in medieval armour, a far cry from the khaki uniforms actually worn on the veldt. But this was still an age when war was considered a colourful adventure for dashing volunteers. Military Cliftonians were beginning to be noticed and the names of Colonel Francis Younghusband, the famous explorer of Tibet, and Colonel Douglas Haig and Captain William Birdwood, both mentioned in dispatches for valour in South Africa, were becoming known. Haig's rise to the top began in 1903 when he was appointed a major-general and sent as Inspector-General of Cavalry to India. Already an ADC to Edward VII, he was introduced to Dorothy Vivian, one of the queen's maids of honour, at Windsor during Ascot week in 1905. The introduction took place on a Thursday, they played golf and Haig proposed and was accepted on Saturday. The wedding took place in July in Buckingham Palace, and Clifton had, through Douglas Haig, reached the heart of the empire.

ARMAGEDDON

In 1906 Haig began three years' work at the War Office, playing a crucial role in the complete reorganization of the British army. In 1909 he became chief of staff in India for two years, and in 1912 he took up the important post of commandant at Aldershot. Meanwhile, Field Marshal Lord Roberts presided over Clifton's elaborate jubilee field day on the 50th anniversary of the school in 1912, noting that about 1,000 Clifton boys had entered the army so far and only 90 the navy. The most popular destination was the Indian Army, followed by the Royal Engineers and the Gloucestershire Regiment.

When hostilities began in the summer of 1914 Haig was given command of one of the two army groups of the 100,000-strong British Expeditionary Force sent to France under the command of Sir John French, and his own troops played an important part in holding the British line at Ypres. Criticism of the French after the Battle of Loos in September 1915 led to Haig's appointment as commander-in-chief of the British forces, a position he held for the next two years and eleven months over an army of more than a million men, by far the largest Britain had ever put into the field.

In February 1916 the Allied offensive on the Somme achieved only modest gains at a heavy cost in

St George

The Gothic bronze image of St George, commissioned by the OC Society, has looked out over The Close since its unveiling in 1905 by General Lord Methuen OC. The knight, in the armour of the late 14th century and with shield and sword in hand, commemorates the 43 Old Cliftonians of all ranks, including one VC, who gave their lives in the South African War.

Field Marshal Earl Haig

Haig's reputation has had its ups and downs. The first to rush into print about him was Winston Churchill, whose volumes of *The World Crisis*, published between 1923 and 1927, were critical of Haig in his own lifetime. In 1929, the year after Haig's death, his loyal former aide Sir John Charteris published a biography defending him. In 1933 Duff Cooper finished his two-volume study, making extensive use of Haig's diaries, which were, it must be said, frequently critical of Lloyd George. The latter, still very much alive, countered with an all-out attack in his *War Memoirs*, finished in 1936. A whole chapter of 21 pages is devoted to refuting criticisms of him made in Duff Cooper's book, and it is extremely entertaining but more the work of an orator and debater than a scholar.

Basil Liddell Hart's *History of the First World War* (1934) was mostly critical, but in 1952 Robert Blake made his name with a masterly edition of Haig's private papers together with a commentary that is supportive of Haig. In 1953 John Davidson produced a study, *Haig: Master of the Field*, whose title tells its own story. In 1963 John Terraine's acclaimed biography, *Douglas Haig: The Educated Soldier*, defended him on almost every point while Corelli Barnett's *The Swordbearers* (also 1963) blamed not only Haig for the disasters of the war, but Clifton, Percival and Newbolt as well. General Sixsmith

Right: *Field Marshal Haig and Field Marshal Birdwood at the unveiling of the Memorial Arch, 30 June 1922. (Pavey/Atkinson album)*

produced an admirably concise and well-argued defence of Haig in 1976, as did Philip Warner in 1991, and since then academic opinion has, if anything, swung even more to the view that Haig had an impossible task and, despite mistakes and bad luck, did remarkably well in the circumstances.

Popular opinion, however, has been strongly influenced by Alan Clark's widely read account, *The Donkeys* (1961), which pursued the line that British troops (lions) were betrayed by the generals (donkeys), and this inspired Joan Littlewood's brilliant musical play, *Oh, What a Lovely War* (1963), which was filmed in 1969. John Laffin's *Butchers and Bunglers of the First World War* had no time for Haig either, as the title suggests, and the debate will doubtless continue to arouse strong feelings: too many men died, too many families suffered. Haig was quick to set up the poppy fund after the war for the relief of needy service personnel and this, at least, all can applaud.

D.O. WINTERBOTTOM
STAFF, 1967–94

casualties on both sides: 650,000 German and 623,000 British and French combined. Haig was heavily criticized by British politicians, but he retained the confidence of King George V and was promoted to field marshal.

The Passchendaele offensive during the summer of 1917 also failed to achieve its objectives, this time at a cost of a quarter of a million British men killed or wounded. These were casualties on a stupendous scale, and the extent to which it is fair to blame Haig for them

has been fiercely debated ever since. What is clear is that he did not waver under his huge responsibility, his officers and men remained deeply loyal, and in November he launched a successful offensive at Cambrai, where he made extensive use of tanks. By October the following year the Germans had been overrun, and on 11 November an armistice was signed, and the politicians who had criticized Haig for making a mess of the war were able to sit down at Versailles and make a mess of the peace.

Because of the deep loyalty instilled by Clifton in its pupils and alumni, the fact that the war effort had been spearheaded by an Old Cliftonian was a source of great pride. During the war years at Clifton, as at similar schools, there was a significant increase in numbers, which rose from 594 in 1914 to 689 in 1918. This was partly because of the high reputation of the School, partly because of the confidence felt in the assured leadership of John King and partly, no doubt, because parents felt that if their 18-year-old son was to be sent to fight in the war, the military training he would receive in the cadet force at Clifton would be a great advantage.

Yet it was a grim time to be at school. Most football and cricket fixtures were cancelled, and festivities in general were curtailed. Economies were made with everything, especially food, paper and heating. Up to 90 per cent of the boys served in the corps, and many spent

Left: *The OTC in the Quad, 1919.*

their summer holidays in lumber camps or digging for potatoes in the countryside. Sixteen masters were away fighting and temporary replacements had to be found. But by far the worst aspect was the unceasing bad news

South Town House Book

An entry into the ST Book records that from ST approximately 320 served in the war; 77 of these were wounded, 15 taken prisoner and 61 killed or died.

It may be of interest for future generations to know how the life of the school has been affected by the Great War.

The corps had hardly gone into camp at Aldershot when rumours of war became hourly more audible (27 July). The crisis had begun with the Austrian note to Serbia on 23 July. Camp suddenly broke out on 3 August. On 7 August came the declaration of War.

The school reassembled on 19 September. Already war had caused gaps in our society. Some boys were detained abroad. Some had already enlisted or obtained commissions. Others left for the same reason during term. One boy – a German – spent a few days at Bedminster Police Court as an interned alien. He was soon released.

Several OCs had already fallen in battle. Numbers now enlisted or became officers in the Territorial, Special Reserve and Service Battalions. Of the Masters Mr Clissold soon gave up all school work for training the territorial engineers and in November – with Mr Langley – was embodied with them. Major Raymer had rejoined the Jersey Militia. Major Burbey commanded the corps until in December he joined the 11th Loyal N. Lancashires and handed over the OTC to Col. Rintoul. Mr H.M. Parr joined the South Staffords. Recruits of the Territorial and service battalions drilled regularly on The Close, borrowing rifles and engineering material. The Downs were similarly used by troops. The sounds of bands and buglers, words of command and the tramp of feet were in our ears all day long.

The War Office having asked that every effort should be made to render the OTC as efficient as possible, considerable changes in our routine were made for that purpose.

1. *The whole of the Upper School, save some 30, joined the corps. The Junior School were instructed in military drill.*
2. *Thursday afternoons 2–5 and whole school days 12.15–1.15 were devoted to drill.*
3. *A special body of boys of 17 and upwards, available for commission, received extra military instruction on Tuesdays and Saturdays 2–3 and some other times. On Sundays 2–5 they went for a route march, without arms, of some 13 miles.*
4. *School hours were altered as follows. On half holidays school ended at 12.45, dinner at 1. On Sundays chapels were at 10.30 and 7 pm, OT at 4–4.45: for the XI and Military Side 11.30. Route marchers were excused.*
5. *All foreign matches, except those with Marlborough and Wellington, were cancelled. Ordinary football was played on Tuesdays. On most Saturdays there were house matches, every house playing every other.*
6. *House suppers were not held. The school concert was held on the last Saturday, no visitors being allowed.*

During term the houses and towns subscribed weekly to Belgian boy refugees in Bristol. Two such boys were admitted into the school in School House. On the last Sunday evening of term the service held at 7 o'clock was so arranged to be in memory of those who had fallen in the war.

about casualties, many of them young men known to boys in the School. By the end of 1914, 1,527 Cliftonians had volunteered for service, and by the end of 1915 the figure stood at 2,250, with 172 killed. By the end of the war a total of 3,100 had served and 578 were dead. Henry Newbolt's comparison in 'Vitaï Lampada' between playing the game of cricket and the 'game' of war had a tragic resonance for the cricket XI of 1914. All had volunteered for service, and five were killed, one died of disease and four were wounded. Five of the masters on the staff were killed, John Percival and John King each lost a son, and James Wilson lost two sons. H.S. Hall and the Rev. Joseph Polack each lost two sons, and five other masters lost one son. 'A gloom and sadness hung over us all,' wrote one master, as the names of the recently fallen were constantly read out in a hushed Chapel.

Among those who survived, the list of achievements was impressive: one commander-in-chief, one army commander (Birdwood), 23 major-generals, 52 brigadier-generals, 5 VCs, 180 DSOs, 14 knighthoods. Many of these were present when a Memorial Archway, designed by Major Charles Holden, architect to the Imperial War Graves Commission, was formally opened in 1922 by Earl Haig, who had agreed that year to become president of the College. It was inscribed with the names of those who had died, as well as the words of Newbolt:

From the great Marshal to the last recruit
These, Clifton, were thy Self, thy spirit in Deed,
Thy flower of Chivalry, thy fallen fruit,
And thine immortal seed.

THE WHATLEY YEARS, 1923–39

John King was due to retire at the age of 60 in 1918, but the College Council was not keen to have a change of Headmaster until the upheavals of wartime had settled down, and he was persuaded to remain in post until 1923, though they allowed him to give up being Housemaster of School House. All five of Clifton's Headmasters thus far had been Oxford or Cambridge dons at some stage in their careers, and the Council now went one step further by appointing Norman Whatley, an Oxford classics don at Hertford College who had no schoolmastering experience at all, although he had been head of school at Radley. When he came to Clifton he was 38 years old and married, with three sons. He was the first of Percival's successors who had not been recommended by Percival himself. The bishop had died in 1918 and was buried, at his own earnest request, in a mausoleum specially constructed below the high altar of Clifton Chapel, rather than in Hereford Cathedral. In 1923 the chairman of Council was Sir Herbert Warren, a distinguished Oxford don, who had been president of Magdalen College and vice-chancellor of the university. Whatley had held the rank of brevet major and had served in the Oxford University OTC and then with the Intelligence Corps in France, being mentioned in dispatches. His military experience developed his abilities to lead and manage as well as to undertake detailed organization, but he was predominantly an academic, and his appointment reflected the Council's desire that postwar Clifton should relinquish some of its status as an army school and build instead on its well-established reputation for academic success.

Below: Wounded soldiers being entertained at Clifton by a cricket match between the School and the MCC, in 1917 or 1918. Boys from The Preparatory School were in their Cub Scout uniforms.

W.H.Y. Titcomb: Faith in Art

William Titcomb (1858–1930), the eldest son of the first Bishop of Rangoon, studied art at South Kensington, Paris and Antwerp. He made his initial reputation in the fledgling art colony at St Ives, where he was based from 1887, and during the 1890s he became that colony's leading figure painter, winning awards in Paris and Chicago.

In 1905 Titcomb and his wife, Jessie, a fellow artist whom he had married in St Ives in 1892, decided to move to Dusseldorf. Having had two children – Frank in 1898 and Loveday in 1900 – this move was apparently made largely because Jessie was of the opinion that German education was vastly superior to anything available in England. However, the four years spent in Germany were unhappy, and in 1909, with German nationalism on the rise, they decided to return to England. Again, the choice of destination was made not on artistic grounds but on educational ones, and they moved to Bristol, living in Vyvyan Terrace. Frank enrolled at Clifton College and Loveday at Clifton High School.

A distinguished figure, Titcomb was warmly welcomed into Bristol art circles, and the Bristol Academy was keen to use his contacts with the Cornish artists to persuade them to exhibit more regularly in the city. Until this time Titcomb had worked almost exclusively in oils, but a commission inspired him to work more regularly in watercolours, and the series of the School, which Jessie Titcomb's diary suggests were done in 1912, included cricket, rugby, swimming and running matches, as well as interiors of the library and Big School. Perhaps the most impressive of these is his depiction of that encounter of intense rivalry, the Clifton–Rugby cricket match, which was later exhibited at the RWA in 1918. Here is the classic vista of the School buildings seen across The Close, enhanced by a group of cricketers sitting on the boundary.

During his first decade in Bristol Titcomb still produced for the Royal Academy a number of significant oil paintings of Bristol scenes. He also depicted the local Boy Scout group on various occasions, perhaps because Frank (and other Clifton boys) had joined, and in 1913 he showed at the Royal Academy a major work, *Cheering the Chief Scout* (Bristol Art Gallery), showing the boys welcoming Robert Baden-Powell in Dowry Square, Hotwells, most probably during his 1910 visit. However, on the outbreak of war in 1914 it was seen as having good propaganda potential and was re-named Send Us.

With outdoor sketching restricted during the war years, Titcomb turned his attention to historical reconstructions and imaginative work. Clifton's painting *The Soldiers' Communion* was his first attempt at a war theme. It shows a group of soldiers kneeling before a makeshift altar set up on planks just behind the firing line. It has been raining, and the Red Cross flies from a nearby flagpole. A Union Jack is the improvised altar cloth, upon which have been set a couple of spluttering candles and a tiny wooden cross. A priest, who is a soldier himself, as his spurs are visible beneath his cassock, administers the sacrament to the reverent congregation, and, although within the sound of the guns, amid battle-scarred trees and with no pomp or religious ritual, the service has a special dignity.

Titcomb used a number of boys from Clifton as models for the painting, while the school's chaplain, Rev. Egbert Ivor Allen Phillips (chaplain 1911–32), modelled as the priest. The best-defined face, that of the kneeling soldier holding a gun, to whom the priest will next turn, was modelled by his own son, Frank, and Titcomb's future son-in-law, Leonard Cogan, modelled for the soldier with the peaked cap.

The following year Titcomb painted another scene from Flanders, *The Message*, which depicts a fatally wounded soldier seeing a vision of his newborn son, so that, in his last moments, he knows he has a son to perpetuate his name, his family and his memory. Little did Titcomb appreciate when he painted this work how soon such considerations would weigh heavily upon himself, for of the boys featured in *The Soldiers' Communion* only Leonard Cogan survived the war. Frank, Titcomb's only son, was among the casualties, crashing in 1917 in thick fog during his first solo flight with the Royal Navy Air Squadron.

The restoration of the painting, funded by Richard and Annette Farrimond, has enabled *The Soldiers' Communion* to be seen in its original splendour in the ante-chapel. It serves constantly as a reminder of the debt that we all owe to those who gave their lives for their country during the First World War, particularly the many former pupils of the School, who had hardly had a chance to put their education to use before being cruelly cut down.

D. TOVEY
OH, 1967–72

Left: *Frank and Loveday Titcomb with their housekeeper.*

Opposite: *W.H.Y. Titcomb, The Soldiers' Communion, Oil, 1915.*

Whatley inherited a school with a record number of 788 boys, and in his first ten years he made radical changes to it. Though he would have been much better off financially had he lived in School House as Housemaster as well as Headmaster, he decided that the posts were incompatible in the modern world, and he chose to live with his family in a school property in Cecil Road. Whatley also inherited two outstanding science teachers in Dr Eric Holmyard, the head of the science department, and William Badcock, the head of physics. He quickly saw that the increase in numbers made the existing laboratory space inadequate, and he also agreed with Holmyard and Badcock's view that the study of science was essential in the postwar world. The Council agreed to the demolition of the Junior School buildings on the Close, and in their place rose one of the most magnificent and best-equipped of school science laboratories, designed by Alan Munby and opened in 1927 by the Prince of Wales. Under Holmyard and Badcock Clifton became a recognized leader in science education, and the long list of their distinguished pupils includes two Nobel prize winners, Sir Nevill Mott and Sir John Kendrew, as well as five Fellows of the Royal Society.

The demolition of the Junior School led to a major re-think about boys aged under 13. Until then boys between the ages of 11 and 13 had been taught mostly by senior school staff, though they had separate day and boarding houses. Boys under the age of 11 were in the Preparatory School (nicknamed the Pre), which by the 1920s was based at Elveden in The Avenue. The Council decided on an ambitious plan to build a fine new Preparatory School for all boys under 13, and it was helped in this plan by the recession after 1929, which made houses in The Avenue cheap to buy and demolish to clear a suitable site.

Below: *The opening of the Science School on 2 June 1927 by HRH the Prince of Wales.*

Right: *Winston Churchill visits Clifton in 1946. When the Head of School presented him with a copy of* Clifton at Bude *he was heard to say 'So You're Head of School are you? Congratulations. I was always bottom of mine.'*

Alan Munby was again the architect, and the new buildings were opened in 1933. After a long search Whatley appointed E.G. Sharp, a prep school deputy head in Eastbourne, as first Headmaster of the new Pre, which soon established itself as a major force in the preparatory school world. However, schools 'tied' to a senior school in this way have always had an ambivalent status because their headmasters are not as independent as those of 'stand-alone' prep schools. Moreover, the arrangement raises the question of whether the function of a junior school is simply to feed the senior school or whether it should be free to send some of its best pupils to other schools. The establishment of the Pre, and its considerable growth and success in the future, made Clifton even more different from many of its rivals and competitors that did not have a tied preparatory school.

Whatley made other changes. Until 1931 boys wore a black coat, a black tie, striped trousers and a house cap. On the grounds of economy, he put the boys into grey flannel trousers and a grey flannel blazer edged with blue, though he did not dare to discontinue the traditional caps. The grey flannel blazers and trousers did not compare well, some thought, with more elegant dress codes at other public schools. Some people say that Clifton has never been a 'smart' school, but this

criticism probably dates back only to 1931. Whatley also completely remodelled the academic organization of the school, creating Blocks I, II and III. Block I was subdivided into the Upper Bench (praepostors), Middle Bench (second year Sixth Formers) and Lower Bench (the rest), a system that was necessary to meet new examination requirements, though it discontinued old traditions and raised hackles among OCs.

At this time a school's academic standing was judged by the number of scholarships and exhibitions (not just places) it gained at Oxford and Cambridge. During the inter-war years Clifton won an average of nine of these awards, with a record 14 in 1932 and another record of 17 in 1937, with 12 in 1938 and 13 in 1939, Whatley's last year. In 1930 *The Morning Post* placed Clifton at number nine in a list of 'the greater public schools', and its academic achievements over the next decade could only have enhanced its reputation. Without question, Whatley achieved what the Council had desired: the modernization of the school and its emergence as a major academic force and recognized leader in science teaching.

Unfortunately, he fell out with the Council in the late 1930s, partly because the economic recession made numbers fall to 630 in 1939 (they had fallen even more

Field Marshal Lord Birdwood

The son of an Indian civil servant and judge, William Birdwood left Oakeley's House in December 1882 at the age of 17 and went on to Sandhurst before joining an Indian regiment. Handsome and charming, he was adjutant of the viceroy's bodyguard from 1893 to 1898, and he married in 1894. He was posted to South Africa in 1899, fighting at Colenso and in the campaigns to relieve Ladysmith. He was wounded and five times mentioned in dispatches. He became a protégé of Lord Kitchener, and between 1900 and 1909 he was his assistant military secretary and then military secretary when Kitchener was commander-in-chief in India. By 1911 Birdwood was a major-general, in command of the Kohat independent brigade, and in 1912 he was secretary to the government of India in the army department. After the outbreak of war in 1914 Kitchener, by then war minister, chose him to command the newly formed Australian and New Zealand contingents (the Anzacs) with the rank of lieutenant general.

In 1915 Britain decided to attack Constantinople (now Istanbul) in order to knock Turkey out of the war, but a naval bombardment failed to secure the Dardanelles, the only access to the city from the Mediterranean. Birdwood's troops then became an important part of an imperial force commanded by Sir Ian Hamilton, who decided to land troops on the beaches of the Gallipoli peninsula rather than, as Birdwood preferred, on the Asiatic coast. The Turks were ready for the assault and put up a fierce resistance, and the Anzac troops, as a result of errors of navigation not attributable to Birdwood, landed in April 1915 at a confined cove surrounded by cliffs, from which they were subject to murderous fire from the Turks. Bolstered by Birdwood's cheerful and enthusiastic leadership style, which made him popular with his men, the Anzacs held this position heroically for eight months, despite suffering thousands of casualties. Birdwood was not among those blamed for the overall failure at Gallipoli, and he was one of the few to emerge with an enhanced reputation, largely because after the replacement of Hamilton he was entrusted with organizing the withdrawal of all the British forces, an operation achieved with great efficiency and few losses.

In March 1916 Birdwood went with the Anzac troops to fight in France. He was promoted to general in 1917 and given command of the Fifth Army in May 1918. According to the *Dictionary of National Biography*, he continued to be 'a brave and resolute soldier and keenly alive to the importance of personal relations ... If not in the first, he was high in the second rank of British commanders in the First World War.' From 1920 to 1924 he commanded the northern army in India and was promoted commander-in-chief in India and field marshal in 1925, but he never became governor-general of Australia, a position he openly coveted. On his retirement from the army he was appointed, to the surprise of many, as Master of Peterhouse, one of Cambridge's most academic colleges, a position he thoroughly enjoyed until 1938, when he retired and was created Baron Birdwood of Anzac and Totnes. He was president of Clifton College from 1931 until his death twenty years later, and he was largely responsible for the appointment as Headmaster of Bertrand Hallward (a Peterhouse don) in 1939.

D.O. WINTERBOTTOM
STAFF 1967–94

drastically in many other schools), and partly because money was short due to all the building projects he had initiated. In addition, he was ill for some time and quarrelled with two of his not very capable bursars. He retired under some pressure in 1939, but his headmastership brought about a significant break with the past, and in many ways he left a new Clifton, shaped very much according to his own vision and priorities.

WAR AGAIN

Although the first aim of Whatley's Clifton was to be an academic school, the cadet corps remained an important feature. Unlike the pre-war corps, however, it was now compulsory, and there was a backlash at first from the boys against its strict discipline, no doubt enforced by masters who had become inured to hardship as officers during the war. Clearly the Cliftonians of 1920 were hoping for a more peaceful future, and as one wrote in the school magazine that year:

> *Then let us pluck up courage and make complaint to those*
> *Who make us carry rifles and wear these khaki clothes,*
> *For since we have all these parades we only hate the more*
> *That ancient institution, the Clifton College Corps.*

Yet under the able leadership of Clifton legends such as 'Jock' Crawfurd and Rodney Gee, the corps won high praise from inspecting officers during the 1920s. By 1929 the long-established engineering course was considered out of date, and the link with the Royal Engineers was abandoned. The Ashburton Shield for shooting was won in 1926 and 1928, with very high scores in most other years, and in 1934 *The Times* announced that the most successful schools at Bisley since 1919 had been Winchester and Clifton.

Earl Haig died in 1928, and a fine bronze statue of him was made by W. McMillan and unveiled on its plinth on the parapet in 1932. He was succeeded as president of the College by J.H. Whitley, a former Speaker of the House of Commons, and in 1935 by Clifton's other field marshal, Lord Birdwood, who had been in command of the Anzac forces at Gallipoli in 1915. A soldier with considerable charm and diplomatic gifts, Birdwood was elected master of Peterhouse, a Cambridge college where young Bertrand Hallward, whose reputation for good looks and intellectual brilliance was already well established, was known to be on the lookout for a headmastership. When Whatley resigned, Birdwood had Hallward lined up to take over in May 1939, confirming the Council's policy of maintaining Clifton as an academic school. At 38 years, Hallward was too young to have fought in the First World War, but he was an expert on the military history of classical Greece and Rome.

The Treaty of Versailles and League of Nations failed to prevent a resurgence of German militarism, and by 1937 the Nazi Party was threatening the peace of Europe. In that year the British prime minister, Neville Chamberlain, appointed an Old Cliftonian, Leslie Hore-Belisha, as secretary of state for war. At first Hore-Belisha went along with the government's policy of appeasement, but after the Munich Conference in 1938 he was one of the first cabinet ministers to change his mind and advocate rearmament. When war broke out in September 1939 Hore-Belisha appointed Lord Gort to command the British Expeditionary Force to France, but military men mistrusted the minister's flamboyance (and lack of punctuality), and Chamberlain replaced him in January 1940.

Meanwhile, at Clifton, Hallward was busy making himself unpopular with the boys for looking far too young and seeming much too confident, and with the staff for reducing their salaries in order to improve the School's shaky financial position. At first Bristol was thought to be out of the range of German bombers, but by May 1940 France, Belgium and the Netherlands were overrun and their aerodromes used by the Luftwaffe. The first bombs fell on Bristol on 24 June, and Clifton boys took refuge in basements while the Council authorized the construction of purpose-built air-raid shelters. On 24 November the Bristol blitz began, and on 2 December a bomb fell on the New Field, missing the Wiseman's House shelter by 30 feet (9.15m) and the Polack's shelter by 60 feet (18.3m). No one was hurt, but the southwest regional commissioner, General Sir Hugh Elles, an OC, advised the Council to evacuate the school.

Hallward rose to the challenge by revealing that he had leadership skills of a high order, and at the start of 1941 he managed to establish 310 Clifton boys and a reduced complement of rather elderly masters in a motley collection of seaside boarding houses in Bude, north Cornwall. So successfully did he organize and inspire this community to work to a high intellectual standard that between 1941 and 1945 the School won an average of 14 awards to Oxford and Cambridge. In 1943 the figure was 21, which put Clifton at the top of the league table, beating Manchester Grammar School, Eton and St Paul's into second, third and fourth places. Patrick Jenkin, later a cabinet minister, was a boy at Bude and has written about the School's time there in Chapter 3.

Meanwhile, in Bristol the Clifton campus became an important focus for soldiering. The Bude hotels had been released by the army in return for the use of the school buildings, and a Royal Army Service Corps Officer Cadet Training Unit moved in shortly after the boys moved out. They were there from February 1941 until September 1942 and were succeeded by a Pioneer Corps Unit. In November 1942 the United States V Corps under Major-General Hartle occupied most of the buildings, and in 1943 Queen Mary visited The Close to see US soldiers playing baseball there. In April 1943 another Old Cliftonian stepped into a highly influential wartime role. This was Lieutenant General Sir Frederick Morgan, who was appointed chief of staff to the Supreme Allied Commander Designate in April 1943, and he did much of the early planning for the D-Day landings, including choosing the Normandy beaches as the main location. In December 1943 General Dwight Eisenhower was appointed Supreme Allied Commander, and he endorsed Morgan's Normandy strategy.

In October 1943 General Omar Bradley moved to Clifton, which became the headquarters of the US First Army, with divisions in Taunton, Plymouth and Warminster. While he was based at Clifton, Bradley's main office was the Housemaster's drawing room in School House, and the Council Room became the heart of invasion planning. Operations and intelligence offices were in the Wilson Tower, while the crow's nest was used for receiving top-secret Ultra messages intercepted from the enemy. As D-Day grew closer the library was full of busy clerks compiling detailed loading lists for the invasion transport, but by early June they had all gone as the greatest amphibious invasion in history got under way. For a while the US Ninth Army under General Simpson trained troops at Clifton, but by September they too had left, thanking Bristol in their subsequent official history for its hospitality and remembering fondly 'Clifton College with its beautiful buildings, tall trees and broad sweep of cricket fields'.

The Clifton buildings were officially handed back to the school in November 1944, and Hallward brought 295 boys back from Bude in March 1945, just a few more than the 273 Old Cliftonians who had lost their lives fighting in the war. Winston Churchill made a brief visit in 1946 and advised the boys to read history. During the next few years Hallward re-established the School's pre-war numbers and basked in the sunshine of a high reputation won by his remarkable success at Bude. In 1948 he left Clifton to become the first vice-chancellor of Nottingham University, and in his 16 years there he laid the foundations of what is today one of Britain's foremost educational institutions. The Council twice looked to him to recommend a successor, and his choices were Desmond Lee (1948–54) and Nick Hammond (1954–62), both former pupils of his and both distinguished classics dons. Under them Clifton successfully pursued its declared aim of being principally an academic school, and in a well-timed burst of brilliance the boys achieved an all-time record of 23 Oxford and Cambridge awards to celebrate the School's centenary in 1962. For them, at least, the pen had triumphed over the sword.

D.O. Winterbottom
Staff, 1967–94

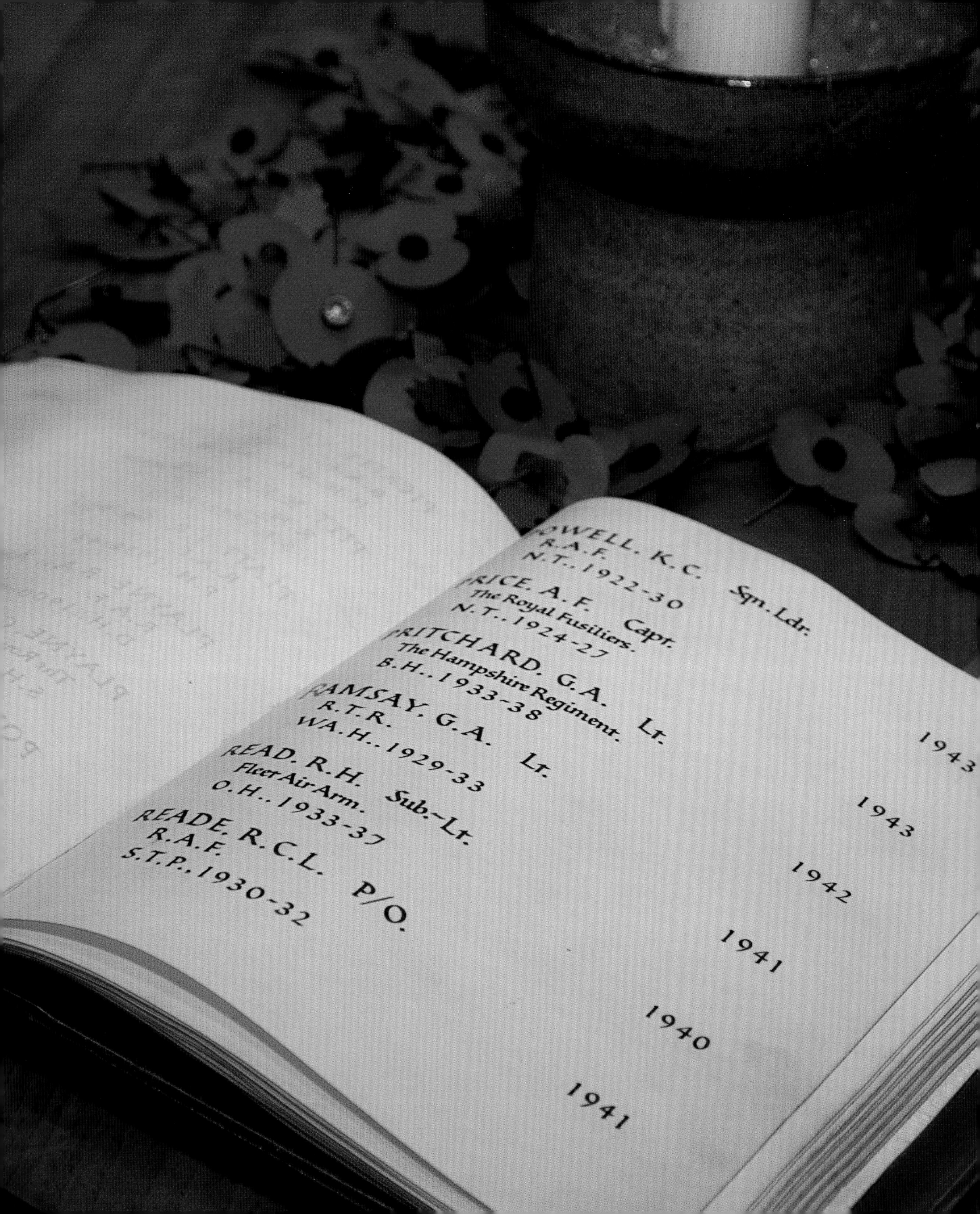

POWELL. K.C. Sqn. Ldr.
R.A.F.
N.T., 1922-30

PRICE. A.F. Capt.
The Royal Fusiliers.
N.T., 1924-27   1943

PRITCHARD. G.A. Lt.
The Hampshire Regiment.
B.H., 1933-38

RAMSAY. G.A. Lt.
R.T.R.
W.A.H., 1929-33   1943

READ. R.H. Sub-Lt.
Fleet Air Arm.
O.H., 1933-37   1942

READE. R.C.L. P/O.
R.A.F.
S.T.P., 1930-32   1941

                                                1940

                                            1941

Remembering

SCOUTING AT CLIFTON

The Cliftonian of July 1910 contains a long letter from General Robert Baden-Powell to Cliftonians. *Scouting for Boys*, published two years before, was based on his experiences in the British army in India and South Africa, and it enjoyed a wide readership. Wanting to promote his ideas further, he wrote about the necessity 'for public school men to have sound bodies and sound ideas and to be leaders of the nation'. He went on: 'I have a very poor opinion of the slopper, as they call him in the backwoods, that is the town-bred loafer who can only slouch about sucking a cigarette and looking on at

football matches. He is the waster who becomes unemployed and unemployable.' Baden-Powell said that he had set up scouting to help these boys, and 'a tremendous lot of these lads are now taking to it and changing into good, useful Britons'. He urged Cliftonians not merely to join the Scouts but to lead and encourage them whenever they could.

The 47th Bristol, Clifton College, Scout Troop, probably the first school troop, was formed in February 1912 by Norton Matthews, then Headmaster of The Preparatory School, with Mr Bull as Scoutmaster, assisted by R.W.J. Pavey, who was running a local troop and had considerable experience of scouting. Pavey, a friend of Baden-Powell, was appointed to the Pre staff in April, and his keenness and enthusiasm kept scouting flourishing at Clifton for many years.

Pavey started as he meant to go on by organizing a camp at the end of his first term at the Pre. The camp, at St Malo in July 1912, was the first time a group of scouts camped in France. They had a tremendous welcome, and *The Times* devoted a whole column to the event. In 1917 a Wolf Cub branch was founded, and the troop became a pack because the boys were then aged 11 and under. Ten years later Martin Hardcastle started a scout troop in the Junior School (11- to 14-year-olds), and in 1930 a Rover Scout crew was formed.

The moral effect of scouting was described in *The Cliftonian* of December 1930 as an antidote 'against the spirit of sniffiness which descends upon the schoolboy at about the age of twelve and in some cases never leaves him; every game and pastime which cannot be catalogued as a sport or as a social accomplishment is childish'.

The Pre camp of 1912

As this is the jubilee year of scouting, it may interest Cliftonians to recall the Pre camp of 1912.

The troop had been started by H.N. Matthews in February of that year, and early in the summer term it was decided to camp in France. It was my first term as an assistant master, and Matthews suggested that I should go to St Malo to find out if a suitable site was available in the neighbourhood. I had spent a couple of summers in St Servan, and I wrote to a M. Pallott, the proprietor of the boarding house, to know if he could help. He very kindly offered to meet me at St Malo and make a tour of possible sites. I duly met M. Pallott and discovered that he had no idea what a camp site was, but he suggested we go to Dinard to see the mayor. We saw the most impossible sites, and I was about to give up when the mayor took us to a proposed building site. It was a field overgrown with brambles and bushes, but the mayor promised to have these cut down and water laid on, and I accepted gratefully.

Matthews immediately got in touch with some high-up official of the LSW Railways and arranged about the crossing: the GWR at Clifton Down promised a through carriage and luggage van to Southampton Dock; a warm welcome was extended from Les Eclaireurs; the French MP for St Malo, M. Geurnier, and the British vice-consul took up the matter with great interest. It was the first occasion on which scouts had camped in France.

Naturally, there was keen excitement among the boys. Between twenty and thirty put their names down. Besides H.N. Matthews, H.A. Butt and myself, E.I.A. Phillips offered

to come as chaplain and Sergeant Bull was sworn as cook. Mrs Matthews was also among the party.

At last the great day came. We marched from the Pre to the station headed by our Union Jack (a present from W.S. Paul OC) and found our carriage waiting and the tents and luggage already loaded up.

By the time we arrived at Salisbury, it was evident that we should miss the boat unless something was done, as the train was over an hour late. Matthews did some hectic telegraphing, and we hoped for the best. As we steamed into Southampton West Station we saw there were hundreds of scouts on the platform. The station master came hurrying towards our carriage and explained that they were the Southampton scouts come to see us off and that a special train was ready to take us alongside the boat, which was being kept back until we arrived. It was a wonderful send-off in spite of the rain, which commenced to fall, and the boat steamed away to the accompaniment of a bugle band and cheers. Then it was discovered that, until Matthews telegraphed from Salisbury, the purser had forgotten that we were coming and the boat was already full. However, the stewards very nobly gave up their accommodation and all was well.

We arrived at St Malo early on Sunday morning to find a great welcome. Every ship in the harbour was decorated, and flags were flying from all the buildings. The harbour master and head of customs came on board and told us that our luggage would be cleared before the other passengers and that a launch was waiting to take us to Dinard. Here the

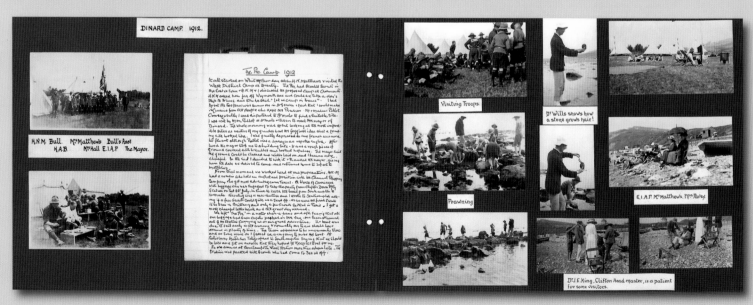

DINARD CAMP. 1912.

H.N.M. Bull. Mc Matthew's Bull's Asst
H.A.B Mc Hall E.I.A.P. The Mayor.

Visiting Troops.

Dr Wills shows how a stone grows hair!

Prawning

E.I.A.P. Mc Matthew's Mrs Paley.

Dr J.E.King, Clifton Head master, is a patient for some visitors.

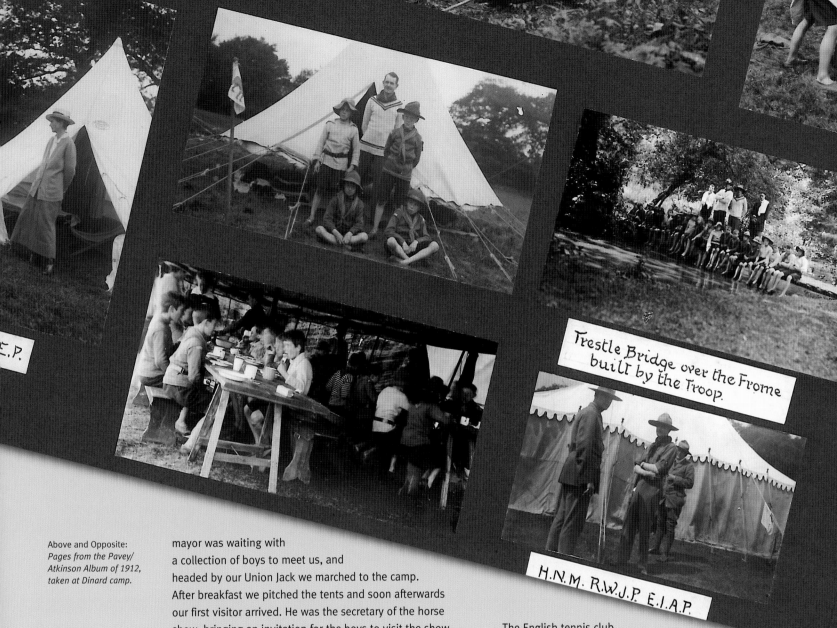

Trestle Bridge over the Frome built by the Troop.

H.N.M. R.W.J.P. E.I.A.P.

E.P.

Above and Opposite:
Pages from the Pavey/
Atkinson Album of 1912,
taken at Dinard camp.

mayor was waiting with
a collection of boys to meet us, and
headed by our Union Jack we marched to the camp.
After breakfast we pitched the tents and soon afterwards
our first visitor arrived. He was the secretary of the horse
show, bringing an invitation for the boys to visit the show
that afternoon. This we joyfully accepted and when we
arrived at the gate we were asked to wait until a certain
event had finished. Then we were invited to march in with
our flag and were escorted round the arena. The band
played 'God Save the King' and the spectators rose in their
welcome. It was rather an embarrassing moment. A grand
stand was set aside for the boys' use, and unfortunately it
collapsed during the afternoon. As far as I can remember,
only S.H. Steadman received any injury, which naturally
spoiled the rest of his camp. We were overwhelmed with
offers of help and hospitality.

The mayor provided an assistant cook for John Bull,
and it was amusing to watch their efforts at conversation.
The new cook could not speak English and Bull knew no
French. The mayor also introduced Matthews to the
provision shops, which were instructed to put everything
down on the mayor's account. He supplied every boy with
a straw palliasse, and there were visions of a mighty bill at
the end of camp.

The English tennis club
invited the camp to tea and to watch the
tournament, but the most exciting invitation came from a
Russian princess who was staying in Dinard. She sent her
major-domo with the request that Matthews should call on
her as she wished to take the boys for a motor drive.
Matthews explained to her that we were rather a large
party, but she replied that she had ten motor cars! So on
Wednesday the camp was taken up the river to Dinard for
tea and then driven back to camp in her ten motor cars.

There were few opportunities for scouting during the
camp, but as a holiday it was an enormous success,
entirely due to the enthusiasm of the mayor. Our visit must
have cost him a considerable amount as the bill he handed
to Matthews on departure came to about £16. The return
journey was uneventful, but the memory of that first camp
lingered for many months and I often look back and marvel
at Matthews's courage and enterprise.

R.W.J. Pavey for *The Cliftonian*
July 1957

43

It goes on to say that with the advent of the rover crew, 'many of the barriers of social reserve have collapsed and now we see day boys and boarders of every House mixing freely to an extent never before possible'.

Scouting at Clifton continued well after the war, by which time young people were being offered so many different choices of activity and adventure that scouting had to adapt, and many school troops and packs closed. At Clifton memorable times were provided by many years of scouting and by its cousins the OTC/CCF and 'night ops'.

R.S. Trafford
Headmaster, The Pre, 1983–93

CHILDHOOD MEMORIES OF CLIFTON

My father became Housemaster of Poole's after his marriage. I don't remember much about those early years, but I do know about the monkey incident. A new polar bear pit had been built at Bristol Zoo, which was next door and just across from our nursery window. This had involved moving a colony of monkeys, and, of course, some got away and roamed all over the place. Early one morning there was a tentative knock on my parents' bedroom door, and a small voice said, 'Sir, please Sir, there's a monkey in the dorm'. And so there was. We were taken to see it, swinging happily along the high rafters and eating a tube of toothpaste filched from the long line of bowls and jugs down the middle of the dormitory. A rather grumpy keeper arrived with a net, and we were glad to see he got bitten by his captive.

I remember, too, that we put up for the night a man who lectured at great length on his many exploits with big game in Africa. He came down for breakfast and said: 'I had the most vivid dream last night after my lecture. Could swear I heard lions roaring. They even woke me up.' My father politely informed him that they were real lions, and it was feeding day at the Zoo today.

I must have been around eight years old when we moved to School House. It seems that things had got a bit out of hand with the current elderly Housemaster, and they needed someone a bit tougher. School House was part of the earliest build, and comfort was not considered necessary for the boys. Cramped little studies were a splendid playground for us in the holidays, but the best game as far as I was concerned was to get a friend round, put on our swimsuits, take our bicycles down to the cellars and turn on all the showers to hot. Then we would ride round and round. We got into trouble for that when we were caught.

Bombs

During the summer of 1940 shelters with three-tiered bunks were constructed, and when term recommenced fire parties were organized. By November 1940 the blitz was being directed on to provincial cities and towns, and 2 December saw a heavy raid over Bristol, during which the area around the School was damaged. All Saints' Church was set alight, and several incendiaries were extinguished in school buildings and Houses. The Preparatory School was saved by a vigilant fire party, but one large bomb fell in New Field between Wiseman's and Polack's shelters, destroying the fives and squash courts and causing considerable damage to Polack's. Another bomb rendered Wiseman's uninhabitable, and another fell opposite Matthews'.

Boys in Wiseman's and Polack's were sent home immediately as they had nowhere to live, and boys began to be withdrawn from the other Houses. Town boys kept going until the end of term, but by then the College Council had decided that because the risk to life was so great it was necessary to evacuate the school and that it would be impossible to run school 'normally'. Parents were refusing to send their sons back, so Clifton 'at Clifton' was beginning to look economically unviable.

The War Office agreed to release some hotels commandeered at Bude in exchange for the Clifton buildings, and day boys from the Upper School were invited to go as boarders. Prep School boarders went to Butcombe Court, 12 miles outside Bristol, and a small number of day boys had lessons in Matthews'. They were all that was left at Clifton. R.K.G. Mackewan (MH 1937–1942) was one of those remaining pupils and remembers 'H.D. (Gilly) Gawne as masterminding the CC 'homefront.' Staff and pupils succeeded in keeping the College flag flying in incredibly difficult circumstances'.

In those days each House did its own catering, and there was an allowance for this, so the food was variable. I always heard that it was good at School House, largely thanks to my mother, who had to run quite an establishment for around 50 boys. On the 'private' side there was a nanny and a nursery maid, a parlour maid and two housemaids. The 'school' side had a steward and two boys (called 'jo boys'), a cook and several kitchen maids, as well as a whole horde of girls from rural Wales, who were always coming and going, to clean the dormitories and all the rest of the boys' side. They were instructed by the House matron, who was a powerful figure. I think that Peter Brook, the House tutor, lived out, but I'm not sure.

I have to mention Douglas Fox here. His history and huge talent are well known, but I have two vivid memories from my childhood. One is of cycling from Canynge Road to College Road behind this rather terrifying apparition, gown billowing in the wind, pursuing an erratic course on a huge, old-fashioned bicycle, a bag of music and the left-hand handlebar in his only hand. And then I remember seeing his left hand: it was very big, and his reach on the keyboard nearly compensated for his not having the other. But in Chapel, when he produced such stunning music on the organ, there was always a rather nervous music scholar there beside him to turn the pages and add occasionally a bit of right hand if absolutely necessary. Masters' families had a small corner in the Chapel, with a separate entrance for a quick exit. We got a splendid view of everything.

Things changed when there was a new Headmaster. In fact, it was a great shock to the staff, who were living a sort of 1918 life. Bertrand Hallward was most irritatingly young, energetic, good looking and full of ideas. It was muttered that he went running with the prefects. I made good friends with his third daughter and often went to play at his house. They had a pianola. Oh joy!

It was not long after this that the war began to get serious. The Zoo released what animals and birds they could, and we were told that in case of a direct hit in an air raid the lion keepers were armed. I do remember camping out one night in School House garden with a morose-looking raven, which didn't know how to feed itself. Sirens soon started going most nights, and we children were put to bed down in the deepest cellars. I remember being utterly terrified that there would be a direct hit, and we would be buried. Our afternoon

walks with the baby and the pram took us past houses in the Clifton vicinity that were smoking ruins.

My father said in his memoirs that in really bad raids he went round the House to make sure that everyone had taken shelter. More than once he had to tell Grace the parlour maid to stop going to the bedrooms to put hot-water bottles in the beds. And one morning he met a man wearing pyjamas and a dressing gown in School House garden. His face seemed to be vaguely familiar, and before my father could say anything, he said with some embarrassment: 'I had better introduce myself. My name is Adrian Boult, and I am conducting the BBC Symphony Orchestra lunchtime concerts in Bristol. I am staying with Douglas Fox, and as there were a good many bombs two nights ago, he said he was sure you would not mind if I slept last night in your basement.' Of course, he was more than welcome to do so.

Peter Brook, who was House tutor and chaplain, took senior boys fire-fighting on the Chapel roof and around the school buildings. I'm sure I saw them with tin chamber pots on their heads for protection, but maybe this was just fun. They did a great job, and probably saved the Chapel.

The trouble was that apparently the Germans saw the playing fields and thought it was Filton airfield, so they targeted us. There was some very serious damage done, and it was a miracle that nobody was killed. A bomb fell on the fives courts with such force that an iron girder flew over my grandparents' house in Canynge Road and landed in their garden. Wiseman's and Polack's were damaged, but mercifully the boys, who were in brick-built

Top right: *June Goodenough (née Mackintosh) and her dog, Vicky, at Bude with Westcliff in the background, 1941.*

Below: *The squash courts were bombed in 1940.*

Right: *Sports teams at Bude, 1944.*

Below: *Water skiing on a door!*

Below right: *R.A. Iles (Pre, ST, 1934–44).*

Below far right : *A gym display at Bude, 1944.*

overground shelters very close at hand, survived. No parents were going to send their boys back to that, of course, so what was to be done? The zingy new Headmaster was up to that, and I am sure it was entirely due to his effort contacting high-powered Old Cliftonians at the War Office that they found some rather bored soldiers stuck away in Cornwall, and he was able to work an exchange. Instead of finding ourselves in some mansion or mental hospital miles away up some valley, we ended up in the marvellous surroundings of Bude. Later in the war, when America came in, they took over the school buildings, and General Bradley sat at my father's desk in School House and started planning D-Day.

J. Goodenough (née Mackintosh)

BUDE REMEMBERED

I went to Clifton in 1940, the first year of the Second World War, as it was thought to be remote from the threat of bombing by the Luftwaffe. In the event, I spent half a term in Bristol before we were bombed out, and the remainder of my Clifton days were spent at Bude.

Others have described how the decision was made to move the school to Bude. When, at the end of a wearisome train journey, we arrived in the dark, we carried our overnight bags the half mile or so to our respective hotels. My House, School House, was on the second floor of the Westcliff Hotel at the end of a row overlooking the bay, Budehaven.

We found ourselves in a hotel bedroom with eight steel-framed beds, mounted in pairs, one above the other, and lashed to wooden posts. For supper we were directed out of the back of the hotel to the Beach Café, where long trestle tables, served by trolleys, had been set up. The arrangements for putting food on the tables for each boy took shape, and though it took a few weeks for the system to settle down I do not remember ever going hungry.

On the next morning, after prayers in the Beach Café, we were addressed by the Headmaster and the

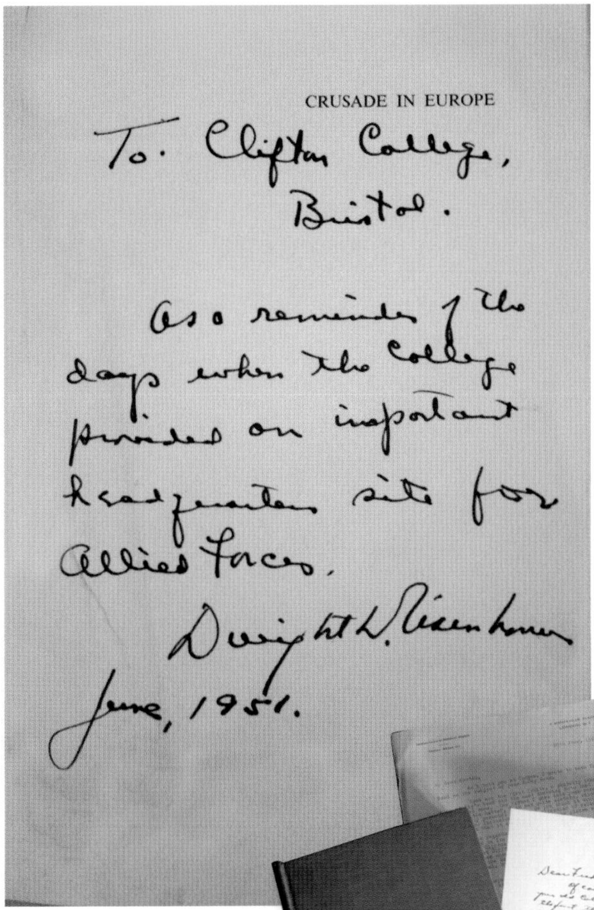

CRUSADE IN EUROPE

To: Clifton College, Bristol.

As a reminder of the days when the College provided an important headquarters site for Allied Forces.

Dwight D. Eisenhower

June, 1951.

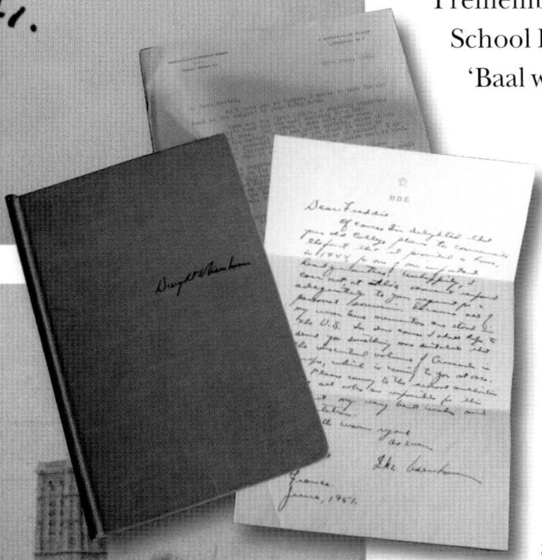

Right: *Dwight Eisenhower presented his book* Crusade in Europe *(1948) in response to a letter from his Deputy Chief of Staff, Lt Gen. Sir Frederick Morgan (BH, 1907–11) who was assisting Martin Hardcastle in his quest for an archive of D-Day memorabilia.*

Below: *A barrage balloon, The Close, September 1940.*

arrangements for daily life outlined. The biggest change was that all classes doing science had to share science laboratories with a local school, and the classes started at 4.30 pm.

We soon settled down to the daily routine. The ground floors of the hotels occupied by the School provided most of the classrooms. The sick room shared premises in one hotel with the Headmaster and his family, and the music staff were able to teach in small rooms in a couple of the hotels. Some of the teachers visited just once a week, and music lessons were taken during classroom hours. The head of music, Dr Douglas Fox, a truly brilliant musician, quickly got the school orchestra and the Choral Society going. Because there was not a great deal else to do in leisure hours, the Choral Society eventually included over half the school. The works performed by the orchestra and the society were hugely ambitious, including symphonies, piano concertos and many major choral works.

I remember the most unlikely boys returning to School House after evening choral practice singing 'Baal we cry for thee' from Mendelssohn's *Elijah*.

During the winters at Bude, we suffered the vagaries of the North Atlantic weather, and we frequently had to move from one room to another lashed by gale force winds and rain. During the summer term, in contrast, we were reminded that Bude had been a popular holiday resort with hugely attractive beaches. However, the boys were forbidden to bathe in the sea without a master's supervision. Instead, we were able to use a sea-filled pool, and swimming competitions took place there.

We played rugby football on more or less flat fields a mile or two along the coast from Bude, and we cycled there. The lines were not marked with whitewash but by digging out small spits of turf along the touchlines and so on, and the game could not begin until all the sheep droppings had been removed by hand. Games were compulsory for all boys, and the House competitions were fiercely contested.

Cricket was played on a flat municipal ground not far from the School, but because it was too small for several cricket games, the school was set the task of digging out one of the banks to extend the boundaries on one side, an activity known to the boys as 'aggers' – that is, it was a sort of agriculture! It was deeply unpopular and largely ineffective but no doubt kept us occupied on days when we were not playing games. Boxing took place in the Beach Café, and athletics happened on the cricket field. The Long Pen was run in the roads round Bude each year.

Sunday Chapel took place in a delightful old church in the village of Poughill, about 1½ miles (2.4km) inland from Bude, and the walk there and back for the whole School was quite an event. Visiting preachers were invited. The school choir led the service, and many boys will have felt the breath of spiritual awareness in that little church. Occasionally, when it was wet, the Sunday service would be held in one of the Free Churches in Bude itself. A mid-week service was also held from time to time in another of the churches. There were confirmation classes every year, and they were held in the cricket pavilion, which is where the communion services were held before breakfast.

Our schooling at Bude was a mixture of improvisation, cooperation, determination and sheer genius. None of us was, I think, conscious of a serious interruption in our formal education. Indeed, the change in our environment acted as a positive stimulus for a change of attitudes, and many of the less desirable features of life in Bristol were left behind, never to be resurrected. Despite the absence of some staff on war service, the School's academic record during the Bude years was outstanding, and in one year Cliftonians won more scholarships to Oxford and Cambridge than any other school in Britain.

During the summer we were encouraged to ride our bikes around the local countryside, something that could not have been more different from the restrictive attitude that I found when I first joined School House in Bristol. Yes, there were accidents on the road – some of them serious – but nobody seemed to regard these as a proper reason for restricting the use of our bicycles at weekends.

My abiding memory is of a first-class education in surroundings as far removed from the academic environment of Clifton at Bristol as could be imagined. To the staff and the people of Bude we owe a huge debt of gratitude.

Lord Jenkin of Roding (C.P.F. Jenkin)
SH, 1940–44

AFTER BUDE: FRIENDS

Bliss, oh bliss! Having spent four years at Bude, I was ecstatic when we returned to Clifton. What a luxury it was to have our own study! Lifelong friendships are created at school, and I shared a study for three years with David 'Ginger' Swift and Gary Zimmerman, Clifton's answer to cricketer Anil Kumble. In those postwar days some parents used to send food parcels to supplement our meagre rations. Swift's usually arrived in tatters, whereas Zim's came by freight train.

It was and is all about friends. Friends made while playing in sports teams and those made in class, sharing

Bottom left: *At the time of the Battle of Britain not everyone could fight, so a Clifton harvesting camp was held at Stow-on-the-Wold, Gloucestershire, in August 1940.*

From Brown's House Book

Easter Term 1945

We have now completed our thirteenth and last term at Bude. We will take back to Bristol a healthy, out-of-doors atmosphere: a friendly atmosphere between Houses as between ourselves; an atmosphere of enterprise and wide-awakeness.

Our last term down here has been an enjoyable one in spite of a widespread 'flu epidemic and the weather, which has been unfavourable for Colts rugger and hockey. A spell of snow, a rare occurrence at Bude, was taken full advantage of by almost everyone. Whilst tobogganing was in full swing the Cornish hills were regarded with feelings far removed from those experienced when we had to cycle out to the Widemouth rugger fields. This ability to occupy one's spare time with some pastime, whatever the weather may be, has been well cultivated whilst down at Bude. Such an ability is a most valuable quality in members of a house or school.

When we return to Clifton our memories of Bude ought not to be entirely pleasant. We must remember that the howling westerly gale raged more often than the summer sun shone. We must remember the enormous inconveniences endured by everyone – especially by masters and others in charge of school affairs.

success and failure. Douglas Bird, cricket captain and quintessential Englishman, could never pronounce the German 'ch' sound, much to the annoyance of Mr Yandell. It was alleged that young Bird excavated a tunnel to the local girls' school for clandestine meetings with his paramour. Johnny Cooper, the all-round sportsman, didn't need a tunnel. He flaunted his conquests openly, much to the envy of the rest of us. 'Rat' Turner and Doug Moorhouse were the *bons viveurs* of our world.

Naturally, masters featured prominently in our life, none more so than the inspirational Guido Lageard, the debonair House tutor, who wove the magic spell of French and Spanish literature over us.

My favourite memory of A.I. Polack, our esteemed Housemaster, centred round him snooping on dormitories to check on any skulduggery. If we caught him prowling he would claim he was 'just looking for the missing cat'.

M. Leek
PH, 1944–49

SPIRIT AND GARGOYLES

The Clifton I encountered in 1960 certainly contained a spirit, an inspiration that derived from Bertrand Hallward, Desmond Lee and Nicholas Hammond, all three former dons who were outstanding Headmasters during the 1940s and 1950s and who, in turn, would have embraced ideals set in the late 19th century by Dr Percival and Canon Wilson, our first two Headmasters.

In 1876, only 14 years after opening, Clifton successfully applied for a Royal Charter, and credit for the School's rapid rise must go to John Percival. Percival regarded the Chapel as the spiritual heart of the School, and its near neighbour the library, which he bequeathed to the School, he saw as an adjunct to the Chapel. He may well have been a chilly autocrat and austere slave-driver, who deplored 'loafing' or 'law tawn' (his Cumberland version of low tone) in his Sunday sermons, but buried inside him was a tender heart.

The outstanding and diverse personalities I encountered in 1960 certainly seemed to owe something to the fine values set by Percival and his successors. Above all, Clifton at its best was not afflicted by any sense of class superiority; there was no sense of 'side'. The highest academic standards were demanded in the classroom, and any tendency to be too games-orientated was fiercely opposed by the scholarly members of common room. Martin Hardcastle had

done much to encourage outward bound activities, such as climbing, potholing and 'night ops', in addition to his sterling work for the Nautical School at Portishead (an approved school). Rev. Peter Brook, with his practical Christianity, his concern for prison welfare and his work as a city councillor – he had pioneered holiday camps for the deprived Southmead area before the war – made sure that the School was aware of local problems. This sense of service to the wider community surely replicated Dr Percival's concern for the poor in the St Agnes area of Bristol and his founding work at Bristol University and at Clifton High School for Girls.

Coming from lowly rural origins, Percival had a natural sympathy with the socially less fortunate that was to be one of Clifton's guiding lights. He was particularly keen on the notion that day boys should not be regarded as inferior to boarders. Clifton led the way in building a proper Science School at a time when classical education prevailed, and music, both instrumental and choral, played a dominant part in school life. The founding of Polack's House, at a time when other schools had a strict quota system for the admission of Jews, is another example of Percival's radical and highly innovative policies.

Bertrand Hallward's greatest achievement as Headmaster was in masterminding the School's evacuation to Bude, where not only was a magnificent academic record achieved, but there was a healthy blowing away of cobwebs in the sense that members of different Houses talked to each other for the first time. Desmond Lee, whose reign as Headmaster was comparatively short (1948–54), was notable for excellent staff appointments and the maintenance of the fine academic record achieved at Bude.

Despite his severe demeanour, Percival did not go for the conventional or conservative in his appointments. It is said that T.E. Brown danced jigs and sang Manx songs when dining with the Percivals after his appointment. Graham Dakyns was known as 'the heroic hurler of dictionaries' from his practice of throwing a Greek lexicon at the heads of inattentive pupils in class. Exasperated by one dullard, he went down on his knees and offered up the prayer: 'Would you were under the green sod and that I was dancing a can-can on your grave.' George Wollaston, the first Housemaster of North Town, allowed boys to call him 'Old Bear' but punished delinquents by locking them in a cupboard. Sir Henry Newbolt spotted that Wollaston was a dedicated teacher and inculcated in his pupils 'a love of books, poetry, pictures, music, travel – every taste that makes life delectable'. Echoes of Wollaston can perhaps be found in Ben Ridler's tribute to his old Housemaster, Harry Edwards (1946–67):

I certainly owe in part to Harry a great belief in the good things of life. A particularly fine Brie springs to mind, reverently transported by Harry to Sir Sydney Barratt's sumptuous table. When the command came, after some glasses of wine, to perform a newly learned Mozart aria, it was not to be refused; but I can now see the carpet of that elegant drawing-room spinning past my head more vividly than I can hear the music I sang.

John Barratt captures the essence of Michael Lane (1947–82):

Boys quickly found that in his manner, in which the saltiness of the quarterdeck mingled with the Delphic mien of an oriental mystic, concealed not only the wisest but also the kindest of counsellors and one who naturally understood them. In argument he often resembled a well-educated highwayman. When at a masters' meeting an eloquent master began his side of the disputation by saying, 'I entirely disagree with you, Michael', 'Good, I rather hoped you would', came the growling, gravelly reply.

No mention of eccentrics would be complete without reference to one of Clifton's finest Fifth Form masters, H.J. Crawfurd (1946–66). He was known for his 'clinics', which were cramming sessions held before breakfast in the frenzied days before O levels. During the Second World War he was seconded to run a dried goats' meat factory in India because the army had apparently confused his name with that of a master-butcher named Crawford. Eventually the dried goats' meat went bad, and a court of enquiry was convened. Hillary's sharp and scholarly mind had little difficulty in clearing himself from a charge of incompetence.

A rather inexperienced master encountered problems with his history set, who had turned their chairs to face the back of the classroom and had interlaced twine between the desks so that there was no access down the aisles. The master was forced to teach the lesson from the back of the class, and when he asked Hillary what he would have done in similar circumstances, Hillary replied: 'I would have had serious second thoughts about my choice of profession.' Early in the autumn term of 1966 Hillary was caught speeding at Temple Cloud. Shortly afterwards he died. Some weeks later a policeman called at No. 4 College Fields: 'Mr Hillary John Crawfurd, Sir?' 'No!' replied the monosyllabic Y.P. Lidell (nicknamed the Yak). 'Then could you put me in touch with him?' asked the constable. 'That presents certain difficulties,' replied Lidell.

Rodney Gee served for 40 years on the staff and lived to be 100. He was awarded the MC during the First World War and was taken prisoner by the Germans when he rejoined the Durhams in 1940. He was a fine cricketer and made centuries on The Close, which he graced until he was nearly 70. He gained a First at Cambridge and was Housemaster of Dakyns' before the war, taking over Watson's when he returned from the war. He had a salty sense of humour and can be heard on the centenary record talking to his English set about injecting prunes with gin.

In Winchester College there is a gargoyle (possibly unique among public schools) of Martin Scott, a former head of History at Clifton, who later became Winchester's Housemaster in charge of scholars and second master. John Thorn, one of Lee's star appointments, who later became Headmaster of Repton and Winchester, described Scott's unlikely role as master in charge of swimming: 'He was adamant that the post required no physical exertion, wet or dry, except for the throwing of a timely lifebelt and the blowing of occasional whistles.' Swimmers had galas in those days, which Martin controlled with an iron but dry, hand, sorting out disputes with grunts of approval or disapproval. The swimming flourished and the swimmers were lucky in their benign leader, but as Thorn dryly notes: 'It was not very professional.'

The multifarious nature of individuals renders it impossible to define a typical Clifton product, which might imply that Cliftonians might be some sort of outward and visible sign of an established ethos. I hope these few disparate gargoyles will serve instead.

T.W.C. Gover
Staff, 1960–2001

Living

4

Opposite: *The Belltower and clock today, at Commem.*

Right: *The Belltower and clock as depicted in a 1898 book of etchings by Edward J. Burrow.*

THE BELLTOWER

What defines a school? To those who built Clifton a school was meant to draw on the ancient and lasting monastic tradition of collegiate learning. When the Chapel was enlarged in 1911, among the carved wooden figures ranged in the hexagonal lantern alongside those of Dr Percival and Dr Arnold were William of Wykeham, founder of Winchester, and Henry VI, founder of Eton. The founders built just three structures when the School opened in October 1862: a boarding house (School House) for the Headmaster and the pupils; a vast towering barn in which all teaching took place (Big School); and a belltower, shaped like a moon rocket, with a clock attached, to control all activity.

The sound of the bell links every Cliftonian back to that very first day. It is the essence of nostalgia because it is deeply lodged in the unconsciousness of every one whose lives it has structured. Those who return are at once, in a flash, borne back to their earlier selves and reminded of what once they were. The sound of the bell is nostalgia personified. That sound could be the sound of release, of freedom, of joy at the end of some dreary and pointless task; it could create panic as it demanded your presence, under punishment, half a mile away; and it could create confusion when rung unexpectedly or as a prank in the middle of the night.

Watches were unnecessary – indeed redundant – because it was the bell that defined the time, and it made one man the controller of the fate of all: the head porter who rang the bell. And that is a profound symbol of a deep truth: the world does not function at the whim of premiers or princes or headmasters, it functions because ordinary people do their job responsibly.

What makes Clifton special?

I suppose there are a thousand individual answers, each valid, to the question 'what makes Clifton special?' But taking a wide-ranging view of the great independent schools of the past 150 years, there is one striking feature of Clifton. The independent schools in Britain can be broadly divided into two categories: those that are boarding schools, and those that are day schools. The boarding schools are inevitably more expensive, and thus had a more exclusive clientele, though all without exception provided support for gifted children without funds and often from a wide geographical base. The day schools were often 16th or 17th century charitable foundations that served a specific local community.

But Clifton has never been either a boarding school or a day school: it has always been both. Among the founders of Clifton was a fashionable local doctor who was appalled by what had happened to his son at a traditional boarding school, but it was a time when none of the local Bristol grammar schools was in a healthy state. He wanted a school that would provide the best education obtainable for the sons of his Clifton contemporaries. When the School opened in October 1862, therefore, it had 60 pupils, 30 boarders and 30 day boys. And as the School's reputation grew and its numbers swelled, the proportion of day boys grew alongside the boarders. The ratio between the two has shifted slightly over the years, but there has never been a time, except briefly during the evacuation to Bude, when one group has dominated.

And this fact has had profound consequences for the way the school is run. Day houses and boarding houses are very different places, run in very different ways. The pupils in them each envy features of the others' existence, though secretly, of course, for each knows their own structure is best. The day houses keep the School grounded in practical reality and prevent the boarding houses from becoming arrogant and isolated. They make sure that the life of the School is continuously monitored by parents, which may be a pain for Housemasters, Headmasters and bursars but also gives them an understanding of how things are actually working, which is often quite different from what they think should be happening. They make sure that local old boys are constantly prowling around, always appalled at the way standards have slipped since their day, but also providing useful contacts in local commerce, industry and government, and frequent supporters of financial appeals.

The boarding houses are cosmopolitan, always in modern times with a substantial number of pupils from distant lands who bring cultural richness, international awareness and a savvy critique of what they are offered based on experience elsewhere. Sometimes it has been America, sometimes Poland, sometimes Iran, sometimes Hong Kong, sometimes Nigeria that has provided students that have inspired their contemporaries. And the boarding houses also have representatives from a wide spectrum of Britain. The majority have always been from the West Country, but

Below: *The minutes of the Council meeting of 3 February 1874, first mention the Grub Shop. Since then it has been an itinerant part of the school fitting in, at first, any shed available and later a basement. Pictured here: the 'Grubber' in the 1950s.*

Above: *The Grubber today.*

Do you Remember the Sixty Club?
The 1960s were heady times: assumptions, beliefs and attitudes were changing fast. In 1962 Clifton was in many ways a traditional school. There were no mid-term breaks, and there was Chapel every Sunday and Old Testament for an hour before Matins for every pupil. Lock-up was at 7.00 pm, and that meant what it said: you did not leave your House on any evening, including Saturday, after that time without specific permission. Uniform was worn at all times, and there was no 'casual dress'. Almost everyone had to play rugger in autumn, hockey in spring and cricket in summer. House matches were key events in the lives of all. The Combined Cadet Force (CCF) was compulsory. There were no television sets or music centres, and if you wanted to use the telephone you

Polack's House for many years provided the panache of London and Manchester business, and there have been long links with Ireland and Scotland, and, once the Severn Bridge was built, with Wales.

And that is why Clifton has been unique, as both boarding and day pupils learn daily from each other, support each other, laugh at each other, compete with each other and envy each other. Boarders smoke surreptitiously in the houses of day friends when their parents are away, safe from the marshal's beady eye. Day boys 'go to the cinema' on Saturday nights with parental leave and join boarders in pubs. The arrangement has made for a happy school, a school of rich variety, a school without obsessions, pomposity or pretension. It is a school that may not be the best at anything but that is good at everything, and second to none at most.

The car, of course, has changed things. The distinction between boarding and day slips when every other weekend the School shuts down and when half-term lasts a week. 'Weekly boarding' and mixed houses, where some are day and some boarders, both of which arrangements go back well into the 1980s, reflect the fact that the needs of pupils, and of parents, are complex and that the process of 'letting go', which once took place when pupils were eight, now happens at 18. And this gives Clifton a unique flexibility, an ability to adapt to individual need that is vital to educational success.

The Wills Family

In the 1870s the five Wills brothers attended Clifton and later supported the school. In 1909 H.H. Wills gave the organ for the newly enlarged Chapel. As a memorial to those OCs who had fallen in the war the large, Gothic-style house on the corner of College and Worcester Road was converted and presented to the school as a hospital, which was even equipped with an operating theatre. This became known as the New San, and a legacy from A.C. Austin OC (1956) enabled the School to purchase No. 2 Worcester Road next to the San. The Council decided that the two houses should be linked by an extension to form an enlarged and modernized Sanatorium, and the new acquisition was named Austin House. These remained in use until the facility was moved back to the Old San in 1988 and Worcester House became a girls' House. Part of this is now the Headmaster's house, and the Wills and Austin bequests continue to offer Cliftonians a wonderful view across The Close.

On the right is the Clifton card from the Wills cigarette card series of public schools. The Imperial Tobacco Company was created in 1901 through the amalgamation of 13 Bristol tobacco and cigarette companies, including that of W.D. & H.O. Wills, the leading manufacturers of the time.

queued at public telephone boxes. Few staff had cars, and the majority were resident in the immediate neighbourhood. Only pupils' surnames were used by staff. There were no women apart from wives and House matrons, although the High School was not far away.

And if that sounds like a restrictive, puritan hell, it was actually, for both staff and pupils, an extraordinarily vibrant and exciting place to be. There was a young and able common room, almost all from Oxbridge and many with Firsts, several with blues. It was led by men who had served in the war (often in the Intelligence Corps), who stood no nonsense and who, for the most part, welcomed those who for them must have seemed callow youths. In the exciting twin elections of 1964 a majority of the staff, I believe, voted for Harold Wilson and were inspired by 'the white heat of the technological revolution'. It was an age when limitless fusion power seemed just around the corner, as did superconductivity; when communications were revolutionized by the Telstar satellite; when there was the promise of computers the size of shoeboxes. (At the time they needed large air-conditioned rooms, and a university was lucky if it had one.)

It was in these conditions that the Sixty Club was founded in 1960. Membership was open to any member of staff and to senior pupils by invitation. It met three or four times a term in the evening at someone's house to discuss a paper presented by a member or an outsider. It was a traditional sort of intellectual club, the kind of thing that was familiar to many from university, and it had no purpose other than to provoke thought among both staff and pupils. The subjects were eclectic, no records as far as I am aware were kept, and no actions were taken, but attitudes were, I know, changed. It concerned itself with the issues of the day, with literature, politics, psychology and education.

For this was a time of ferment in education, as grammar schools and the 11+ exam were attacked, and the concept of all-in comprehensive schools was developed. The city of Bristol was in the lead in this process, forcing its many ancient and excellent grammar schools to become independent and hence a potential threat to Clifton, and building a ring of new schools on the edge of the city. Staff and pupils discussed a range of measures to liberalize the school, to end compulsion in many areas and, instead, to provide choice – in clothes, in games, in Chapel services, in the CCF, in the curriculum itself, which became much more complex and gave a much wider

range of opportunities. Efforts were made to involve pupils directly in decision-making, at first in the Houses through House councils, and then in the School with an elected School Council. American educational ideas were important in this process, and the long link with Milton Academy in Boston, which allowed the swapping of staff for a year and pupils for a term, was hugely fruitful for both parties. The two schools were similar in their structure, composition and academic standards, but they did everything totally differently, though the end product was more or less identical: a well-rounded, confident, articulate individual. A vivid illustration of the idea that there are a dozen ways to skin a cat. Alas! Student democracy never caught on at Clifton.

Clifton was at the cutting edge of educational change. Its science staff were revolutionizing science teaching by pioneering Nuffield science. Modern

Above: *Princess Elizabeth visits Clifton, March 1950.*

Left: *The visit of the Prince of Wales, 1974.*

Above: *Boys' study,*
c.1960.

of Thomas Malthus, there was a greater awareness of, and belief in, Christian chivalry and *noblesse oblige.* The role in society of those gifted with intelligence was to enable society to function effectively for the general good. Education was to fit men for the civil service, military service or ecclesiastical service or, perhaps the most significant form of service of all, to become themselves teachers in school or university. And those indeed were the roles that the vast majority of OCs achieved in the first century of the school's existence.

In 1963 the CCF was compulsory for every pupil and occupied the entire school for two hours every Monday afternoon. This situation had been created by the desperate needs of the First World War, reinforced by the Second, but it was already clearly dated. Britain's military role in the world was diminishing by the hour; even National Service was a thing of the past. There were no alternative activities.

January 1963 was the coldest month at Clifton since records had begun to be kept there in 1881, and February was the coldest since the dire winter of 1917. The freeze-up began on Boxing Day and lasted throughout the Easter term. Brown's House boys flooded their yard with water and played ice hockey daily for two months. The distribution of coal by large lorries from the Clifton Down coal yard was, for most dwellings, still vital to keep water hot and hearths burning. But because the roads were ice bound (this was before the days of gritters) the coal lorries could not get to homes on the steepest Clifton streets. By the end of January some homes had used their last shovelful of coal, and Clifton College was asked if it could help. The School had one transport vehicle, lovingly called the laundry van and used primarily by the Boat Club, but also by the sailors to get to Axbridge Reservoir, and for the theatre tour to Denmark with *A Man for All Seasons* (before there was a theatre, of course). So a small party of naval cadets – it was natural for the senior service to take control – was organized to drive to the coal yard (now a Sainsbury's), pick up sacks of coal (how were they paid for?) and, skilfully navigating the icy roads, deliver their precious cargo to desperate householders.

And this was the simple start of social service activities, which became Monday afternoon activities when the CCF became voluntary in 1968.

R.L. Bland
Staff, 1961–96

languages expanded beyond French and German and had their own language laboratory. The opening of the Redgrave Theatre (at a total cost of £60,000) in 1966 transformed drama, and English teaching became fully professional. For generations it had been one of a group of 'form' subjects, along with Latin, history, geography and religious education, taught by humanists. The transformation of morning Chapel from a rather boring hymn, reading, prayer, to a student-led theatrical event made national news, and much that was hugely innovative and dramatic was to result.

In the 1960s anything was possible, and everything was debated. A wave of transforming radical liberalism swept across Clifton and the land, and the Sixty Club was a key part of it. I don't know when it last met, and I don't know when the wave slipped back into the ocean of ideas, but they were heady days.

Social Service

I dare say it is now called 'outreach', but Clifton's commitment to serve the local community has long and deep roots. The ethos of the great 19th-century independent schools was that of service; it was based on a muscular Christianity, an understanding expressed vividly in the pope's title of *Servus servorum Dei* ('the servant of the servants of the Lord', for those whose Latin has slipped a bit). Although, perhaps influenced by the utilitarianism of Jeremy Bentham and the views

60 YEARS ON

On my first day at Clifton I arrived at Temple Meads Station and was transported by taxi to Wiseman's House. My trunk, which had travelled in the luggage van of the train, was delivered later the same day. Most boys arrived by train at that time, although some parents were able to drive them there.

Fresh from being a day boy at a preparatory school more than 100 miles away, I was a little scared, although I knew that it was not likely that I would be tossed in a blanket or roasted like the unfortunate young 'uns in *Tom Brown's Schooldays*. But I was welcomed by the Housemaster, 'Jock' Crawfurd, a man who had, as I realized in later life, an incredible empathy with boys. With a few well-chosen words in the weeks that followed he showed that he was keeping an eye on me and that everything would be all right. I am sure that things work in the same way nowadays.

But something has changed, and that is the living conditions. In the 1950s we slept in dormitories, with room only for a chair between the beds – the chair was used for placing clothes on at night. On Saturday evenings we would be issued with clean shirts, socks, pyjamas and underwear for the following week, and the clothes that we took off, and the sheets and towels that we had used, went into large laundry hampers to be sent off on the following Monday. Our shirts had separate collars with collar studs, and those who did not like to reach Saturday with seven days' grime on the white cotton had the option mid-week of doubling the collar over the other way. It would then show a hem around the edge, but at least it would be clean.

Hot water for baths was provided after games on three afternoons each week, Tuesdays, Thursdays and Saturdays. There was a big communal bathroom with six or seven baths in the basement of the House, and there was a row of showers too, but only cold showers were allowed, because hot ones took too much water. This may seem strange, but it should be remembered that except for the first to arrive in the bathroom after games, who might be lucky, it was normal to have two boys to a bath, and as soon as one got out, another would take his place, running in a little more hot water to reduce the increasingly soupy nature of what remained. This was economical. For the first week or two I was embarrassed by the sight of so much nudity and very shy because it was not what I was used to, so I found some excuse to delay my bath until the bathroom

was emptying, but in doing so I ran the risk of having only lukewarm water, and it was not long before I ceased to worry about my nakedness or anyone else's.

A promotional black-and-white film about Clifton that used to be shown at the time showed a scene with boys taking cold plunges in the morning, leaping into and out of a bath one after another, but I think that this was staged, because I can't remember anyone except for a few obsessional keep-fitters going in for this kind of thing, except maybe in a heat wave in summer.

The row of toilets that lay in the basement beyond the bathroom was monitored in the after-breakfast rush hour by a House Sixth, whose duty it was to hand out three sheets of hard, folded toilet paper to each boy as he came along, economy once again being the order of the day.

There were two boys to a study, except for the Head of House, and I can't remember that this created any problems, because we did not have a great number of possessions.

Main meals were organized in Big School, beginning with a breakfast of porridge with milk, a high-cholesterol fried dish, toast, marmalade and tea or coffee. Sugar was still rationed at the time, and it was the weekly duty of one of the House Sixths to collect a large biscuit tin containing the week's supply of sugar for the whole House, and then use a mug to divide it

Above: *Old School House exterior meets new Watson's House interior.*

Opposite: *Boys' study, c.1970.*

The conditions under which today's Cliftonians live have changed for the better. This is in accordance with the community's standards and expectations. But as far as I can tell the basic spirit of the School hasn't changed, in spite of technological advances and a more comfortable way of life.

An anonymous Old Cliftonian

BEST SCHOOL?

For me Clifton is not perhaps the 'best school of all', a debatable claim, but I can vouch for it being the best 'college' of all, using the word in the sense of a place of higher education in a collegiate setting, a mini-university in fact. In terms of offering its pupils (although I prefer the term college students) a broad and deep introduction to the humanities and, indeed, the sciences, Clifton College did a better job than the four universities I have attended so far, and that includes both Oxford and London (the others were Toronto and Tehran), not to mention a stint at Cambridge during National Service to learn Russian. This is even more true if the *mens sana in corpore sano* factor is included in the rating system.

I began my Clifton education in 1945 at the age of ten, after learning the three Rs at a village school in Devon, where a no-nonsense Yorkshire headmistress had begun the day with mental arithmetic, a good way to get the grey cells moving. We also learned English history and spelling from rhymes such as 'In fourteen hundred and ninety-two/Columbus sailed the ocean blue' and 'I before E, except after C'. She put me down for a scholarship exam for a place at Clifton, partly funded by the London Livery Company of Clothworkers, which was open to boys from West Country primary schools. I won my place, but the scholarship did not cover the total costs, which my mother, a country doctor with three young boys to support, could not afford. She wrote to Bertrand Hallward, then Headmaster, who generously arranged for the fees to be reduced, so off I went to Clifton as a boarder in the Pre.

Even at that age the curriculum was tough. We did not just do maths and English, but French, Latin, some Greek and lots of classical history, altogether rather like Shakespeare's education. My knowledge of when Columbus set sail was little help here, although I have once or twice impressed professional historians and philologists by referring to the invasion of the Jutes, which was to change the language of Britain for ever, as 'in the mid-fifth century, if I'm not mistaken' thanks to

with great care into about 60 portions, distributed among the individual jam jars that each boy had. On the other hand, there seemed to be an adequate supply of jam. Butter, too, was rationed, but there was a larger supply of margarine. I remember when I went over to Big School for afternoon tea that a good combination to quell hunger was a slice of bread spread liberally with margarine and then with jam, topped with a few slices of cheese. I don't want to suggest that we were underfed, but growing boys have enormous appetites.

Another Old Cliftonian once remarked to me that as a part of his legal training he had to visit a boys' reformatory institution or borstal, as they were called, and thought that the conditions under which we lived at school were not dissimilar. That may be true. I do not think that during my years at the School the living conditions had changed a great deal from what had been normal in the early 20th century or even the 19th century, except that we ate together in Big School instead of being dependent on the talents of the Housemaster's wife, which had been the practice in earlier times.

Miss Robinson's 'Hengist and Horsa, covered in brine/Landed in Thanet four forty-nine'. Trivial pursuits can prove useful.

When Hartnell's reopened I was moved there, having managed to annoy the Housemaster of Butcombe with some out-of-place humour, always my weak point. There I came under the wonderful Major Read, who in time made me his head boy. He had served in the Indian army and was addicted to backgammon, but had no one to play with, so he taught me the rules and strategy. Years later, in Iran, where the game began and is still hugely popular, this gave me a headstart. But my jokes and japes got me into trouble again, and in the summer of 1948 he moved me to the Upper School, largely, I suspect, to appoint my much more reliable friend Graham Rooth as head boy.

This meant that I spent only one term in the Fourth Form. That autumn, now in Dakyns', I became the youngest student in the Fifth Form, which was run by the remarkable 'Tubby' Merrick. He gave us a superb education in English and Latin, with Harry Edwards teaching us French, while German, advanced maths and some basic science were also on the menu. We all did well in the last year of the old School Cert. The whole class passed, in nine or ten subjects, mainly with credits or distinctions, before moving on to the new A levels. Many of my classmates were to achieve academic glory, including our late college president, Professor John Barron, who became a distinguished classical scholar and head of an Oxford college. Graham, my best friend, won a scholarship to Cambridge to study modern languages, but after graduating he decided to become a doctor, which with great difficulty he managed to do, finishing up as a highly regarded consultant psychiatrist. Both, I am sure, would give credit to Mr Merrick for their later achievements. Oxbridge, if we wanted it, was our oyster.

Classmates included my other best friend, Mark Harrison, a mathematics guru, who won the Long Pen in record time. At Oxford he switched to the obscure school of PPP, with one of the Ps standing for psychology and another, perhaps, for philosophy. As College Harry, he was famed as the only undergraduate who could outrun the proctor's bulldogs late at night, including once swimming across the Cherwell before climbing into his college. The multi-disciplinary Clifton background and a sceptical attitude to authority undoubtedly had something to do with his becoming the Arts Council's

chief contract administrator for the convoluted National Theatre project, and learning the cello at Clifton probably helped too. Christopher Fildes, who for two years pretty well wrote the entire *Cliftonian* himself under a series of noms de plumes, went on to become the wittiest British writer on economic matters, with a well-deserved OBE. All this was just one year of a single class.

Meanwhile, Clifton was not forgetting our healthy bodies. We played a lot of sport, and membership of the CCF was compulsory. We drilled in the quads and learned to read maps and plot routes on the Downs, useful skills when National Service was the next step for most of us. Dakyns' was a 'sporty' house, and our Head of House, Tom Penny, was also captain of cricket and rugby and Head of School. In the long summer evenings we played 'tip and run' or French cricket (with a stump as bat, a tennis ball and your legs as the wicket) on The Close. Not being much of a sportsman, I enjoyed trying to run out or bowl this great athlete, which he took in good part.

Above: *Boys on the way to their classes pass under the Memorial Arch, 1950s.*

Opposite: *The Grubber, in the basement of the Coulson Centre. This room became the temporary Worcester House Hall after the fire of 1995; it is now a design and technology classroom.*

Music and poetry played a large part in our education. Not only did we sing all the hymns in the Clifton hymnbook, but we also took part in the annual House Song competition. I can still sing from memory our ambitious efforts at 'Die beiden Grenadiere' and 'Erlkoenig', with words by Heine and Goethe, and music by Schumann and Schubert, respectively. And at weddings and funerals I often belt out more decibels than the rest of the congregation put together, unless there's another OC present. Grateful thanks to Douglas Fox for Clifton's wonderful musical tradition. Under maestro Merrick we had sailed through Chaucer's *Prologue to The Canterbury Tales* and a couple of Shakespeare plays, which I still know almost line by line. Half a century later *Richard II* proved useful during my five years in an Iranian jail, when I managed to recall almost all of the king's prison soliloquy, 'I have been studying how I may compare …'. Harry Edwards was House tutor at Dakyns', where he introduced senior boys to the opera, something I came to love, with his LPs. Our Housemaster, 'Yak' Lidell, also taught the older boys bridge, and we even got a glass of sherry during the rubbers.

Clifton has a reputation for acting, especially now with the Redgrave Theatre. Michael Redgrave himself and Trevor Howard (see Chapter 6) had both been in Dakyns' and visited regularly. More recently there has

been John Cleese. In the summer, IIb, the modern languages Sixth Form, used to put on a French play in the front quad.

I did French and German A levels, and although we read a great deal under Guido Lageard and Bernard Yandell it was a pity that they both taught us in English, not their native tongues. Language laboratories hadn't been invented, so despite a good knowledge of both literatures I could not then speak either language confidently. I left Clifton at the end of 1952, aged 17, and got a job in an Austrian hotel translating the menus and helping visitors who didn't know German. Six months later I was in the army, where the languages acquired at Clifton got me on to the Russian course at Cambridge, then into the Intelligence Corps as a Cold War interpreter.

With the end of empire and, indeed, of National Service, Clifton became less important as a training ground for service personnel, although when I last counted there were three admirals on our board of governors. It is also pleasing that the once-despised First World War commander-in-chief Douglas Haig has recently been rehabilitated by military historians as a great strategist.

Art was my weakest subject. Our tutor had a rugby trial for Scotland, but he was also a fine artist and was supportive of those with talent, such as my housemate Paul Banning, who later switched from being a prize-winning furniture designer to become a highly acclaimed landscape painter. But for hopeless cases like me he had no sympathy. He would set up, say, a bowl of flowers and tell us to draw it, in complete silence, while he retired to his studio to work on his own projects. On one occasion, when my first draft was even more of a failure than usual, I leaned across from my easel and quietly asked to borrow a friend's rubber. Out came our tutor, almost frothing at the mouth, to order the boy who had spoken to stand up. Following Clifton convention, I did so, quaking. I was brought forward and in front of the whole class beaten quite hard on the bottom, with whatever the manic artist had to hand. The pain soon wore off, and I won not a little street cred from my mates. He did nevertheless institute a scheme of loaning high-quality prints of paintings by mainly modern artists, so for a fortnight we could have a Monet or a Picasso to brighten up our dismal studies.

That was by no means the only beating I got from masters and prefects in the late 1940s, and I'm ashamed

Food

The US army had converted Big School into a dining room during the Second World War, and on the school's return from Bude it was decided to abandon 'House feeding' and adopt a communal dining system. Miss Thomas, the caterer at Bude, returned to Clifton with the school and coped resourcefully in difficult circumstances with poor facilities and rationing. She retired in 1958.

In 1953 the minutes of the School Food Committee noted: 'The question of fish for meals was raised. It was felt that on the days when fish was served it was desirable that larger helpings of it should be served. In opposition to this was the fact that wastage on fish days was enormous. Finally, it was agreed that the present helping was sufficient and on the whole satisfactory. If boys wanted more there was always an opportunity for "getting" seconds. It was also felt that fried fish would be preferable to smoked haddock for supper. Miss

Thomas said that she would have a fry when she had enough fat. More pork and liver was felt to be desirable, but Miss Thomas said that this matter was entirely out of her hands. She took what the butcher had to give her and this depended on the Ministry of Food. It was also thought that, at lunch, helpings should contain more meat and less potato. There was also a suggestion that high table were not getting enough to eat. This said, Miss Thomas was Mr Carter's (deputy hall warden) responsibility, and it was entirely his fault if high table starved. Mr Carter looked suitably chastened, and it was finally agreed that a dish of potato should be placed on high table for those who felt especially hungry. This, it was thought, was impracticable for the whole school because (a) there were not enough dishes and (b) by the time it had been placed on the table the potato would be stone cold.'

MINUTES OF THE SCHOOL FOOD COMMITTEE, 1953

Above: *After the return from Bude, the school ate together in Big School.*

Above: *Nicholas Hammond DSO, during his wartime service with the SOE in Greece.*

has been educated at a public school and served in the ranks of the British army is perfectly at home in a Third World prison.'

The two things I most wish for Clifton in the 21st century are a continuation of its high and wide intellectual standards, combined with sporting activity and other extra-curricular activities, not necessarily competitive, although that probably helps. One of my regrets is that when it was my daughter's time for secondary education she was the wrong sex for Clifton.

Last year, as a governor, I met for the first time some recent OCs, including several young women. The setting was the rather formidable House of Lords, but I noted their easy confidence, with no sign of shyness or arrogance. All seemed to be doing well in their various fields, even though in a couple of cases these had little to do with their formal studies. They were polite and friendly. They reminded me of Kipling's ideal:

If you can talk with crowds and keep your virtue
Or walk with Kings – nor lose the common touch

And I wouldn't mind betting that at least some of them could also 'fill the unforgiving minute with sixty seconds' worth of distance run'. If my evaluation is right, much or most of this must be because they were products of 'the best college of all.'

J.R.S. Cooper
Pre. DH, 1945–52

to say I later administered a few myself, although as House prefects we were restricted to the use of a gym shoe. Luckily, the parent of one boy, believed to be a psychiatrist and possibly my own absentee father, persuaded the Headmaster, then H.D.P. Lee, to end this system, much to the fury of the traditionalists.

None of the OCs mentioned here, or many others besides, would, I think, deny the major role that Clifton played in developing their character and potential or refute my theory that the School encouraged lateral thinking, contrarianism and out-of-the-box ideas, even while we learned the value of discipline and cooperative action. In my own case I'm quoted as saying on the day of my release from jail in Iran: 'Anyone who

THE 1950s

With 50 years of hindsight the dominating influence on the Clifton of my time must have been its then Headmaster, Nicholas Hammond, although to the average Cliftonian of his era this would probably have appeared an unlikely judgement. He was not a charismatic or dominating figure. Rather, he was a quiet, benign and authoritative influence over what was clearly a golden age for the academic achievements of the School. There was certainly a sense at Clifton in the late 1950s of Oxford and Cambridge being closer than their geographical distance would suggest. It was a notably academic and cultured institution.

Nick Hammond came to Clifton from Cambridge, where he had been senior tutor of Clare College. In its 2001 obituary *The Times* referred to the bright coterie of Cambridge scholars that Hammond drew to the School.

Two of those who taught me history were Martin Scott and John Thorn, the former progressing to become second master of Winchester and the latter following in his wake to become headmaster of the same school. John came from Corpus Christi and Martin from King's, as had Tom Wells, who taught us English. Tom was a double First and double blue – and an England rugby trialist at full back – who went on to be Headmaster of one of New Zealand's leading private schools.

As Nick Hammond swept with his flowing gown past Field Marshal Earl Haig and on towards morning Chapel with a firm step and tilted smile, the aura of the quadrangled world of Cambridge (at least for me) accompanied him. But he had been no mere occupant of the fields of academe. These were still postwar years, and many of us had whiled away our years at prep schools reading the wartime adventures of escapees and resistance heroes. What we at Clifton were not told was that our mild-mannered Headmaster was one of those men. Maybe those in authority over us knew little themselves. Why did the *Independent* on his death write 'warrior, sportsman, schoolmaster, long-distance walker … anything but the stereotype of the scholar'? Why 'warrior'?

Would we have reacted differently to his presence if we had known that he was the wartime Colonel Hammond who had been parachuted in the spring of 1943 into the inhospitable mountains of northern Greece under the auspices of SOE, charged with organizing acts of sabotage by the resistance against the occupying Germans? By the summer of 1944 he had become acting commander of the Allied Military Mission and had been awarded the DSO. After the war he received the Order of the Phoenix from the king of Greece. His book *Venture into Greece: With the Guerrillas 1943–4* was published in 1983, perhaps a little late to engender fans among the schoolboys of Clifton.

I must admit to possessing an ingrained Cambridge bias. I had been at King's College School, Cambridge, from where I was despatched to Clifton with a bursary, funded by the College, in 1955. Six months before arriving I knew nothing of Clifton – my brother was at Wellington, where my father had been – but I was delivered into the care of the suave Harry Edwards, not by chance another King's man who had also grown up in pre-war Cambridge. Harry had just taken over Watson's House, as rumour had it because no other master was prepared to face the challenge, its

reputation at the time being in such disrepute. Harry's elegant, burgundy-coloured Alvis sat in the Watson's yard, a statement of style (lifestyle, they would call it today). Harry was firm and fair and up to the challenge.

Theatre and music thrived. We played *The Crucible*, *Endgame* and Synge's *In the Shadow of the Glen* and were never out of the first two places in the House drama competition. Cambridge entrance in 1959 would be eased by a discussion of *Endgame*. House competition-winning producer of *The Crucible* was the urbane Waris Habibullah (later Hussein), who himself took the Cambridge theatrical world by storm before becoming the first and formative director of *Dr Who* and the first Indian to direct at the National Theatre. The theatre was supplemented by clandestine visits to the Tatler Cinema, Bristol's then home of art cinema, where Bergman's *The Seventh Seal* transformed our lives and no doubt a quick fag was inhaled. Fagging was, of course, another matter.

Focusing on life below the stairs (although I think they were actually housed in the attic), I do not know if Harry Edwards himself would have taken credit for the appointment of his German au pairs. But certainly one year they induced a Zuleika Dobson-like effect on almost all the inhabitants of Watson's. One was a brunette, and pretty enough, but the other was a blonde and heart-stopping to any adolescent. Her name to us was simply Elke, but I am slightly ashamed to have discovered some years later, while by chance reading a women's magazine, that she subsequently metamorphosed into the film star Elke Sommer. Miss Sommer spoke in the article of the fun she had had while being an au pair at a school in Bristol. Unfortunately, she had not had any of that fun with me, but many of us in Watson's at the time had their suspicions. These fell unanimously on Mike Johnson. The reason was that Mike came from the then colony of Kenya. He was always bronzed and self-confident and even then we knew what happened out there.

From Watson's the physical entrance to the School was, of course, through the Memorial Arch. The two world wars were the

Joys of being a Housemaster.

A. Paul. '57.

"You do approve of free love, I hope, Mr. Edwards?"

"But you don't let them have HOT water, surely!!"

When you say that, Mr. Edwards, do you mean you are a sort of 4th Day Adventist?"

"But in his report, I thought you said he was puerile and shallow minded?"

"Goodbye darling – now dear Mr. Edwards is going to show you round the whole school."

Above and opposite:
Cartoons in Watson's Maltese Cross, *by Anthony Paul, 1957.*

taste of scandal and the racing results as they sauntered through towards supper in Big School and with the middle bench bravado of jackets unbuttoned.

If our centre of loyalty was to our House, Big School was for us the focus of the School itself, where we became as one with our boarding colleagues. (The lives of the day boys never really impinged on us; they did not share the intimacies of our lives.) Most important events happened in Big School, under its high, aspiring ceiling and the gaze of former Headmasters. We experienced the sublime – the one-armed Dr Douglas Fox introducing his friend Dame Myra Hess for a Sunday evening concert – and the challengingly absurd – on Watson's tables O.J. Beament winning the hardboiled egg-eating contest with, I think, a never-to-be-equalled 22. There was also occasional absurdity outside, the fire escape playing its part on one occasion as a stage, with the assembled school below, for the satirical fireworks of an exuberant John Cleese (some day boys took the limelight).

The evident difference between Clifton and the other schools that our contemporaries and relatives attended was the unique contribution made by Polack's House. The Jewish intellectual, cultural and particularly musical contribution was disproportionate, engendering a respect that has lasted for life. It provided a bridge to London, bringing a metropolitan buzz to a more reticent West Country school.

It may have been the Polack's edge that drew Nick Hammond to Clifton. Whatever it was I was fortunate enough to do Sixth-Form essays under his critical eye, which no doubt had something to do with the fact that I went on to Clare College, not King's.

J.F. Platt
WaH, 1955–60

recent past to us rationed war babies. The First World War was only 40 years behind us – Captain Palmer, the bandmaster, recounted tales of regimental life in Ireland with the Black and Tans – and the Second War was only ten – many of our warrior fathers were not yet middle-aged. Remembrance Sunday was a major event, even daunting for us buglers lined up in front of Captain Palmer.

The Memorial Arch comes to mind, in the rain, on dark November evenings with Taffy the news vendor sheltering beneath it – diminutive and Welsh, with cloth cap and evening newspapers tucked under his arm, chirping 'pink un, green un' to the passing sporting sophisticates. The loucher older boarders were waylaid, on the cusp of their adult lives, with the

OUTSIDE THE CLASSROOM

All my best memories of Clifton are of activities and moments spent outside the classroom and often outside the School bounds. They are also closely linked to the bonding of friendships through discovery and adventure.

I was lucky enough to join School House in 1955 and to have Martin Hardcastle (Cassy) as my Housemaster. Cassy was a wonderful man, who inspired and enthused us all to search, to encounter and to enrich our young lives through a wide range of unusual activities. He organized the Venturers, potholing in the Mendips, trips to Steep Holm and the Farne Islands and, best of

Left: *Steep Holm, 12 May 1957. Standing, left to right: Ferryman, Mr Hardcastle, Baynes, Benson, Whitty, Mandeville, Ispahani, Lees. Sitting, left to right: two assistant ferryman, Chaston, Sibbald, Mr Lane, Parsons, Edwards.*

all, those exciting 'night ops'. Something akin to cops and robbers or MI5 versus the Gestapo, these night-time adventure games took us in groups of two or three, in disguise and on foot, by bike and by bus, over the Downs, the Suspension Bridge and parts of Bristol, with our hearts pounding lest we should 'get caught'.

Cassy was a central figure in the end of term House entertainment. On one occasion he chose me to play his lady companion-cum-servant (he himself playing an ageing spinster) in a sketch in which we exchanged flippancies ('have a Bismuth …'), while sitting in a conservatory overlooking the English Channel. I learned to knit for the part, maybe at his suggestion. These House entertainments helped us discover each other's aptitudes and talents. School House won the House art, the House singing competitions and the House play (at least twice) while I was there. I remember Douglas Fox and Mr Prentice as talented music teachers. I played second violin for the School orchestra but rarely had the time or inclination to practice, and so I was moved back a desk every year. I remember imitating the bow movements of the desk in front and trying to play as quietly and as unobtrusively as possible. There were School entertainments (with a magnificent John Cleese as Hitler haranguing the audience in the quad from Big School), School plays with staff participation, the Q Society cricket matches and the Film Society. (I nearly had a gruesome poster I designed for *The Fiends* censored by a prudish praepostor.) And there were the

Clifton Morris Men. Initiated and directed by Ian 'Act' Lindsay, we danced for House entertainments and Commem, practised in front of, and behind, Earl Haig and were invited to dance and sing for a week's tour in Austria, by a kind English professor, Dr Kapitan. I remember getting lost for 24 hours in Amstetten, drinking white wine while overlooking the Danube, getting turned out of our youth hostel beds early in the morning in Vienna and, like most of the group, having a crush on Maria, Dr Kapitan's lovely daughter.

I also remember singing the words to the School Song very loudly and with a broad grin, thinking 'this is perhaps a little exaggerated – but fun'. In retrospect, it was certainly the best out-of-school of all.

R. Lees
SH, 1955–60

'SECRET' PUBBING

Let's not beat about the bush: a great many of Clifton's boarders, certainly in the 1960s and 1970s, used to be illicit teenage 'regulars' in Bristol's numerous pubs, virtually all of which in those days were tied to the city's Courage Brewery.

It was hardly surprising at weekends, in a bland era when we boys had no television, no computers and no mobile phones to occupy us, could not socialize with girls and parental contact was still kept to a relative minimum. Even permission to wear casual clothes in Bristol was an innovation.

I was just one of many boys in Oakeley's who liked to seek out a few pints of Courage Full Brew as and when pocket money allowed, but I was anxious not to cause embarrassment to my widowed mother by being caught in the act, either by College staff or praepostors, let alone being subjected to severe disciplinary action. It was apparent from the periodic catches and punishment of my contemporaries that visits to many pubs incurred just such a 'real and present danger', particularly on certain days and at various times. 'High risk' in Clifton were notoriously the Coronation Tap, the Portcullis and the slightly more distant Port of Call on Blackboy Hill. All geographically obvious really. In town the Llandoger Trow or the Hatchet Inn were certainly dangerous territory, but if there was nothing likely to be of theatrical interest to College masters being performed at either the Bristol Hippodrome or the Old Vic, I might occasionally nip cautiously into the Bunch of Grapes in Denmark Street or up to the first-floor bar of the Naval Volunteer in King Street (which had a useful escape stair route to the rear).

A source of some irritation to my contemporaries (over the years 1969–71) was that I appeared to know

Below: Boys in the JCR, 1970s. This was situated in the present Health Centre.

of safer premises, of which I would never release details. This was entirely correct. So, belatedly, I now finally reveal that there was no way that any member of the Clifton staff was ever going to find me contentedly seated behind a pint at the diminutive (and basic) 17th century Seven Stars tavern, which was located in an alleyway just off St Thomas Street a few yards from Bristol Bridge, a tavern so appropriately well concealed within darkest Bristol that much of the evidence upon Bristol slave trading activity was discreetly gathered there in 1787 on behalf of William Wilberforce.

There, the secret's out, fellow OCs!

However, by the time we left Clifton in July 1971 growing trust had led to about a dozen of us responsible seniors (and the odd praepostor or two, including myself) having the confidence to party together regularly at the Adam and Eve in Hotwells. We were not caught, and my privileged knowledge of the whereabouts of the Severn Stars was hence rendered obsolete – until now disclosed!

N. Mitchell
Pre, OH, 1962–71

Left: *'Q' Society cricket, summer 1959. Baynes, Annett, Lees, Harrison, Allen, Williams.*

AMNESTY INTERNATIONAL

The year 1964 was a seminal one for many at Clifton. The Cold War was in full swing and the country had its first Labour government for 13 years, albeit with a wafer thin majority. The Conservatives had won the School mock election, but in Polack's the Liberals were the victors. The new Housemaster at Polack's, Ernest Polack, had come straight from the racist Republic of South Africa and, with his House tutor, became the School's only socialist team. Many saw Polack's as the most radically aware House for politics and cultural issues and thought there was a stronger left-wing emphasis than elsewhere in the School.

Indeed, Polack's itself underwent its most prolific and intense 'intellectual and political awakening' in 1964 with a new spirit matching the excitement of national politics and international focus on race issues. For the next five years racial tensions surfaced in Bristol, and there were Sikh boycotts of the buses. The Housemaster–tutor team encouraged fierce debate and keen interest in issues of the day, including the Six Day War in 1967.

My first week at Clifton was also Ernest Polack's first as Housemaster, and he was already talking to boys about

apartheid. Within a few weeks I became the youngest member of the Anti-Apartheid Movement in Britain and avidly fell into the shadow of the older boys who were the fierce debaters of political and social issues. As they started to leave school to go on to university, I searched for a way to sustain the momentum and was introduced to Peter Berenson, who had founded Amnesty International.

I returned to Clifton inspired, rattling off my ideas to my Housemaster, and with his support I set up Amnesty's first ever proper school group. As Simon Rocker later wrote in the *Jewish Chronicle*: 'Typically, it was a Polackian who had started the school's Amnesty International group.'

Our first prisoner of conscience was a black South African, a member of the banned ANC, who was a political prisoner. We wrote letters to the prisoner, his family, the British government and the South African government. We needed to fund our work, so we set up a loan scheme from parents and raised £500 (a large sum in those days) in interest-free loans, subsequently repaid on time.

One of our prisoners was a Spanish Jehovah's Witness who refused to do military service. So we created the first Amnesty International Lecture at Clifton with a talk on the Spanish Civil War given by group member Ian Black (who now writes for the *Guardian*). The group paid for an advertisement to be placed in newspapers asking British tourists to Spain to protest against political imprisonment when they left. I also organized an art exhibition, which included works by Lowry, Ingres, Hitchens, Piper, Picasso, Dufy, Utrillo and Kollwitz, the proceeds going to fund the group.

Within three years two of the group's prisoners (in South Africa and Gabon) had been released, and in addition to our Spanish case we adopted prisoners of conscience in Greece, Poland and Singapore.

Robert Nadler, the group's secretary in 1969, wrote in the House magazine: 'The group stimulates the intellect and gives boys a chance to come face to face with a political situation other than our own. It gives us an idea of the suppressing policies of many countries

around the world, all of whom signed the United Nations Charter on Human Rights. Amnesty gives us a chance to involve ourselves and to feel we can help.'

D. Blausten
PH, 1964–69

THE MARSHAL'S CANES

From a box behind the door,
Daily does the Marshal draw
Four old canes with much use curved;
They their time have amply served.
One has a handle, two have none,
The fourth has only half a one.
What they are made of no one knows,
Could the Marshal e'er disclose
Such an awful mystery?
If you try to bend them, they
Any angle will retain,
And not seek their shape again.
They have served a generation,
This is no exaggeration,
As perchance you might suppose.
Time it is their life should close.
To bark a shin, or crack a head
At calling over, they were bred;
And so vile's their reputation
They deserve incarceration
In that box behind the door,
And ne'er show their faces more.

F.L.C.
The Cliftonian, 1876

NIGHT OPS

Whenever Old Cliftonians of a certain age and a certain type find themselves in nostalgic mode their thoughts will invariably turn to 'night ops'. These night operations were, I believe, the brainchild of Martin Hardcastle, Housemaster of School House in the 1950s. Their name tells you they were usually nocturnal, but 'ops' was an understatement for the most astonishingly wide-ranging and imaginative stunts arranged for the participation of boys, often taking full advantage of the fact that Martin was quite well connected. One of his more spectacular involved boys spending a night aboard a naval destroyer, a rendezvous with Martin himself, top-hatted in Downing Street, arranging to have the boys arrested and detained at Scotland Yard

The Marshal

During the history of the school there have been 13 previous Headmasters and only eight Marshals. The role of the Marshal is a very special one, and *The Cliftonian* of February 1924 noted: 'Of all school officials there is only one who has his finger in every pie, who is apparently ubiquitous, omniscient in school matters, unforgetful, indispensable – the Marshal. Names, faces, rooms, Chapel lists and Chapel places, call-overs, absentees, delinquents to see the Headmaster in the break, all the tiresome, necessary details of school life are everlastingly his care.' Always appointed from the services, the job description of 1982 likened the role to that of a village policeman: 'His policing role relieves the teaching staff of the burden of enforcing the more routine

In memory of the School Marshals

JOHN SKELTON	1864-1881
GEORGE WILSON	1881-1897
JOHN SHAW	1897-1923
ALBERT MOSS	1924-1941
JAMES FRENCH	1946-1972

aspects of school discipline: the friendly relations between boys and staff owe much to the fact that the enforcement of discipline outside the classroom is not seen as the masters' prime concern.' Little has changed in this role, and many Cliftonians have cause to be grateful to the steely and steady way in which successive Marshals have helped them through their school days.

and ending up having tea with the Duke of Beaufort at Badminton. It took three days, that one!

Night ops usually involved some story line of espionage or contraband, with Third Formers as participants maybe travelling on trains to remote stations or walking in the dark across Mendip, Brean Down or in the Wye Valley, making liaisons with accomplices and agents, known, unknown or in disguise and ending with much hilarity and well-cooked sausages around a fire or in a warm kitchen somewhere. It was always good to have a final focus: a dusty, cobweb-festooned tunnel leading to a secret underground staircase up to the warmth of the kitchen at Crowe Hall, that fort at the end of Brean Down or an open fire in an old railway tunnel below King's Wood. Adventures would be compared, and boys would show off about how brave and daring they had been or how demanding their task was to complete. Boys frequently got lost in distant fields (or felt more lost than they actually were) and rapidly came to realize that the senses heighten in the dark. That dreadful noise was just a fox barking, those bulls were actually tranquil cows, that ferocious dog was a jolly fellow simply saying hello, that crashing in the branches was a frightened pigeon taking flight.

Recent ops involved journeys across the River Axe by boat in the dead of night, a journey hidden under a tarpaulin in the back of a lorry, being held up at gun-point on a train near Highbridge by a French temptress or being hidden unseen in the back of a Land Rover, which was then arranged to be stolen. Frequently, participants never knew their whole task right from the start. Instructions had to be collected on the way, dead-letter boxes were used, identities of contacts unknown to boys had to be confirmed by secret signs or passwords. Failure to seek such confirmation could lead to tricky situations. One group of boys who thought that the policeman who stopped the van was fake and remained adamant that the semtex (or cocaine or whatever) was real, only slowly and reluctantly came to the understanding inside Frome police station later on that it was the other way round: the policeman was real and the semtex was fake.

Tom Gover, Michael Lane, John Barratt and others nurtured night ops, but Martin Hardcastle's other nocturnal pursuits organization, the Never Again Club, died out. Members, in number those who could fit into his car, used to take on stunts on Saturday nights that

Left: *D of E training camp at Dyffryn, 2009.*

were so demanding or alarming that they swore never to do them again. That was until about Tuesday, when they started to thaw out (probably both in body as well as spirit), by Wednesday they were actually enjoying the past memories, and by Thursday they were planning the next one. Night ops almost survived to the turn of the century but, alas, they have gone and along with them an immense amount of indescribably good fun and adventure. And I write as one who has been taken by Martin to climb the side of Cheddar Gorge at night (for goodness sake), but who is now prevented from walking a group of pupils on even quite low parts of the Brecon Beacons for even quite short distances on a lovely summer's day in broad daylight by legislation called Health and Safety.

S.J.M. Reece
Pre, ST, 1958–69; Staff, 1973–

Left: *Martin Hardcastle on his way to an abseil.*

THE SANATORIUM

I started at Clifton in September 1985 with some trepidation, having had no experience of life in a boys' public school. When, during my first week, a boy was transported solemnly up College Road at 1a.m. on a door, having injured his neck in a pillow fight, I realized it was not going to be dull – and so it proved. The move from Worcester House to the Old/New San was to take place within a year, so a lot of planning was involved and the aim was to open up the San to the whole school, both staff and boys. Having visited a number of other schools by way of research, we were able to achieve excellent accommodation and facilities at the San, and we were lucky to enlist the services of

Below: *The Health Centre, 2009.*

Peter Scott as a GP, who knew Clifton well, having had two sons at the School. In addition, Bryan Williams, an educational psychologist, joined our team, and we had our own dental surgery run by Jon Myrvold (which I think was unique at the time). With a fully qualified nursing staff, we provided 24-hour cover for all.

The arrival of the girls in 1987 presented a great change for the staff, the boys and the San, and it was a challenging time for us with a very different range of problems. Pastoral care became a vital part of our duties, and many a problem was solved by our very good line in chocolate cake.

I was never quite sure whether it was a good or a bad thing to be so close to the rugby pitches on The Close and to see the injuries as they happened. It was useful on one occasion, however, when a boy who had been discharged from Frenchay Hospital the day before with concussion was spotted playing in a match – he was removed from the pitch by the nursing staff, much to the astonishment of the master in charge.

There are many happy and extraordinary memories, including the young man from the 1st XV who was admitted with an injury, snoring blissfully and clutching his teddy bear. Then there was the Pre pupil who found boarding very difficult and was encouraged to go to school clutching a hand and saying very soulfully 'please could we walk very slowly …'. We were lucky to work in such a diverse school, which required us to provide a wide range of skills and support.

M. Newman
San Sister, 1985–2002

The New Old San

After a spell of 65 years on Worcester Road, the Sanatorium has returned home to the original building, now no longer known as the 'Old San', but just 'The San'. The whole thing has been completely modernized and now offers smart up-to-date facilities – a splendid improvement, even if the JCR was rendered homeless as a result.

Preparations were made for the first move to Worcester Road in 1921. Just as all was ready, a patient – one A.R. Jackson (WaH) – was admitted and promptly developed pneumonia. The move had to be postponed for two weeks until he was fit enough to travel. Extraordinarily enough, the first patient to be treated at the San after reopening this term was Duncan MacLaren (WaH), A.R. Jackson's grandson. Duncan was suffering from a colourful allergic reaction to penicillin, the very drug that, had it been discovered then, might have speeded his grandfather's recovery.

THE CLIFTONIAN, 1986

FREEDOMS

Looking back I now realize that Clifton gave me a freedom that I didn't realize or appreciate at the time: a freedom to do what I thought was right even though my actions were sometimes against the rules of the School, sometimes against its ethos. I was tolerated and survived, and the School put up with me.

I've no idea if Clifton is 'the best school of all'. What I do know is that Clifton reinforced an underlying belief that decency, tolerance, a consciousness of inequality and some sense of public service were important, and it provided the atmosphere that allowed me to be 'out of step'. Nobody tried to change who I was and for this I am genuinely grateful.

W.J. Stephen
Pre, ST, 1942–50

Learning

5

Opposite: *Physics lesson in the refurbished Science School, 2009.*

THE CURRICULUM AFTER 1945

The essence of any school is what happens in the classroom: what is taught and what is learned. Exactly what was taught at Clifton and therefore the shape of the curriculum was based on the general public school emphasis on a classical education. Percival and many of his successors, however, were innovators, and the School's liberal philosophy ensured that there was more to it than that. Needless to say, none of them would recognize (or perhaps approve of) today's curriculum. So much has changed in the last 60 years. Independent schools are less independent, and autonomy over the curriculum has been eroded; social attitudes and expectations have changed; and educational legislation has increased to levels undreamed of in the mid-20th century.

The return from Bude in March 1945 brought many challenges for the School. The infrastructure had to be reclaimed after four years of wartime occupation, and there were significant problems with staffing and pupil numbers. Almost certainly, there was a sense of loss after the innocence of life in north Cornwall. Nevertheless, life had to continue, and Bertrand Hallward took on the task of postwar consolidation with tremendous energy. Externally there were other challenges too: the election of a Labour government in July, the Fleming Report (1942) and the Burnham Committee on salaries.

The year 1945 must have been very unsettling. Tyranny had been defeated, but the postwar situation was still uncertain and challenging. Cliftonians faced the prospect of National Service and a world of the atomic bomb and the Cold War. The old order had been swept away and a new order was emerging, and public schools faced questions about their place in society and their values, at a time when some people were even raising the possibility of abolition.

The Headmaster set out to meet these challenges and took the opportunity to refashion the curriculum. In *Clifton after Percival: A Public School in the Twentieth Century (1990),* D.O. Winterbottom described the changes. All boys in Blocks II and III (the Fourth/Fifth and the Thirds) were to study science, thus continuing Clifton's tradition in this area. Thereafter, this became a choice between general science and more specialized science in Block II. Forms were graded according to ability in Latin and English. A D-stream existed, which did not study Latin but instead took geography in the School Certificate. In Block I (Upper Fifth and Sixth) boys specialized in examination subjects of their choice but also followed non-examination courses in scripture, English, current affairs and a modern language. The current affairs programme was a new departure. There is a progressive feel to this programme of study.

Hallward's other key reform was to set up scholarships and bursaries for boys whose families could not afford a public school education. As noted by J. Gathorne-Hardy in *The Public School Phenomenon* (1977), the Fleming Report had advocated that 25 per cent of pupils at public schools should originate from state schools. When it came to implementing the scheme, however, the cost proved prohibitive. Hallward recommended to the Council that ten per cent of the annual intake should be of boys from elementary schools. From 1939 the Clothworkers' Company

Generations of Phelps

My father had been closely connected with Clifton since my grandfather, Philip Ashby Phelps, was appointed as a teacher, presumably by Percival, to teach Art. He was ordained and later became vicar of St John's in the city. My father, Edwin Ashby, was head of school in 1890–91, going on to Oxford and into the ICS. I joined the school in the summer of 1940, 1D with dear Miss Imlach, to be evacuated that winter to Butcombe Court. Subsequently, my three sons followed my footsteps to Watson's: J.A. in 1975–81, E.J. in 1978–83 and W.T. in 1984–89.

If I was asked to single out one master who inspired me it would be S.H. (Oss) Steadman. He took the Fourth (top) Form at Butcombe and taught us Classics. He was also responsible for Drama and created an outdoor production of *A Midsummer Night's Dream*, with me as Puck. The production is commented on in *The Cliftonian*. On our return to Clifton he produced two plays, casting me as Emil in *Emil and the Detectives* and Raina in Shaw's *Arms and the Man*.

J.P. Comerford (Pre, BH, 1943–50) remembers SHS as being 'considered something of a maverick by the staider element of the staff' and recalls accompanying him on several amusing camping trips on the Thames from Folly Bridge to Lechlade. Later SHS withdrew from teaching and became librarian, but he subsequently led a group on an informal tour of Greece, highlighting the glories of the country with great skill. He was almost a good enough classicist to persuade me to read classics at university, but not quite, and in many ways I now regret my decision to read maths!

C.E. PHELPS
PRE, WAH, 1940–50

contributed to another scholarship, and this had provided for about 40 boys by 1946. These were all-round pupils who could contribute to, and benefit from, the school in many ways. Despite the relatively low numbers, Hallward and the Council do appear to have been committed to widening participation and, of course, attracting bright pupils to the School.

Hallward's successor, Desmond Lee, was another Cambridge don. If Hallward consolidated Clifton after the war, Lee's challenge was to move the School forward. In 1951 O and A levels replaced the School Certificate, and this change required significant planning and thinking, especially with the complications of the initial rule that set a minimum age for the completion of O levels. Lee, a distinguished classics scholar, placed great emphasis on the teaching of history, and this department, under some eminent leadership, flourished in these years and produced many successful Oxbridge applicants. Under Lee school numbers went up significantly, and academically the school was strengthened.

In the next decade, under the guidance of Stephen McWatters, this impressive reputation continued. The year 1963 saw the introduction of grades for A level in place of the distinction, pass or fail. This, allied to the growth in free university education and competition from the grammar schools, meant that public schools had to make academic work central to their business. Up to this point the number of A level distinctions had

been excellent, but there was also a significant failure rate at both A and O level. To combat this, a number of measures were put in place to liberalize the curriculum. A new emphasis on the teaching of English was established, and extra time was made for English in the Sixth Form, and the department went from strength to strength. Mathematics was a spectacular success, with a high number of distinctions. Religious Studies teaching also underwent an overhaul, and teachers volunteered to teach this rather than being press-ganged. O level scripture was taken by all boys in the Fourth Form.

The other key curriculum decision made at this time was to stop the selection of boys into arts or science streams by postponing this choice until O levels, and this meant that most boys had to study science to O level. Biology (at the time the poor relation in the sciences) benefited enormously from a greater emphasis and new teaching facilities and laboratories. In 1971 Clifton continued to lead the way in the sciences by becoming the first school to teach Nuffield syllabuses in physics, biology and chemistry. Geography and economics were established as full A level subjects. General studies and business studies were promoted. Parents' conferences were also introduced, and the reporting scheme was changed. The opening of the Redgrave Theatre in 1966 was significant for the status of drama in the School, and Clifton can, as Winterbottom remarked, 'fairly claim to be a pioneer of drama'. Two years later a new

Technology Centre was opened for engineering and technical skills.

Oxbridge entrance continued to be a measure of success for schools like Clifton, which managed to hold its own on this front – 1950, for instance, saw the School placed sixth in the academic league tables. By the 1980s pressure on Oxford and Cambridge to broaden their access and increased competition made application more difficult, although in the late 1980s and early 1990s there were some remarkably successful years. More recently, the School has established a strong Oxbridge application process with a good number each year taking up places.

The traditional public school emphasis on classics and mathematics had never entirely been the Clifton way (especially with its tradition in the sciences), but by the early 1970s the curriculum was very different from anything envisaged in the age of Percival. The last 20 years have seen even more significant changes in the school curriculum in light of increased government intervention and legislation. Perhaps the most significant development was the 1988 Education Act and the advent of a national curriculum. This also brought the end of O levels and the introduction of

GCSEs, which placed more emphasis on coursework. This meant that the Fourth Form could no longer be rushed through the religious studies syllabus in one year, so the subject became a two-year GCSE option studied by a few. More recently, it is has become a compulsory subject at GCSE, taking its place alongside mathematics, science, English and a modern language as the core subjects for all pupils.

In this period of change Clifton became fully co-educational (perhaps the most significant moment in Clifton's recent history), and the School embraced the assisted places scheme, introduced by the Conservative government in 1979, making some ten places a year available. This, allied to some other generous funding, allowed a significant number of pupils access to a Clifton education. The School's commitment was signalled by the appointment of Stuart Andrews, then Headmaster, as deputy chairman of the national Assisted Places Committee. But the scheme was controversial, with some arguing that it deprived state schools of bright children. Others pointed out that the number of children from working-class backgrounds taking advantage of this scheme was low. However, Clifton benefited from an influx of bright pupils through the scheme. The scheme was abolished when Tony Blair became prime minister in 1997.

Curriculum 2000 brought more change and an overhaul of the A level qualification, the so-called gold standard in the British education system. The result was the creation of a modular A level qualification, which has been successful in broadening the number of subjects studied at a higher level, but this has been refined in 2008. The GCSE syllabus is now being developed into a modular form as educational reform moves relentlessly on. ICT has grown into a key element of the School's curriculum, not bolted on but increasingly intertwined in all that is taught, and the facilities for this are impressive. Change seems to be the order of the day.

The last 60 years have shown a school that is not frightened to adapt and change. Innovation is welcome. Teaching and learning are varied, and pupils enjoy their studies. Without being complacent, Clifton recognizes and values a curriculum that challenges every pupil.

J.S. Tait
Staff, 1996–

Below: *Lord Robert Winston cutting the periodic table cake at the opening of the newly refurbished Science School in 2008.*

BOLD SCIENCE

Clifton College was born at a pivotal moment in the development of modern thought: Charles Darwin's *Origin of Species* was less than ten years old; Karl Marx was writing *Das Kapital* in the Reading Room of the British Museum; and Sigmund Freud would soon embark on a journey into the unconscious mind. Victorian England was poised for a revolution in rational thinking. Thus the young John Percival was bold and innovative to incorporate science into his vision of the new Clifton.

His teachers were imaginative and creative. Herr Leipner built a garden of rare and unusual plants in what is now the North Quad at the same time as Gregor Mendel was counting pea plants in a monastery garden in Brno. W.A. Tolden, A.M. Worthington, J. Perry and A.W. Reinold were early teachers of science at Clifton, and all became Fellows of the Royal Society. They inspired through their example of being practising scientists.

Richard Threlfall (Pre SH WaH, 1873–80) was an early pupil, who pioneered physics at the University of Sydney and later became a distinguished chemical engineer in the explosives industry, despite losing two fingers in an accident with nitro-glycerine while working at Cambridge.

The august science magazine *Nature* declared in 1871: 'Foremost if not positively the first amongst those schools where science is taught stands Clifton College.' The article includes an impressive woodcut of the beautiful new library, which originally housed a museum for the specimens of animals and birds that adorn (some might say clutter) the biology department to this day.

Years pass, but bold and innovative teaching remains a powerful force. W.A. Shenstone invented silica glass in his laboratory, now the Prichard Room, and each time a scientist uses a beaker or a test tube we celebrate his invention. He also ran popular (and lucrative) practical science classes. Reginald Punnett (SH, 1889–91) attended these classes in chemistry and physics, and he also joined the Scientific Society, where he discovered a fascination for fossils and marine worms. At Cambridge he became the world's first professor of genetics, helping to secure Mendel's legacy and strengthen Darwin's theory of evolution. He was also the inventor of the Punnett square, so beloved by science students across the world.

Science became a dominant force within Clifton and had outgrown its premises in rooms 16, 17 and the 'crow's nest' (each now filled with banks of ICT equipment). The purpose-built Science School, which was paid for by public subscription, was opened by the Prince of Wales in 1927. It was a 'palace' for practical science teaching, where the bold and innovative flourished. With characteristic foresight, the foundations of the Science School were built strong enough to allow the biology department to be added on the top floor in 1962.

E.J. Holmyard (1891–1959) was head of the science department between the wars. He had a deep knowledge of the historical development of chemistry from its roots in alchemy, and he invited a distinguished alchemical scholar to attempt a 'transformation' in the labs at Clifton and recorded the (unsuccessful) outcome with wry humour in *The Cliftonian*. He taught C.H. Waddington (WiH, 1919–23) alchemy during one summer holiday. The symbolism of the egg fascinated Waddington, who became one of the most rigorous experimentalists of his generation, studying how eggs and embryos develop. Waddington's ability to think deeply and question Mendel and Darwin's orthodoxy led him to investigate how the environment might alter the activity of genes. His theory of 'epigenetics' is set to become one of the dominant ideas in genetics in the next decades.

The Papyrus from Oxyrhynchus

The College had a connection with this extraordinary discovery because Bernard Pyne Grenfell (Pre, Junior, ST OH, 1878–88) won a scholarship to Queen's College, Oxford, and became a leading Egyptologist. Together with Arthur S. Hunt, he excavated the site at Oxyrhynchus, 160 miles southwest of Cairo. There, sifting through mountains of rubbish, they found pieces of Greek and Roman texts and documents. In 1908 he became Professor of Papyri at Oxford and spent his life collecting, translating and preserving the fragments. His father, John Granville Grenfell, taught chemistry and physics at Clifton and was Housemaster of OH from 1884 until 1889, helping to found the Scientific Society. The Clifton fragment of papyrus now resides in the Percival Library.

A Young Master's Experiences

I was very rude to a distinguished member of the College Council when I noticed him writing a letter in my Sixth Form Geography set instead of listening to my words of wisdom. He was 17 years old at the time, and I had just joined the staff fresh from my own education in the army and at Oxford. Some of the staff had taught at Clifton before the war or at Bude, some had returned from war service, and a few, like me, were beginners. It was a happy and supportive common room, with a sprinkling of engaging eccentrics, one of whom told me proudly that he had not been beyond Pembroke Road for four years. One evening at supper in the refectory (now room 8) I asked Douglas Fox, the distinguished director of music, who had lost an arm during the war: 'Does that old organ in Big School still work?' 'Old organ! That's a Father Willis,' he shouted. 'Come with me!' Supper abandoned, he took me upstairs and played to me for a magical half hour. A senior master, whom I had respectfully addressed as Mr X, took me on one side to tell me, in hushed tones: 'We're very informal here: you call me X – and I call you Fromant.' Somehow, I survived my first term.

Desmond Lee was a formidable Headmaster, who piloted the school adroitly through the period of postwar change until he was head-hunted by Winchester. The rigidities of the House system were mellowing after the freedoms of Bude, helped by communal feeding in Big School. We still lunched in House groups, and meals were cooked in the basic kitchens installed by the US army during its occupation of the buildings. Trolley-loads of food were pushed (raced) to tables by the House fags, and a perfunctory Latin grace was the signal for serving to begin.

Every boy played games three afternoons a week, and inter-house rugby and cricket matches roused more interest (and occasional arguments) than inter-school matches. We travelled to Beggar's Bush in the 'biscuit tins', the lightly constructed buses that were allowed to cross the suspension bridge with full loads. They were already museum pieces, expertly maintained by the groundsmen.

Life was spartan in many ways in the 1950s. There was no heating in the dormitories, and only two colours of paint were available (brown and green), but there was a great sense of freedom and adventurousness. We took boys climbing in the Gorge and caving in the Mendips, 'night ops' at weekends saw them scattered over Bristol and the surrounding

countryside. Health and safety risk assessments hadn't even been thought of, but we all survived. Every Sunday morning Chapel was compulsory, after a form period in which form masters were required to teach the Old Testament. Not all did, preferring to teach their own subjects. A clergyman visiting my classroom seemed rather puzzled to hear a lesson on the physical geography of South America. After Chapel the boarding Houses took it in turn to host sherry parties, and since everyone lived near the School these were popular. It was the custom for new masters to be invited to dine in most of the boarding Houses during their first term, and this was a wonderful way of getting to know everyone. On one occasion I ate a nourishing supper in the Refectory, only to remember that I had been invited to a rather daunting formal dinner on that same evening. I jumped into my dinner suit, arrived just in time and manfully ate my way through seven courses!

J.D. FROMANT
STAFF, 1951–88

Above right: Dudley Fromant teaching Geography in Room 16, which is now part of the Percival Library. Today it has a mezzanine floor and a bank of computers. See photo on pages 82–83.

J.C. Kendrew (WaH, 1930–36) and N.F. Mott (Pre, SH, 1918–23) discovered 'hard science' at Clifton – the exhilarating (and slightly frightening) challenge of working for exacting, precise, questioning teachers. Mott revelled in the mathematical aspects of physics. Kendrew taught himself German to read a university-level textbook in German that was issued by Holmyard to the Sixth Form. The technical German was useful

when Kendrew helped to found the European Molecular Biology Organization in Heidelberg in 1964.

A.B. Pippard (Pre, SH, 1930–38) was as entranced by the music at Clifton as by the science, but achieved greatness as the Cavendish Professor of Physics at Cambridge University. C.A. Coulson (ST, 1923–28) excelled at chemistry and mathematics and became an influential lay-leader in evangelical Christianity.

J.M.M. Pinkerton (WaH, 1932–37) built complex electrical circuits while he was in the Fourth Form at Clifton, and became the chief designer for the world's first computers for J. Lyons & Co.

If the discipline was tough and unforgiving it was also beneficial, for the Science School can claim to have produced two Nobel laureates. Mott was awarded the Nobel prize for physics in 1977 for his research into solid state physics, which has allowed the electronics industry to flourish. Kendrew carried out research into the molecular structure of proteins, especially myoglobin, an oxygen store found in muscles. He received a Nobel prize alongside Crick and Watson in

1962. In fact, Clifton can boast a third Nobel laureate. The mathematical economist J.R. Hicks (WiH, 1917–22) received the Nobel prize for economic sciences in 1972. In his biography he said: 'To the mathematical training I received at Clifton, in particular, I owe a great debt.'

I.B. Hopley, Clifton's head of science from 1965 to 1987, reckons that when he started teaching physics in the late 1950s 'the syllabus was one hundred years out of date'. The Nuffield science courses in the 1960s and 1970s, pioneered by Hopley, M.D.W. Vokins, R.L. Gliddon, P.L. Bright and K.W.C. Watson, changed all that. The new emphasis on practical science through

Below: *The old science laboratory, now rooms 18, 18a and 19 in the East Cloister and part of the geography department.*

The Briggs Family

John (ST 1989–96), Brian (ST 1995–7) and Adam (ST 1994–2001) Briggs are brothers who attended Clifton in the 1990s and the early years of this century. They are part of a scientific family. Their father, Derek, is a world-renowned palaeontologist, who is currently director of the Peabody Museum of Natural History at Yale University. We asked the 'boys' what they were doing in July 2008 and to reminisce about their formative experiences at Clifton.

John Briggs

John is a research group leader at the European Molecular Biology Laboratory in Heidelberg, using electron microscopy techniques to study the structures of viruses and cells, especially the HIV and Ebola viruses. He studies biological questions, even though his A levels were in physics, chemistry and maths. He writes:

'At Clifton I was inspired by my science teachers both inside and outside the classroom. I particularly remember David Harrison, who taught me maths for the first three years. He came into our first lesson and terrified the classroom with a clear explanation of how we would behave in his classroom, after which we did some problems in silence. After that the lessons became fun, relaxed and inspiring, an environment he could keep under control because we remembered how things would be if we went too far! He helped a few of us through the AS exam during our GCSE year. Outside of the classroom he supervised us for the Duke of Edinburgh Gold award, including treks through the Brecons and the Lakes, and ran the Chess Club. He had incredible enthusiasm for everything he did. Maths is so essential to the kind of science I do now, which is becoming increasingly technical and inter-disciplinary, and I am very grateful to him for making clear that maths (and mathematicians) don't have to be boring! My chemistry teachers also taught more than just scientific skills. Anthony Newman was an

inspiring Housemaster. I remember him driving some of us across the country for a visit to Cambridge when we were looking for universities, as well as dispensing valuable life advice in his role as Housemaster.'

Brian Briggs

Brian has just finished his DPhil on wildfowl ecology and conservation and is working with a tiny company called the Environment Bank, aiming to improve the system by which developers mitigate or compensate for their environmental impacts. He leads a successful Oxford-based band, Stornoway, writing his own songs. Brian writes:

'I have been keen on wildlife since I was small, but I remember two things in particular about my time at Clifton that really fuelled my interest in ecology and conservation. One was walking around the leafy Clifton streets in the summer with Simon Reece listening to blackbirds and attempting to map out their territories. The other was waving my tie at the lady at the Bristol Zoo back gate and wandering round the gardens during lunch breaks – the newly opened bug house was one of the many highlights on offer.'

Adam Briggs

Adam has completed his medical elective in Zambia and New Zealand and has just finished his BMBCh on the graduate-entry course at Oxford. He will work in northeast London as a junior doctor. He is doing an academic job, which means that in his second year he will get some time dedicated to research in public health and primary care. He hopes to combine medical work with research throughout his career. Adam writes:

'I've always been interested in science and maths, and particularly inspiring aspects of my time at Clifton include exploding metals in lower sixth chemistry lessons with Anthony Newman, interspersed with the occasional motivational conversation. This type of chat happened throughout my early years in the Upper School and concerned not just chemistry but also music, sport and leadership, and certainly helped to generate an enthusiasm to do well and achieve.

'From a more science-oriented angle, I remember inspiring conversations with Neil Ingram in his office discussing aspects of genomics and the potential of proteomics and its relation in particular to oncology – this was my substitute for studying A level biology!

'The one other teacher whom I particularly admired was Gerard Coulson. I can't put my finger on it exactly, but he was a teacher who pushed us incredibly hard in maths but always maintained an informal relationship, which in my situation made for a productive and enjoyable learning environment. Hugh Monro would be another man who believed in the all-round ethos of Clifton, which certainly benefited me.'

N.R. INGRAM
STAFF, 1991–2008

'enquiry' matched the hunger for discovery of a generation forged in the 'white heat of technology' that wished to explore the moon. This was the era of great textbook writing: T.B. Akrill, G.P. Rendell and their co-authors all made significant contributions at this time. The successors to the Nuffield courses – Nuffield Coordinated Sciences, Salter's Nuffield Advanced Biology, Salter's Chemistry and Advancing Physics – have continued to be influenced by a newer generation of Clifton teachers, such as D.R.B. Barrett, M.I. Dixon, N.R. Ingram, T.A. Meunier, T. Reeves and D. Richardson.

The educational landscape at Clifton is not so different now from that of a mid-Victorian school. Then and now 'every child matters', and a broad and balanced science education is available for all. The challenges remain the same, as is the imperative that science should be as practical and 'hands-on' as possible. All the students who have chosen to study scientific subjects at university are a testament to that philosophy, and so too are those who passed through the Science School and who decided that their main interests lay elsewhere.

John Cleese became a famous comedian but wished he could have studied psychology at Clifton. Adam Phillips became a celebrated psychotherapist and popular writer. His books, including *The Beast in the Nursery* (1998) and *Darwin's Worms* (1999), allow Freud, Darwin and Mendel to meet within the terrors of the unconscious mind.

The biology department was refurbished in 2001 with the generous support of the Harry Crook Foundation, with chemistry and physics refurbished in 2008. The Science School now embraces digital technology. The establishment by D. Futak of a computer-controlled telescope on the roof of the Tribe fulfils an ambition for practical astronomy that began in the early years of the last century.

The 'new-look' Science School will engage the pupils of the next generation in contemporary science, with a flourishing psychology department added to the traditional canon of physics, chemistry and biology, whilst rooted in the bold and innovative practical traditions of the past. The Science School at Clifton will continue to be 'foremost amongst those schools where science is taught'.

N.R. Ingram
Staff, 1991–2008

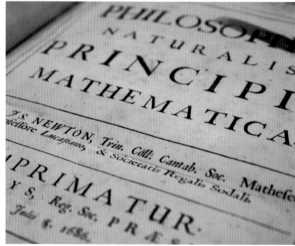

Above: On the Origin of Species by Means of Natural Selection, *by Charles Darwin. First Edition, London 1859, The Stone Library.*

Left: Philosophiae Naturalis Principia Mathematica, *by Isaac Newton, Second Edition, Cambridge 1713, Stone Library.*

STONE MEMORIAL LIBRARY

The Stone Memorial Library is a dedicated science library holding in excess of 5,000 volumes, and it was built as an integral part of the new Science School, opened in 1927. The then head of science, Eric John Holmyard, was convinced that the historic and cultural aspects of science were uniquely important, and the Stone Library was his personal project. He regarded it as 'one of the principal foci of our work' and as important as a laboratory. Holmyard had read chemistry and history at Cambridge, and his attitudes underpinned Clifton's pioneering spirit in science teaching. This spirit still persists and is still supported by the Stone and its librarians, who continually update its stocks and keep up with the requirements of modern curricula.

You will find books on butterflies, ferns, quantum physics, alchemy, philosophy and ancient science as well as topics of popular interest, such as the God versus Science debate. You will find old books, standard school text books and shiny new volumes full of wonderful pictures in addition to any science book you could wish for to help with your studies. Many pupils now come for books for their coursework research, and many more have found the Stone a peaceful place to browse and work. There are several gracious wooden shelf sets, and the wooden tables (the originals) have been retained during the recent refurbishment. Fine antiquarian books are held in safekeeping. We now have several computer terminals to allow a complete research experience, although not so many as to detract from the Stone's abiding identity as a library.

A portrait of Lieutenant Henry Brassington Stone (OC), who was killed in action in the First World War, hangs on one wall, and the Stone Library was funded as a memorial to him. There is also a portrait of Holmyard, looking down on our efforts. We hope he would still consider our science library as, possibly, among the 'finest in the world'.

R.M. Williams
Staff, Stone Librarian, from 2001–

Right: *Six Headmasters, July 1990. Standing, from left to right: Stephen McWatters (1963–75), Stuart Andrews (1975–90) and Nicholas Hammond (1954–63); seated, from left to right: Bertrand Hallward (1939–48), Hugh Monro (then Headmaster elect) (1990–2000) and Desmond Lee (1948–54).*

LIGHT TOUCH AND SCIENTIFIC AWAKENING

During their first meeting Stuart Andrews warned my parents that Clifton exposed pupils to a port city as well as the country. Every conceivable temptation was available: Britain's highest density of public houses, several girls' schools on the doorstep (co-education started during my lower sixth year) and affordable trout reservoirs a mere 30 minutes' cycle ride through Ashton Park. I'm sure there were plenty of other advantages, but what attracted me, as an eight-year-old, was the zoo next door with its white tigers, wolves, rhinos and other charismatic mega fauna, all for 2p entry on display of a blue Pre tie.

While most of our parents were worrying about the Cruise missiles at Greenham Common, school fees and how much Steer & Geary would charge for a uniform, the really important deal was the new reptile house that was under construction. Shortly after its opening, an invincible young Cliftonian took on a large Nile crocodile in a tie-flicking contest. He lost, and to avoid further amputations the zoo built a bigger wall. Today the zoo doesn't have any proper crocodiles, but Clifton is every bit as full of invincible youth.

My College sentence was to five years in School House, progressing from Third Form collective study and dormitory to the legendary basement, where previous generations of Fourth Formers had lived until the Council condemned the place. During this time I discovered I had a truly scientific bent, which the school allowed to develop. Science and technology were more than available outside lessons. Biology was still satisfied by the zoo, which was now charging 10p to enter, but they did have the world's first nocturnal house, which went some way to making up for the increase.

Through the rather peculiar Technical Activities Centre, a fume-filled underground dungeon of work benches, ironmongery and milling machines, Clifton set up a unique satellite project, which was acclaimed in *The Times Educational Supplement* no less. Harnessing some specialized radio equipment and several computers, which were probably less powerful than that in the average refrigerator today, we predicted flight paths of orbiting satellites and had motorized antennae and various dishes chasing them across the sky, decoding their pictures and the other data they transmitted. In the process we intercepted plenty of East German shipping messages, and during Commem displayed real-time pictures of the Chernobyl smoke cloud drifting westwards.

Shortly after that publicity, the Science department deemed it useful to conduct a serious research project, the sort of thing that a university might do, and settled on cat-nip. Within months the small team had managed to both extract and synthesize the magic potion that sends cats dotty, a feat well beyond 1980s A level chemistry. The school's Scientific Society, which met on Friday nights, was abuzz with mammalian semiochemistry, gerbils' Harderian glands and polysyllabic chemicals that offend normal English pronunciation. World experts came and handed out wooden ice-lollipop sticks dipped in the filthy stench that sends pigs into salivating lust frenzies, detailed film of which accompanied the sticks, and then to top it all the Zoo allowed access to the lions' cage. Hours of video showed the pride poking and prodding an ice cream carton doped with cat-nip.

The arcane specialities didn't stop at science. Ignoring major sports (primarily because I was awful at them), Clifton provided some superb alternatives. Fencing under the eagle eyes of Bill Bailey kept us continually on a par with the great universities. Rackets was taught by a world champion. Fives was considered almost mundane, and crowning them all was real tetrathlon, with Russian pistols. Of more conventional shooting, I recall the Clifton versus Zimbabwe match, which was held with the official blessing of President Banana himself.

I doubt if that's what all schools offer. I recall Clifton as a serious institution with a very light touch, which I couldn't possibly appreciate until many years later.

R.M.G. Witherow
Pre, SH, 1979–89

MATHEMATICS, 1939–2008

Did you enjoy mathematics when you were at school? Your chances of saying 'yes' are good if you went to Clifton. Why? The answer lies in the quality of staff who have taught in that department, and throughout the period there have always been nine or ten graduates of the subject, all capable of teaching in the Sixth Form. But Clifton has also had its share of less able pupils, and for them there have been teachers like Rory Gillespie to inspire them to unlikely success.

The measure of academic success in the public eye has always been unsatisfactory. From the 1940s to the 1960s success was judged almost entirely on how many pupils got into Oxbridge. Later the measure depended on the number of A grades at Advanced Level. It is true that by these measures Clifton comes out well, and recently there have been over 30 A grades each year. But these measures tell only part of the story of Clifton's success.

A mathematics department requires leadership, preferably from someone of high academic standing, and from 1939 to 1958 there was P.C. Unwin, a Cambridge wrangler, who was remarkably successful. He was followed by Dr A.J. Willson, a fellow of St John's College, Cambridge, who went on to be a professor at the University of Leicester. He was followed by J.B. Evans,

a former goalkeeper for England at hockey, and then John Hersee, who eventually left to run the School Mathematics Project, in its day an innovative national project that has had a lasting influence on the content of mathematics at school level. He became leader of the UK International Mathematical Olympiad Team and finally chairman of the IMO board. Then came Tony Hughes, with a First from Oxford, followed by Christopher Bradley, a fellow of Jesus College, Oxford. When Bradley came to Clifton in 1981 pupils never did more than three subjects at A level, which meant that virtually no one did both mathematics and further mathematics. He persuaded the then Headmaster, Stuart Andrews, to allow a fourth A level, as long as it

Below: *Computer suite in Room 16 (see also photo on page 77).*

was further mathematics. The subject enjoyed a vogue and is still popular, attracting up to 20 of the best scholars each year.

During this period distinguished pupils, such as Andrew Cates, Ben Preston and David Chow, went on to Oxford and Cambridge to get Firsts; Cates got a Smith's Prize at Cambridge for his research in fluid mechanics.

The department was now so strong that there was no point in an external appointment and the internal appointments of John Barrett and Mike West followed. David Cook was appointed from outside as Mike West's deputy, and he was followed, when he moved to Badminton, by the present head of department, Gilbert Simmons. He has taken Clifton on to the widely respected International General Certificate (IGCSE), which many other public schools now support.

C.J. Bradley
Staff, 1981–2003

CLASSICS – AND NICK HAMMOND

John Percival was well aware of how to promote a school in the public eye. A school's intellectual quality was judged by its pupils' successes in gaining scholarships and exhibitions at Oxford and Cambridge, initially in classics and mathematics, later in a much wider range of subjects. There were no league tables measuring standards across the whole school. Matters continued in this fashion until the 1980s, when Oxbridge decided to abandon entrance awards and instead give awards on the basis of first university examinations. Under the old system there is no doubt that the standards of scholarship among the cleverer pupils were exceptionally high. At the same time, because academic success was measured by the performance of the most able, a school such as Clifton could admit pupils of wide range of ability and did so to the benefit of all.

With four classical Oxbridge dons as Headmasters between 1923 and 1962 – Whatley, Hallward, Lee and Hammond – one would expect high standards. All four taught classics, but even at this period a Headmaster's time for teaching was limited, and the burden of teaching fell on the classical staff. Head of classics from 1952 was David Gaunt, a scholar of Shrewsbury and Clare College, Cambridge. He came to Clifton after distinguished war service at Bletchley and remained until 1964, when he took up the post of reader in classics at Bristol University. Interestingly, David had been taught at Clare by Nick Hammond, as had David Douglas,

senior classics master at the Pre, and Geoffrey Hardyman, who joined the Upper School staff in 1957. David's terms of employment freed him from the customary necessities of acting as our House tutor or taking games. Apart from running the Archaeological Society, he concentrated exclusively on teaching classics, almost entirely to the classical sixth post-A level, which would normally consist of between five and 12 pupils. He set the subjects for the composition prizes and the syllabus for the Dakyns' Prize and Hugh Lucas Scholarship. The prize compositions were carefully inscribed into a compositions book, which the author of this article found languishing in a cupboard in the Sixth Form room and is now restored to the Percival Library. Weekly prose and verse compositions, alternately Greek and Latin, were demanded, and these were kept by each

pupil in special prose and verse books, on the left-hand-side the passage to be translated and a fair copy, on the right-hand side, of the pupil's version. Every pupil would spend an hour a week going through his compositions with David in College Fields – he had an upstairs flat with a study on the half-landing. These details are mentioned because they show a little of the care and devotion shown by David to the teaching of Classics. He set out to obtain Oxbridge awards for his pupils and would spend endless time deciding which college to aim for with a heavy bias, it has to be said, to Cambridge (Clifton as a whole at this stage sent far more pupils to Cambridge than Oxford). The number of awards gained during his tenure is impressive. Clifton's tally of classical awards would put it easily in the top ten schools in the country, not far behind Westminster (regularly visited by the most learned classicist of the day, Eduard Fraenkel), Manchester Grammar School and Rugby.

Distinguished Cliftonian scholars of this period include Gerald Toomer (a fellow of Corpus Christi, Oxford, before he changed his academic interests to Arabic mathematics), Roger Dawe, an expert in the manuscripts of Aeschylus, and the late Professor John Barron, president of the College and formerly a professor of Greek at King's College, London. T.F. Higham was for many postwar years University Orator at Oxford, composing many witty Latin speeches for degree days.

While it is absolutely right to give pride of place among staff to David Gaunt, he was well supported by others. Ollie Grove, Robin Hone and John McKeown took charge of the Classical upper fifth. Alister Cox, who became headmaster of the Royal Grammar School, Newcastle, was a painstaking scholar who had charge of the lower sixth. David Gaunt's traditions were ably continued by Robin Barton, assisted by Geoffrey Hardyman and Tony Record. By the 1990s, however, the numbers of classicists had begun to shrink, although there are some indications that there is now a reverse trend, and the current head of Classics, Bill Huntington, is as distinguished as his predecessors.

What of the Headmasters? After Bude, Hallward briefly returned to Clifton before leaving for Nottingham in 1947. By all accounts he was an inspired teacher. Desmond Lee taught the Sixth Form, although it is suggested that he did not inspire. Both men were administrators rather than scholars. The same would not be said of Nicholas Hammond, however, who was in the first rank of Greek historians. Seldom can a school have had such a remarkable head. His war record behind the lines in Greece showed him to be a person of enormous bravery and resourcefulness, yet he was essentially a simple man (the reason perhaps that he could get on so well with Greek shepherds in the Greek resistance), the son of a Cornish minister, who moved to Scotland and obtained a free scholarship to Fettes. In the 1930s, while a classics don, he walked the length and breadth of Greece. The knowledge he gained was put to good use both in the war and in scholarship. He knew that Herodotus was right when he described how the Persians advancing up the pass at Thermopylae crunched the dry leaves under their feet: the leaves fell at the start of the year, not in autumn. He also guessed correctly where Philip of Macedon's capital was.

Opposite and right: *Language Labs past and present.*

The Percival Library

Dr Percival decided that the early arrangement of the library being housed in Big School did not stimulate a scholarly approach to reading and research, which required a silent study environment. Partly at his own expense, therefore, a library was built; there is a plaque in the newly restored window bay area recording his 'generous gift'. Initially, in 1870, the building extended only part of the way along the north side of the South Quadrangle. *The Cliftonian* of that year stated that 'the new building in which it is intended to place the library and museum is now rapidly approaching completion'. Charles Hansom, who had already worked on the design of a library for Ushaw College near Durham in 1851, designed this first phase along with his brother, Joseph.

The Council report of 1875 saluted 'a voluntary movement' by masters, pupils and a few friends of the Headmaster to add a museum, with classrooms underneath, and to 'create a cloister to the buildings thus extended'. A fund had been opened in 1874 to complete the north range. The east wing was completed to the staircase in 1880, and the Wilson Tower with the Council room, also designed by Hansom, was added between

1888 and 1890. Wilson, the second Headmaster, also contributed generously to the building works from his salary of £2,000 a year.

During the Second World War the Percival Library was taken over by clerks typing loading bills for the D-Day invasion. Corps and division commanders used the Council room for their planning of the D-Day landings, and drawing-pin holes from this time are still just visible in the oak panelling. The Council room did not become part of the library until after the Second World War, when Sixth

Left: *Bust of Nelson in the Percival Library.*

Below: *Percival memorial mugs and jug, Ashtead Pottery. The pottery, based in Ashtead, Surrey, ran from 1923 to 1935 and was set up with the aim of providing employment for ex–servicemen mainly from the First World War.*

Below left: *Percival's Library.*

Above: *Percival Library after refurbishment by Mark Webber (OC)*.

Percival Library, and their contributions still form part of the collection today. In 1963 David Reed was appointed to the school as cataloguer and assistant librarian, while Rodney Gee was librarian. He became the first professional librarian and undertook the first major recataloguing of the collection.

After the librarianship of David Reed, the library has been the domain of a number of schoolmaster-librarians on half a timetable, and first Geoffrey Hardyman and then Robin Barton carried on the model of good practice established by Reed, cataloguing to Dewey Decimal standards and adding scholarly items to stock. In 1998 a part-time information scientist, Anne Mossman, was appointed as librarian. A beginning was made on the computerization of the catalogue, and plans were started for the refurbishment of the library.

The new century has seen the advent of a new librarian, no longer in charge solely of the Percival Library but with overall responsibility for all libraries within Clifton. Instead of one librarian, the College now has seven library staff. The School decided to integrate the older technology of the printed word with the newer information technology, and this was successfully achieved by architect Mark Webber OC in his sensitively upgraded Percival Library, which was reopened in 2002. This places reading and all forms of research back into the centre of life at the school. An old geography classroom now complements the library as a computer suite, and the Council room has become a reference and enquiry area with newspapers and periodicals in many languages.

Today the library is a busy and welcoming place. Students enjoy working in an area that is bright, cheerful and well stocked. Audio-visual items as well as a wide range of fiction and non-fiction are on offer. It is busy all day, and Sixth Formers find it a positive place to study. The Percival Library now incorporates both the best of Clifton traditions and the latest in modern facilities. This integration of information technology with more traditional book-based resources will help develop the scholarly, enquiring minds of the future. The listed wooden shelves are still there with plaster busts on top, and the wonderful view along the library is much the same but appears different with subtle lighting and vibrantly coloured carpet. It remains a most inviting place to work.

A. ALLAN
COLLEGE LIBRARIAN, 1990–

Formers were allowed to use it for study. This tradition ended only in the late 1980s.

In 1954–55 oak shelves for the Council room and new furniture for the Percival Library were purchased in memory of Cecil Francis Taylor, librarian and second master during the 1930s. Stanley Steadman OC, 'the most scholarly man in the place' according to Martin Scott, was appointed librarian in 1947 and remained so until 1962. Both Taylor and Steadman left substantial legacies to the

Left: *Depiction of the Sixth Form room from 1898 book of etchings. Many of the original fixtures and fittings remain (see also photo on page 179).*

At Clifton Hammond taught A level ancient history. Using only three periods a week he regularly achieved the best A level results in the country. Using his Cambridge lecture notes, he taught a technique for answering the A level questions. Four essays were required in two hours, so there was little time, and Hammond insisted that you took a view at the start of the essay and supported it with facts and quotes. You could easily see if your essay was any good because each correct fact received a tick. Great effort was required to get the material down, but there were occasional breaks. In these, Hammond would digress on to subjects such as wild shepherd dogs in Greece and how to kill them.

For those taking Oxbridge scholarships Hammond used to take each candidate on his own for a whole morning each week in his study for composition. Masters, secretaries and the Marshal would come in and out, and Hammond would give instant decisions before immediately returning to what really interested him, the composition. For this he had a remarkable facility: 150 lines of Shakespeare would appear in best Sophoclean iambics in a morning. One doubts whether any other school would have offered its classical scholars such an education.

While he was at Clifton Hammond kept up a stream of scholarly articles and wrote his *History of Greece* while on sabbatical at Princeton. The burden of school administration, teaching and scholarly work was enormous, but Hammond survived because he thought remarkably quickly. However, in the School's centenary year the offer of the professorship of Greek at Bristol was too tempting, and he accepted. His departure was marked by a record number of Oxbridge awards for Clifton (surpassed in that year only by Winchester and Manchester Grammar School). Clifton lost a remarkable Headmaster who may have come to Clifton by accident. Rumour has it that when consulted by Sir Christopher Cox on suitable candidates, he decided to take the job himself.

A.R. Thornhill
Pre, NT, 1951–62

IMAGINE!

The Upper School was blessed with a colourful cast of teachers. Mostly from Oxbridge, the staff were all people with a 'hinterland', other skills and passions that meant they could have done anything with their lives. Many were rich, at least in the 1950s, when the staff car park contained a slew of Rolls-Royces and Bentleys (or so I recall Dudley Fromant telling me). By the 1980s teachers were less well off. When a new member of staff moaned about his lowly salary, an old-timer retorted memorably: 'Good heavens! Don't you have a private income?'

George Cross (what a wonderful name) could have had an alternative career as an Oxford don or as a Basil Fawlty hotelier. Some of the staff, such as Peter Knight, not only arrived at the School with a (legendary) previous career (as an ex-international rugby player), but went on to follow a new vocation, as a priest. Others, like Michael Lane and Len Brown, also left to take up the cloth.

The chaplains, Stuart Taylor and John Rankin, made a powerful and fun-loving priestly duo. I doubt to this day that they realize just how much influence they had on the School. Their boundless good humour, limitless energy and vivacity helped make Clifton feel a happy and humane place. How could any schoolboy ever forget Mr Rankin screaming from the sidelines during a rugger match with Marlborough, 'Strike that man down, Lord!'? Clearly, in this Anglican's view, God was not just an Englishman but an Old Cliftonian.

Eccentrics were in no short supply. Tom Gover's classes were pure theatre of a manic kind. His ravings against the 'Irish swinging on [his imaginary] classroom chandelier' and 'Johnny foreigners' generally belied a keen intellect and kind heart and a total commitment to Clifton and its ethos.

Brian Worthington, head of the English department, was another giant, not physically, but by force of his personality and intellect. A stickler for punctuation and punctuality, he instilled not only good manners and good grammar, but a great love of English literature in all whom he taught. Gifted with a genius for understanding the limits and possibilities of each of his pupils, Brian's teaching skills helped make and shape the likes of the BBC sports commentator John Inverdale and the outstanding Shakespearian actor Simon Russell Beale.

In my case, Clifton helped me identify my great passion: politics and history. In no small part this was due to my two A level teachers, Derek Winterbottom and John Barratt. Whereas Derek was structured and disciplined in his approach, 'Johnny' (as he was affectionately known) was colourful and chaotic, but no less effective. His approach was to make every history lesson fun. A keen traveller and unashamed imperialist, he would have been a great district governor in Malaya.

His book *Through Lightest Africa* is a wonderful account of his eventful travels through the continent just as the old colonies gained independence.

A brilliant storyteller, John would reduce every major historical event to a gripping drama, with every pupil hanging on his every word. As each tale reached a crescendo you could hear a pin drop in the classroom. That is unless John's Staffordshire bull terrier (which came to every class) was snoring or, more likely, dashing around the desks. Imagine that happening today.

J.S. Bradshaw
Pre, OH, 1976–85

ALTERNATIVE LEARNING – T.C.W.G.

The board rubber flew through the air, and we new Third Formers began to realize that these would be rather different English lessons. Three board rubbers were positioned on the front of the elevated desk in the Sixth Form room, and with little or no back-lift Tom would propel them at unsuspecting miscreants. The missiles did not always meet their target. I remember one studious and completely innocent individual taking one in the teeth. The apology predictably took the form of black jelly babies. I seem to recall that injury put Tom off slightly for a day or two, and punishments took the form of being sent to the 'Chinese toilet', a small room packed full of books adjoining the classroom. It was off-the-wall stuff, politically incorrect, challenging and infinitely memorable. However, while lessons with Tom were certainly theatrical, this stimulated the learning experience rather than overshadowing it. The texts of Chaucer, Dickens and Shakespeare were good on their own, but with Tom as impresario – exhorting us to read extracts as if we were part of the drama – they really came to life. Come to think of it, Dickens would probably have been pleased to claim Tom as one of his own.

The disappointment of ending English lessons with Tom was short-lived, because my Fourth Form rugby term was spent with him as coach of our unbeaten team. Mao Tse Tung and Nagasaki played on the wings, Château Lafite was our most successful penalty call, and 'rooting warthogs' was the main instruction from the sidelines. I am sure our success was partly down to the opposition's confusion, but the coach had engendered a brilliant enthusiasm and team spirit. It was great fun.

J.R.E. Trafford
Pre, WiH, 1983–92

Creating

6

Opposite: *Duncan Grant, Still Life with Flowers and Omega Vase, 1914. Oil on Canvas. Cecil Taylor Bequest, Clifton College.*

THE LITERARY LEGACY:
Writers and Teachers

Any consideration of Clifton's literary past must almost inevitably begin with the figure of Sir Henry Newbolt (ST NT, 1876–81), the staggeringly popular poet of the early 20th century, who memorialized the spirit of the public school as community and moral foundation, with the recurrent note of patriotism and sacrifice, as exemplified in such pieces as 'Clifton Chapel', 'Commemoration', 'He Fell among Thieves' and, most notably, 'Vitaï Lampada'. The refrain 'Play up! Play up! and play the game!' has attained proverbial status, even if its authorship is often unrecognized. Like Kipling, Newbolt has been charged with jingoism, but his stock may be rising. Clifton, under the guise of 'Downton', features in his novel *The Twymans: A Tale of Youth* (1911). He also wrote the words of the remarkable School Song, ('The Best School of All'): actually an Old Cliftonians' song, it probably owes its survival to the splendid if difficult tune composed for it by Sir Hubert Parry.

One of Percival's first Housemasters, T.E. Brown (1830–97), at one time enjoyed something of the same status. His poems in the Manx dialect retain a resolute following in the isle, but his non-dialect poems have not worn well.

Sir Arthur Quiller-Couch (DH, 1880–82), universally known by his early adopted pseudonym 'Q', was a poet and prolific novelist, whose *Oxford Book of English Verse* remains the most celebrated of all anthologies of English poetry. More notably, he was (effectively) the first King Edward VII Professor of English Literature at Cambridge. The plan to found the chair had to overcome some initial opposition; a leading voice of dissent was that of Q's Clifton contemporary, the Hegelian philosopher J.M.E. McTaggart, who opined that 'a professorship of such a subject … would not only be useless but positively harmful to the university'. In the event, Q's 32-year tenure of the post was brilliantly successful; he left a faculty with firmly established academic standing and a reputation that extended far beyond the confines of Cambridge. His signal strength was as an appreciative critic; always for whom there was a sense of the beauty and power of great literature and the profound enjoyment it offers. His uncompleted autobiography, *Memories and Opinions* (1944), contains a not wholly uncritical account of his time at Clifton.

I.A. Richards (NT, 1905–11), nurtured by the Pre, was a pupil of Q's at Cambridge, becoming an internationally influential literary critic with *Principles of Literary Criticism* (1924) and *Practical Criticism: A Study of Literary Judgement* (1929). Richards is also a link with the other great Cambridge influence on English studies, the formidable partnership of F.R. and Q.D. Leavis. In the 1970s both Leavises lectured and gave seminars to Cliftonians.

Among more recent novelists the best by far (if one excludes L.P. Hartley, author of *The Go-Between*, who fled to Harrow after a single term) is Joyce Cary (1888–1957), who left Clifton in 1906. *The Horse's Mouth* (1944) is a wonderfully rich novel in the picaresque tradition, its archetypically chaotic artist-hero combining elements of Stanley Spencer and Augustus John, with a touch of Blakean mysticism. By turns funny and moving, *Mister*

Sir Henry Newbolt

Newbolt was born in 1862, the year that Clifton College opened, and he always felt that this gave him a special affinity with the School. His father, a vicar in Staffordshire, died in 1866, and his mother eventually moved to a house in Worcester Crescent in Clifton because she had been recommended to send her two sons, Henry and Frank, to the School because of its growing reputation under John Percival. Henry was a day boy in North Town and rose to be editor of *The Cliftonian*, captain of the corps, captain of the shooting VIII, Head of House and acting head of School. He left in 1881 with a classical scholarship to Corpus Christi College, Oxford, where he got a First in Mods but, to his shame, only a Second in Greats. He qualified as a barrister in 1887, and in 1889 he married Margaret Duckworth, a daughter of the squire of Orchardleigh, Somerset. His wife had literary interests, as did her close friend Ella Coltman, and they encouraged Newbolt to write poems and short stories, an interest that had been encouraged at school by the second master and poet, T.E. Brown. In 1897 Newbolt produced his first bestselling book of poems, *Admirals All and Other Verses*, which included 'Drake's Drum' and 'Vitaï Lampada', his poem about a schoolboy cricketer who leaves school, joins the army and is killed leading his men in desert warfare. Its opening and closing lines – 'There's a breathless hush in the Close to-night' and 'Play up! play up! and play the game!' – were soon famous throughout the English-speaking world, and Newbolt became an international celebrity. In 1899, after a visit to Clifton, he wrote 'The Best School of All', which was adopted as the School song after Sir Hubert Parry set it to music in 1908.

Newbolt gave up his life as a lawyer and devoted himself to full-time writing, producing some 40 publications, including poems, novels, adventure stories for boys and history books, specializing in naval affairs. He was knighted in 1915 for services to the nation, which included producing inspirational poems and providing advice to the Admiralty and other government departments, and in 1922 he was made one of the first Companions of Honour. He was an influential member of the Clifton Council from 1919 until 1937, the year before his death, and also president of the Old Cliftonian Society.

D.O. WINTERBOTTOM
STAFF, 1967–94

Johnson (1939) depicts the hapless African clerk of the title with unforced warmth and humanity.

C.H.B. Kitchin (Pre, ST, 1908–14) and L.P. Hartley (OH, 1910) met at Clifton; with tastes in common they became lifelong friends. Kitchin is still remembered for his detective story *Death of My Aunt*, but he also wrote a number of stylish, witty, serious novels, sadly now out of print.

The *métier* of T.O. Beachcroft (Pre, NT WaH, 1912–21) was the short story: he produced a large number of accomplished examples, as well as writing a critical monograph, *The Modest Art: A Survey of the Short Story in English*. His involvement with the British

Council included editing the invaluable *Writers and their Work* series.

Geoffrey Household (DH, 1914–19) was a prolific writer of suspense stories somewhat in the John Buchan mould; a recurrent motif (as in *Rogue Male* (1939) and *Watcher in the Shadows* (1960)), being that of the hunter and the hunted. A careful craftsman with a sense of style, he described himself as a 'sort of a bastard by Stevenson out of Conrad'.

M.R. Ridley (Staff, 1900–03, 1905–09) came back to Clifton as a master for six years before returning to Balliol as a fellow and tutor in English. In addition to the general editorship of *The New Temple Shakespeare*,

Sir Arthur Thomas Quiller-Couch

Born in Bodmin in 1863, Arthur Quiller-Couch was the eldest of five children. After attending Newton Abbot College in Devon, he won a scholarship to Clifton at the age of 17. His father found educating such a large family a burden, and it was fortunate that Q was awarded an entrance scholarship to read classics at Trinity College, Oxford. By the time he had graduated his father had died and there were considerable family debts. To earn money he moved to London and started working night and day writing articles, short stories and poems for various Fleet Street publications, including *The Spectator*. By the time he was 25 he had written three novels, and in 1888 his novel *The Astonishing History of Troy Town*, a thinly disguised account of life in Fowey, was published.

He had first visited Fowey in 1879 to take advantage of the sea air, and he grew to love the town. One of the attractions was Miss Louisa Amelia Hicks, to whom he became engaged and finally married, in 1889, once he had managed to pay off the family debts. His literary career continued to develop, and at first they lived in London. However, overwork led to a breakdown and he was advised to leave the city.

From then on his life centred on Fowey, although he was often away. Arthur and Amelia moved to The Haven and brought up their two children, a son, Bevil, and a daughter, Foy. Q kept in touch with his journalist and literary friends, including Sir James Barrie and Kenneth Grahame. He was involved with the Fowey Yacht Club, first as honorary secretary and, from 1911, as commodore. Appointed a JP in 1907, he was knighted in 1910 and became the King Edward VII Professor of English Literature at Cambridge in 1912, later pioneering the English tripos. He now divided his time between Fowey and Cambridge, travelling by train between the two as he never owned a car. He always expected his room at Cambridge to be filled with flowers, especially his favourites, peonies and chrysanthemums.

He was a leading member of the TA from the time of its formation. and during the early part of the First World War he formed and trained a battalion of the Duke of Cornwall's Light Infantry, putting the recruits through their initial training. His son Bevil went to Oxford and fought in the war, only to die of influenza in January 1919. Q described his sorrow as a figure of Grief sitting on the hearth stone.

Soon after the formation of the Cornwall County Education Committee he was elected to its membership and served as either chairman or vice-chairman for the next 30 years. During this time he visited 300 schools and devoted much time and energy to the goal of providing secondary education for every child in the county. He worked tirelessly for Fowey, which elected him as mayor in 1937, and for Cambridge.

Q died in 1944 when the countryside around Fowey was packed with troops and ships in crowded inlets waiting to invade France. Although most of his books are now out of print, his influence on the teaching and reading of English is an abiding legacy. Clifton always had a place in his affections, even if it was not that of Cambridge or, above all, Cornwall, the county of his heart, and it is as a Cornish gentleman that Q would probably wish to be remembered.

C. TRAFFORD

he edited *Antony and Cleopatra* and *Othello* for the New Arden edition, and his lively *Keats's Craftsmanship* remains a standard work. In a different field, he made an unwitting contribution when Dorothy Sayers borrowed his youthful good looks for her aristocratic fictional detective Lord Peter Wimsey.

Another master, Bernard Groom (Staff, 1923–40), whose dedicated teaching inspired a number of distinguished former pupils to endow a munificent English prize in his name, continued the scholarly tradition. He went on to become professor of English at McMaster University, Canada; among his publications were *A History of English Literature* and the New Clarendon edition of *Macbeth*.

The Twymans: A Tale of Youth

Newbolt's largely autobiographical novel tells the story of Percival Twyman, who went to Downton (Clifton), and about his entry and time at school. The foreword was addressed to Q, saying that he too will remember the events in the story: 'What I have to tell you of these will be, I hope, not less new than familiar, for though you and I were fated to look upon the same faces and the same fields of youth, it is not possible that we looked upon them with the same eyes.' He describes Percival's first view of Downton (Clifton) as he arrived to take the scholarship exams:

'Last of all came the drive from the station to the school. It was at first uninteresting: but presently the drowsy-paced cab emerged from a terrace into the glare of a wide white road which at first descended by a gentle slope. On the left side of it stood a row of substantial houses, taking the sun comfortably on their backs among lilacs and laburnums; on the right was a long range of black paling with a guard of netting above it, and behind both a line of young lime trees. Even now, while the leaves still hid the view from him, Percival heard again and again the sweet crack of bat on ball: then as he drew level and looked between the trees he saw that which took his breath with an entirely new delight. In the distance were buildings – large and stately they seemed, but he hardly thought of them – in front lay a wide green sward, level as a lawn, flooded with low sunlight, and covered in every direction with a multitude of white figures, standing, running, walking, bowling, throwing, batting – in every attitude that can express the energy or the expectancy of youth.'

Above: *Boris Ord.*

Below: *Clifton College Orchestra, 1935. Douglas Fox is in the front row, centre, and David Willcocks is in the back row, second from right.*

However, it was not until the 1960s that Clifton, as in many academic areas, led the field among the great boarding schools by establishing the first separately staffed and trained English department. Initiated under the inspirational joint leadership of Reggie Watters and Nigel Dodd, who assembled around them a brilliant young team, a blend of imaginative approaches and innovative curricula revolutionized the teaching of the subject. The old dispensation, with English taught by form masters, suddenly seemed part of an almost unimaginable antediluvian past. Reggie's style was quiet, measured and authoritative, with his deep love of the subject apparent in all he did. He was an expert on Coleridge (on whom he later wrote an excellent short book), and when he left Clifton in 1967 it was appropriate that it should have been to become head of English at Christ's Hospital, Coleridge's old school. Nigel, in common with many of the best , brought something of the actor's art into the classroom, and stories (some doubtless *ben trovato*) of his more unusual methods abounded. He had been known to conduct proceedings lying on the floor; an apple was produced (and duly consumed) as an aid to a disquisition on *Paradise Lost*; and an A-level set spoke with awe of a whole 90-minute double period devoted to the patient exfoliation of the multiple layers of meaning in a couple of lines of *Hamlet*.

When Nigel left in 1969 he was succeeded by Brian Worthington, another great teacher, who over the next three decades (1970–2000) presided over what the present Headmaster has called 'the formidable English Department' with rare skill, playing to the strengths of its very different members, with results that gained English at Clifton a national repute. From what had become the largest A-level department in the school record numbers of pupils went on to read English at Oxford and Cambridge and other major universities, culminating in the *annus mirabilis* of 1974, when an astonishing 13 Oxbridge places (including six awards) were gained. Brian's edition for the Penguin English Library of Mrs Humphry Ward's *Helbeck of Bannisdale* brought to notice an unjustly neglected book.

D.S. Reed
Staff, 1963–83

ROW. – D.F.CALLANDER, G.R.DUNN, R.G.M.BAGGOTT, J.L.BRAITHWAITE, C.P.LEWIS-SMITH, W.R.COLE, D.V.WILLCOCKS, P.F.MIDDLETON.
ROW. – K.R.W.EAGER, A.J.POTTER, D.T.PIPER, E.C.DE CHAZAL, L.W.DOBSON, A.G.COMER, J.WAY, D.H.FORSTER, A.M.G.TROWER, J.H.HETHEY, F.M.COUSINS, B.V.JACOB, R.E.H.CHARLES
TED. – A.L.MACLEOD, W.F.BALMER.ESQ, F.B.FINTER.ESQ, N.AMBACHE, M.ALEXANDER ESQ, D.G.A.FOX ESQ, M.H.HARDY.ESQ, G.S.MOWAT, V.P.LIDELL ESQ, W.H.OLDAKER.ESQ, L.J.PAGE.

150 YEARS OF MUSIC

Many extraordinarily gifted and famous musicians have been associated with Clifton over the years. These have included directors of music and their assistants, Old Cliftonians, and famous composers such as Sir Charles Villiers Stanford and Sir Hubert Parry. The musical reputation of Clifton has always been extremely high, and during Douglas Fox's time as director of music, a principal of one of London's music colleges was quoted as suggesting that Clifton should be the first choice of school for the education of a musically gifted boy. It was during the time of Arthur Peppin, Clifton's first official director of music, that Parry wrote, in 1908, the wonderful tune to the words of Sir Henry Newbolt, which we now know as 'The School Song'. Its dedication mentions Harry Plunket Greene (1865–1935) who, during the two decades leading up to the First World War, was renowned throughout Europe as one of the finest singers of German Lieder. Stanford wrote one of his most famous works, *Songs of the Sea* (five settings of verse by Newbolt), for him.

In the early days many other musicians known well beyond the confines of Clifton, such as C.S. Lang, F.W. Rootham and W.N. (later Sir William) McKie, served the Music department. One of Peppin's most distinguished pupils was the renowned Dr Boris Ord (ST, 1904–14), director of music at King's College, Cambridge, and the greatest choirmaster of his time. Later of course, D.V. (later Sir David) Willcocks (WaH, 1934–38) followed in Ord's footsteps. Sir David, who was born in 1919, has been for many years one of Britain's most distinguished musicians and is known to every person who has ever sung choral music or Christmas carols in a choir. He is still conducting choirs and orchestras all over the world in what has been an astonishing and fruitful career. Perhaps Sir David's most memorable return to Clifton was in November 1995, when he conducted the Choral Society with the English Chamber Orchestra (no less) in Fauré's *Requiem*.

The link between Clifton and Cambridge colleges continues with the recent appointment in 2007 of Andrew Nethsingha (WaH, 1981–54) as director of music at St John's College. Andrew learned his trade at Clifton with Gwilym Isaac, and at the young age of 34 he was appointed director of music at Gloucester Cathedral.

Below: *Douglas Fox taking orchestra practice.*

Douglas Fox

The story of music at Clifton is inseparably bound up with the personality of Douglas Fox (1893–1978). Douglas was the first boy ever to be elected to a music scholarship at Clifton, and he went on to gain a scholarship to the Royal College of Music where he was highly thought of by the most eminent musician of the day, Sir Hubert Parry. His next step was to gain an organ scholarship to Keble College, Oxford, but then came the First World War and disaster for Douglas: he was so seriously wounded that his right arm had to be amputated. However, such was Douglas's character that he triumphantly overcame this terrible blow and embarked on a brilliant career as director of music, first at Bradfield and then, from 1931 to 1957, at Clifton. He was an inspirational teacher for all those musically talented young men who passed through Clifton during these 26 years, and no fewer than 30 of them gained awards at Oxford, Cambridge or the London College of Music.

Douglas's own performances were memorable. In her biography of her brother, Winifred Fox lists his professional performances of the famous Ravel *Concerto for the Left Hand*, mainly during the 1940s. These were with the top orchestras of the day under conductors such as Sir Adrian Boult and Sir Malcolm Sargent. When Douglas himself conducted at school concerts, he managed to turn the pages of the score with extraordinary dexterity so as not to interrupt the flow of the music in any way. And then, of course, there were his legendary recitals, and for a period of about 60 years Douglas performed these all over the country.

Douglas was not a major innovator in terms of music at Clifton, but he was responsible for several developments, including the revival of the House Singing Competition, and there were some extraordinary performances of choral music during his time, such as Mozart's *Requiem* at Bude in 1942 and Beethoven's *Missa Solemnis* in Bristol Cathedral in 1946.

His services to music were duly recognized by the award of an OBE following his retirement. Perhaps the mainspring of his achievement can be identified as his sheer musical integrity, and this is surely the way in which any musician would most like to be remembered.

C.R.P. KINSEY
STAFF, 1972–2006

Top right: July Verkade as piano soloist at the School Concert at St George's Brandon Hill, 2008. St George's is Bristol's premier music venue and was the brainchild of Harry Edwards.

He conducted many fine performances at the Three Choirs Festival with the Philharmonia Orchestra. Playing in the orchestra, as he has done for many years as principal bassoon, was Meyrick Alexander (ET, 1965–69). Robert Codd (DH, 1953–62) held the same position with the BBC National Orchestra of Wales until his recent retirement.

Ian Partridge (OH, 1952–56) and Christopher Purves (Pre, ST, 1971–79) have been successful singers. As a young man Partridge took part in a BBC television master class with Sir Peter Pears, and his recordings of music by Handel and Finzi are great treasures. His recording (accompanied by his sister Jennifer) of

Schubert's song-cycle *Die Schöne Müllerin* is widely regarded as the finest available. Ian is coming towards the end of his career now, but approaching the apex of his career is the brilliant baritone Christopher Purves. He has taken the lead roles in a number of Welsh National Opera productions, including Alban Berg's *Wozzeck*, and has performed with distinction abroad and made many recordings. He is now much in demand worldwide.

Martina Topley-Bird (OH, 1998–2001) has become very well known, having been nominated for awards in the world of jazz music, and Laura Creese will, I think, soon be making a name for herself, possibly in the world of musical theatre. While she was still at Clifton she sang the lead role in a performance of *Carmen* (produced by Rachel Skinner) and was outstanding.

Singing continues to flourish at Clifton. Douglas Fox revived the House Unison Singing Competition in 1936, although the repertoire has changed considerably over the years. However, the essential element – that of the involvement of almost every pupil in the School – has continued, and this type of choral singing is a valuable experience for even the least musical of pupils. Over the years there have been some highly accomplished 'a cappella' groups, of which Anthony Newman's OK Chorale in the 1980s was certainly one of the best. It made a number of recordings and even performed at the Edinburgh Festival.

Evan Prentice, who served Clifton's music for 19 years, the last ten as director (taking over from Douglas Fox), improved and extended the scope of school music in many directions, including a radical reform of the instrumental competitions, which catalysed an enormous increase in instrumental activity. Evan died tragically from an accident in 1966 when on the point of taking up a lectureship at Bristol University.

Joseph Cooper (NT, 1926–31) won a music scholarship to Clifton and gained an organ scholarship to Keble College, Oxford. To millions of television viewers in the 1970s he was known as the genial host of *Face the Music*, with his dummy keyboard and hidden melodies always likely to confuse panellists such as Joyce Grenfell and Richard Baker. This was one of the most successful programmes ever produced by BBC2, and Joe made many friends all over Britain with his popular lecture recitals about favourite composers and latterly with concerts presented under the title of 'An Evening with Joseph Cooper'. When he died, he remembered Clifton in his will with a generous bequest for a music scholarship, and his complete library of music books was given to the Percival Library.

Other distinguished pianists from Clifton's past include Paul Armstrong (NT, 1967–71), Jeremy Vowles (Pre, NT, 1970–77) and Charles Matthews (Pre, OT, 1973–83), another pupil of Gwilym Isaac. Charles is brilliant on the organ as well as the piano and is developing a promising career, which includes composition as well as keyboard. Charles and Jeremy learned their trade during the 15-year musical directorship of David Pettit in the 1970s. David is a man of enormous energy and brilliant keyboard and conducting skills; his rehearsals at Clifton were never dull. He had married the distinguished clarinettist, Angela Malsbury, whose performances of the great clarinet works frequently enriched the concert life of Clifton.

David's successor, John Davenport, continued to follow David's path by choosing adventurous major choral works for the Choral Society as well as taking over the baton of the Bristol Concert Orchestra (a leading amateur ensemble) from him, and he managed to tempt the professionals of the Bournemouth Sinfonietta for a short residency at Clifton in November 1988. This included a splendid performance of Mendelssohn's *Fingal's Cave* in Chapel, conducted by John. This was given at a morning service with the whole school present. John Marsh (Staff, 1980–94) taught at Clifton during this period and contributed to the department at every level, also writing for both school choral and orchestral groups.

Clifton has never been short of gifted string players. Peter Tanfield (Pre, ET, 1969–78) has built up an impressive career as a violinist leading professional orchestras and as a member of the distinguished Dussek Piano Trio. More recently, the violinist Liv-Marie Fletcher is just starting out on her career and is building up an impressive repertoire. She is particularly strong in the music of the great romantics, and a performance in Chapel of the famous Bruch concerto stands out. Still younger is Ha Young Jung, an extraordinarily gifted player on the double bass, and many will have listened with amazement to Julia Hwang, perhaps at the Prom on The Close or at St George's, Bristol. All these players have been guided in their careers by the irrepressible Richard Crabtree, himself a distinguished viola player as well as a brilliant teacher. Michael Partington (Pre, OH, 1980–85) is a young man who is forging a notable career on the guitar – his website includes an impressive list of recordings and also engagements on both sides of the Atlantic. Other distinguished string players from Clifton include Rachel Walker, one time principal viola of the National Youth Orchestra, and Joseph Crouch, the current principal cello of the Academy of Ancient Music, one of London's leading ensembles playing on original instruments. Chris Grist, another cellist, is the leading light in the string ensemble London Concertante.

Music has continued to flourish in recent years under the wise tutelage of John Heritage and James Hills in the Upper School as well as David Crabtree and David Pafford at the Pre. James Hills has masterminded the hugely successful annual Prom on The Close, which has brought to the Bristol public not only internationally famous musicians but also the best of Clifton's own music-making. In recent years James and John have ensured that Clifton's musicians have had the opportunity of performing at one of Britain's top music venues, St George's, Bristol, a building saved for the nation by one-time Housemaster of Watson's and devoted music-lover, Harry Edwards. The wonderful acoustic of St George's ensures that the Clifton College Orchestra always sounds splendid when it plays there.

The musical tradition continues with vibrant instrumental and orchestral playing, tremendously talented swing and wind bands, and all kinds of singing at a very high standard.

C.R.P. Kinsey
Staff, 1972–2006

Above: *The Chapel organ.*

singing and renderings of the School Song. It gave splendid service for nearly 100 years, surviving the exigencies of errant birds, volatile school buns and aspiring youthful organ enthusiasts. In the early 1970s, with the need for greater dining space, it was dismantled one summer vacation and stored in a room beneath the Chapel.

In 1973, through the magnificent generosity of Dr J.H. Britton CBE, president of Clifton College, the organ was restored, with some modifications, by the firm of Daniels of Clevedon to a similar position on the now upper floor of Big School. It had new casework and a mobile console, and it was opened by Christopher Robinson, the then organist and master of the choristers of Worcester Cathedral.

Sadly its condition gradually deteriorated, and in 2005, again with a need for dining space, it was dismantled and eventually sold to the parish church of Bridgnorth, Shropshire, where its fine sound now fills that lovely church.

The original Chapel was, unlike the present magnificent building, simpler and straight-sided, with a chamber on the north side in which stood the organ. This was given in the 1860s by John Percival, the first Headmaster. Little is known about this instrument, but it was modest in size and was possibly again by the Father Willis firm.

The highly original extensions to the Chapel in the early 20th century meant that the organ had to be relocated, and the opportunity was taken to build a new and much larger instrument, in a splendid case, in the west gallery (originally occupied by lady worshippers). The work was undertaken by the firm of Harrison & Harrison of Durham and was the gift of H.H. Wills OC in memory of his brother. It was opened in 1911. This instrument of four manuals and pedals and some 40 speaking stops, with its noble and full-bodied tone, truly fulfilled its purpose of accompanying fine choral performance and lusty congregational singing. It also nurtured and inspired the budding talent of many of our most distinguished organists. It gave magnificent service, with few problems, until it underwent a major rebuild in 1979. It is a fine example of British organ building and will no doubt continue to inspire, support and nurture singers, players and listeners for many years to come.

Dr J. Marsh
Staff, 1966–94

Organs

The organs of Clifton College, the one formerly in Big School and the one in the Chapel, are important and historic instruments, equal in interest and size to those in many of our major public schools.

The organ in the splendid Gothic Revival Big School was given by the Clifton College Choral Society in 1873 and was built by the famous firm of Father Willis. It stood in two cases, one either side of the large, arched window at The Close end of the building. The right-hand case contained the pipes and action for the two manuals and integral console, while that on the left-hand side contained the pipes for the pedal department. Its tone was refined and beautiful, and it accompanied countless concerts, sessions of school

Good Songs

This book's title naturally conjures up memories of some rousing performances of the School Song at Christmas concerts and OC reunions. The words and music are easily remembered, possibly because it is Clifton's good fortune to have the best school song of all. The combination of Sir Henry Newbolt's words and music by Sir Hubert Parry means that Old Cliftonians around the world have it imprinted on their minds.

The singing of the 'Dorset Carol' at the carol service was also memorable, but the provenance of this carol is somewhat obscure. It was always sung with enthusiasm by the school at the end of the service, but it seems to have been peculiar to Clifton, and those of us who have included it in other services have discovered that it has no magic anywhere else.

During my 15-year tenure of the post of director of music and organist, the music could not have survived without the generous and passionate support from Headmasters and colleagues. Appointments to the staff of anyone who could sing or play the viola were always welcome, and the involvement of everybody in music at Clifton meant that we had some tremendous and memorable occasions in the Chapel. I remember particularly the unique year when Easter was exceptionally early, and we spent it at school. The Harrison organ had been away in Durham for six months having a partial rebuild, and its voice was heard again on Easter eve at the service of the blessing of the New Fire and Paschal candle. It was a magical moment for me at the beginning of the service, watching the spread of the candlelight around the Chapel and then hearing the singing accompanied by the full organ. If I remember correctly, the Pre choir's wonderful performance of Fauré's *Requiem* on the Good Friday meant that this thereafter became a welcome annual event.

The annual choral concerts in the Colston Hall, attended by the whole school, hold many special memories for me, and we were often able to attract some distinguished soloists to join with the Choral Society, which was made up of boys from the Pre and Upper Schools, members of the teaching and ancillary staffs and girls from Clifton High School and Badminton School. Among the many famous choral works we performed, I remember Elgar's *Dream of Gerontius* and Bach's *St Matthew Passion* as being particularly fine (as well as the parties afterwards).

The House competitions and other concerts had their high moments as well, and it has been with pride that we have seen some of our young musicians go on to forge careers in music and other artistic disciplines. The musical environment that was created through the cooperation of staff and boys was a springboard for their success, and I could not have had two more brilliant assistants during my years at Clifton than Gwilym Isaac, who ran the music in the Pre with such skill, and John Marsh, who managed to assist both of us and teach, as well as being closely associated with the music of St Mary Redcliffe. It was a first-rate triumvirate, and we are still in communication with one another. We hope that all those who enjoyed taking part in the music-making remember it fondly as an exacting and satisfying discipline and that it continues to be an important part of their lives.

D. Pettit
Staff, 1966–81

Left: *Nicholas Bromilow, winner of The Worshipful Company of Musicians Prize, 2009.*

Opposite: *Lyre engraved in sandstone on the face of the Joseph Cooper Music School.*

INSPIRATIONS

The greatest Clifton inspirations for me came from a number of outstanding individuals. In mathematics the teaching of Christopher Bradley and Granville Sykes was remarkable, and we were also fortunate to be taught in very small groups indeed.

In music I was constantly stretched by my brilliant organ teacher, Gwilym Isaac. His congregational practices in the Pre used to keep me on my toes. He would play the piano, I would play the organ, and 500 boys would sing. Mr Isaac, who liked his organ pupils to think of him as a god, always tried to catch me out by starting off in a different key. The opportunity to play at daily services was a great preparation for my subsequent career in cathedral music. Accompanying 700 teenage boys singing Stanford's *Te Deum* in B flat is not an experience one forgets.

Charles Matthews, two years above me at Clifton, is one of the most outstanding musicians of his generation, and he was the best possible role model, although I will never have even a tenth of his talent. And page-turning in the organ loft for John was always memorable. If he thought a piece was too long, he would improvise with one hand and feet (shades of Douglas Fox a generation earlier) and flick through the pages with the other hand until he found a passage he felt like playing – no one downstairs had any idea. John Marsh showed us all how to enjoy music-making. The only occasion I can remember him being truly angry was at the end of my first term, when my inept percussion-playing managed to wreck his performances of both a Rachmaninov piano concerto and one of Elgar's *Pomp and Circumstance* marches. Counting hundreds of bars of rests is hard when you are not used to it, and what made it even harder was trying to prevent the cymbals from hitting the brass buttons on my smart new school blazer.

It was a time of musical discovery for me. I vividly remember the excitement of many hours spent listening to LPs of the great orchestral works, always encouraged by John Davenport. Sitting alone by the record player, my ears were opened to the world of Schumann, Bruckner, Mahler, Tippett and so many others. That certainly contributed to my determination to try to find opportunities to conduct orchestras later in life. It was also exciting to discover some of the great choral works for the first time – *The Creation*, Verdi's *Requiem*, *Elijah* and so on – either singing or accompanying the Choral Society.

The history of the School was always in my mind. Not only had my grandfather and his father been in Watson's House, but I was also much aware of the giants of church music who had been at Clifton in the past, such as Boris Ord, Sir David Willcocks and Richard Popplewell.

The dedication of the staff was always apparent. Here were people who had, in many cases, devoted their whole careers to Clifton and its pupils. This taught me a lot about the importance of passing on knowledge to the next generation and about loyalty to an institution.

Other memories include sitting my French O level exam in the zoo ballroom (what on earth was it used for at other times?); bowling a double wicket maiden in a House sixes match (excellently arranged for the worst six sportsmen in each house); having to get out of the bus and run across the suspension bridge on the way to games at Beggar's Bush; spending lots of time lying in the sun on the Downs listening to the 1983 Cricket World Cup on the radio, when I should have been revising for O levels; and that fabulous Parry tune for the School Song at 'The Best School of All'.

A.M. Nethsingha
WaH, 1981–85

Above: Newly refurbished room in the Music School with School House in the background.

Drama and the Redgrave Theatre

Clifton's drama, which already had a proud history, entered a new phase in the 1960s with the building of the Clifton College Theatre. It was the first purpose-built school theatre in the country, as opposed to a multi-purpose hall, which until then had been customary for school drama. Eton followed some months later and modelled its theatre in large measure on what is now known as the Redgrave Theatre. The Redgrave Theatre itself was modelled on the Mermaid Theatre in London, now sadly defunct. With its unadorned brickwork and raked auditorium, it provides to this day wonderful acoustics and sightlines for every seat in the auditorium. It is hard to believe, with the benefit of hindsight, that until the 1960s it was usual for the stage to be raised and the auditorium to be flat.

One need look no further than the Pre school hall, which served as the stage for the Upper School until the new theatre was built in 1966. In 1962 a group of pupils wrote an impassioned piece for the centenary book, bemoaning the fact that it was next to impossible to produce good-quality drama in such conditions. They unwittingly introduced a revolution in drama in schools generally, by prompting John Hersee, later head of mathematics at Clifton but also very much a man of the theatre, to press the then Headmaster, Stephen McWatters, and the Council to build a theatre

on the space that was then part of Wiseman's House, on an area that is, amazingly, smaller than a tennis court.

I still marvel at the ingenuity. There are no wings and no fly-tower (ancient lights problems), but the theatre is a magnificent space in which to present plays. Nowadays, it is equipped more or less to professional levels in terms of lighting and sound equipment, and the restrictions on space have to be resolved by the set designer at an early stage. The Bristol Old Vic Theatre School, which uses it as its main base, shows just what extraordinary standards can be achieved in set design despite the difficulties.

The Redgrave Theatre opened with a flurry of activity, but rather oddly it soon became 'dark' for much of the year. This was because John Hersee, the brilliant mastermind of its building, was also the licensee, and he erroneously believed that he personally had to be

Trevor Howard

Trevor Howard went to The Preparatory School in 1921 and on to Dakyns' when R.P. Keigwin was Housemaster and Rodney Gee was House tutor. He was an outstanding athlete and was in the 1st XV, 1st XI and the boxing and athletic teams, and he played an excellent game of fives. But cricket was his first delight. He was a member of the MCC and was the only actor who always stipulated in his contracts that he would never be called upon to perform when a test match was being played at Lord's. He enjoyed his schooldays but curiously never acted at Clifton. It was at the suggestion of a member of the English staff that he tried for a scholarship to RADA and was successful.

Howard was a great actor, who preferred cricket to other relaxations and who disliked the international jet-set, infinitely preferring a visit to his local pub to a glittering, cosmopolitan party. He knew how much he owed to the loyalty and love of his wife, Helen Cherry, over 40 years of married life. He would have been delighted when she became the first female honorary OC. As an actor he had few equals and, in the words of Barry Norman, 'was a man totally incapable of giving a phony performance'.

Sir Michael Redgrave

The College Theatre was renamed the Redgrave Theatre on the death in 1985 of arguably the best-known OC actor, who was described in *The Times* obituary notice as ranking 'indisputably among the greatest half dozen British actors of the century'. Michael Redgrave came to Clifton in 1922 and was placed in the modern side (no Latin), which was then at a low ebb. However, he flourished and went up to Magdalene College, Cambridge, to read French and German before switching to English. He was *proxime accessit* for the Winchester Reading Prize and had undoubtedly gained a great deal from his Clifton Housemaster, R.P. Keigwin, of whose work he later gave public readings.

Even at school it was quickly evident that he was an outstanding actor. School plays were then performed in Big School, acting was not highly regarded, and actors were so drilled that they were apt to grow like their parts. Redgrave's greatest triumph was as Lady Mary in James Barrie's *The Admirable Crichton*, when he became so moved that he produced real tears. Other memorable parts were Captain Absolute and Lady Macbeth.

present at every performance. When, in 1970, he handed over the administration to Christopher Jefferies (who did a wonderful job for more than 30 years), it became clear that this was not the legal requirement. At much the same time, the Little Theatre, part of the Colston Hall and a regular theatre for amateur companies, closed. There was thus an opening for the Redgrave Theatre to offer its facilities to amateur companies in Bristol and the West Country.

Under Nigel Dodd's enthusiastic leadership of the English department, in 1969 Clifton hosted a major conference for schools on drama and theatre in education. This was quite an eye-opener for this young teacher. It was the 1960s, and the idea of actually putting on plays by established playwrights was anathema – the only respectable kind of drama was that improvised by pupils. It was left to John Hersee himself to argue that there might possibly be a case for presenting plays by real playwrights, and he was received by the audience of drama teachers from all over the country with a somewhat frosty silence. Others were literally howled down for such reactionary views.

Despite this, Clifton persisted in being reactionary and presented high-quality drama in these magnificent

surroundings. With the new-found income from lettings to amateur companies, Christopher Jefferies embarked on a programme of updating the theatre's facilities. It had been built on a shoestring for the incredibly small price of £37,500, because John Hersee, Michael Vokins and others (including large numbers of boys) fitted it all out: seating, wiring, carpeting and so on. There were no technicians in those days (I was the technician in my spare time), and I longed for the day when our income would be sufficient to employ a trained one. (This happened only in 1979, when I

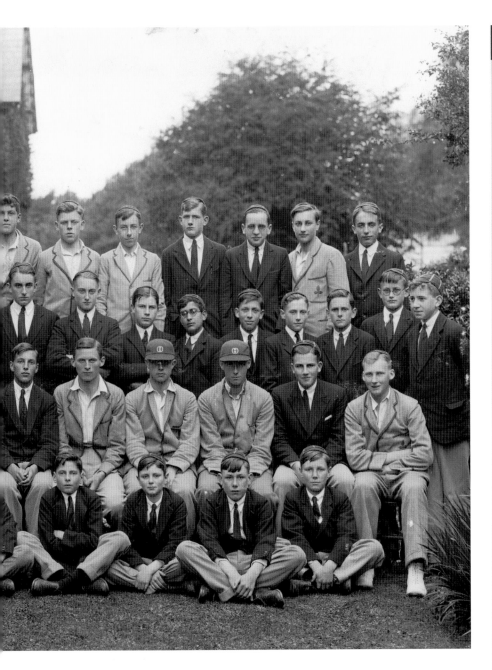

Brief Encounter

Trevor Howard arrived at the back door of Dakyns' at about the time Michael Redgrave was departing through the front door in 1926. These two Dakyns' boys were to become leading British actors for some 40 years, but playing very different roles.

In 1984 Rita and I invited Trevor Howard and his actress wife, Helen Cherry, to lunch in the House and to meet some Dakyns' boys. They enjoyed meeting everybody and had a fine time perusing the House Books of the period, which contained a full account of Trevor's exploits in athletics, boxing, cricket and rugby. There was not much evidence of acting or school work, but there were photographs of the rugby XV with Trevor proudly wearing his colours cap and sporting a moustache. He was also impressed to find that Michael Redgrave had achieved earlier acclaim for his portrayal of Lady Macbeth in the school play. Michael had also won the major school music award, the Kadoorie Cup, playing a piano solo.

The highlight for Trevor was when, accompanied by boys, he found his study with a large peg on the back of the door. He remembered how he had kept his raincoat and trilby hat on that very peg to add to his disguise when he was making regular nocturnal visits to a Clifton bar for a stiff gin or three. 'Nothing much has changed,' he declared with a twinkle in his eye, and we were all amused at this deliberately ambiguous statement. He was a household name for so many years, playing strong characters in films, and we suspect that it was that same hat and coat that launched his famous career when he played opposite Celia Johnson in the 1945 classic film, *Brief Encounter*.

R.L. GLIDDON
STAFF, 1969–76

Above: Dakyns' House photo, 1926. Michael Redgrave is seated second left in the second row. Seated centre is Housemaster R.P. Keigwen (1920–35), see page 126. Seated left of Keigwin is C.H.R. (Rodney) Gee, later Housemaster of Dakyns' (1935–40) and Watson's (1946–55).

Right: Trevor Howard and his wife Helen Cherry with Rita Gliddon on their visit to Dakyns' House.

became a Housemaster and clearly could not afford the time to run the technical side of the theatre in addition to my other duties.)

In the meantime, ignoring the overwhelming message of the 1969 conference, boys were enthusiastic in putting on plays, even those written by dead playwrights. The House Drama Festival, an event instituted in the school calendar in the Bude days during the Second World War, flourished as always and continues to do so. Some of the most impressive drama productions I have seen (amateur or

professional) were during the festival, and they led many Cliftonians to pursue a career in the theatre, television or films.

The School play, the main production of the year, was directed by a wide variety of teachers. The modern languages department produced regular productions in French, Spanish and Italian, and they were often of excellent quality. The junior play at Commem in June (now May) was a fine introduction to acting for younger members of the Upper School.

In 1987, when Heather Henderson became director of drama in the Pre, she immediately transferred productions to the Redgrave Theatre, where they have remained ever since. Her reasons were exactly the same as the 1962 Upper School protesters': why use an inadequate multi-purpose hall when you have the magnificent facilities of a purpose-built theatre available? Since then, Butcombe has also used the Redgrave, and so the long tradition of fine Clifton drama is set to continue.

The theatre hosts all productions in the College and is the base for almost all amateur companies in Bristol and the west. It has become more or less a repertory theatre, with most weeks of the year (apart from maintenance work in the summer) filled by a huge variety of drama.

Until 1993 drama was always part of the English department, and Nigel Dodd and then Brian Worthington (successive heads of English and drama) directed many fine productions. But in 1993 all schools were developing their drama policies, with the growth of the academic subjects of theatre studies at A level (not yet A2) and GCSE's drama and theatre arts. I was appointed the first director of drama, but most of the teaching was undertaken by Sue Shousha (now Sue Slator), John Hartoch (of the Bristol Old Vic Theatre School) and, in the early years, by Derek Weeks. In 2003 Simon Miller took over as director of Drama and developed the department with great distinction.

A key figure in Clifton's drama was Tony Cottrell (Staff, 1978–85). An Old Cliftonian who left in 1967, he returned to teach modern languages, but he was always a great man of the theatre, whether as director, writer, actor, set designer and builder, or stage manager. In his time at Clifton he was influential in developing new ideas and different groups, including the Bristol Independent Schools Drama Organization (BISDO).

Left: *Redgrave Theatre*.

Below: Fiddler on the Roof, *School play, 2007.*

He was a stalwart of the annual Christmas staff productions, often as writer and director, especially of several award-winning pantomimes.

It is somewhat invidious and indeed hazardous to pick out Cliftonians who have flourished in the theatre, films or TV in this period, but among many are Simon Russell Beale, widely regarded as the finest actor of his generation, Simon Shepherd, Roger Michell, Neal Foster, Steven Clarke, Peter Coe, Neil Constable, Julian Firth, Clive Panto, Mark Hill, Chris Hunt, John Inverdale, John Bonham-Carter, Christopher Purves, James Redmond, Adrian Penketh, Andrew Wilson, Angus Scott and Steve Scott.

D.C. Henderson
Staff, 1968–2003

Above: *Simon Russell Beale (as Caius Cassius) in the 2005 production of Julius Caesar at the Barbican Theatre in London.*

Always Ask a Busy Man

These were the words ringing in my head as I walked back to Watson's House after an anxious meeting with Mr Worthington, head of the English department and the teacher who exercised the greatest influence over me during my time at Clifton.

I can't remember now the exact day, but the meeting must have taken place during my last year at school. A few days before, Mr Worthington, with characteristic forcefulness and daring, had announced that the School play that year was to be *King Lear*, and he suggested that I should take the title role. I had agreed, partly because it seemed an exciting prospect and partly because, frankly, I didn't seem to have much choice. I then felt a surge of panic. How could I possibly rehearse a play like *King Lear* and sit my Oxbridge entrance exams at the same time?

And so I asked to meet Mr Worthington. My anxieties were dismissed, and, I'm happy to say, he proved to be right. I enjoyed playing King Lear immensely, and I managed to scrape into Cambridge, due in part to the fact that I had now a reasonable knowledge of at least one major Shakespearean tragedy. That could only have helped.

Being busy is one of the things I remember most about my happy time at Clifton. I went up as a music exhibitioner and so had duties – singing, playing, conducting – that had nothing to do with my increasing interest in English literature and in the theatre, which took up a lot of my time. I made a feeble contribution, too, to the school swimming team. All this activity revealed new paths. Music was, and remains, a central love of my life, but that was, in a sense, to be expected. I came from a musical family and had been to choir school. What was new for me was a whole world of literature and, especially, the thrill of studying Shakespeare.

I had always assumed that I would train as a doctor, like both my parents, but Mr Worthington's charismatic teaching seduced me into taking English at A level and reading English at university. The rigour of his approach – indeed, of all his colleagues in the department – would form the bedrock of my professional life as an actor, so much of which has been spent studying the work of great writers.

And then there was the theatre. Mr Cross, my wonderful Housemaster, recommended me for a small job in the production of the House play during my first term, and Mr Worthington followed this up when he cast me as (a rather frumpy) Desdemona in my first School play. They also suggested to my parents that I might think of a career in the theatre. Subconsciously, a decision was made then and I never looked back.

S.R. Beale
WaH, 1974–78

ART

It could be said, with some justification, that the artistic careers of Henry Tonks (WiH, 1877–79), Roger Fry (SH, 1881–84) and Peter Lanyon (OH, 1931–35) flourished despite, rather than because of, their education at Clifton. The arts were considered of little importance to the brutalized environment of the 19th century public school. Fry recalled the 'hygienic hideousness of the new limestone buildings' and nurtured a 'sullen revolt' against his school and its corporate ethos. But a mark of Clifton's early liberal atmosphere was its comparative tolerance of those creative eccentrics and the encouragement they received from a series of aesthetically minded masters.

Both Tonks and Fry left Clifton to pursue scientific careers. Tonks (1862–1937) became a doctor, simultaneously developing his skills as an anatomist and draughtsman. In 1892 he left medicine and became a teacher at the Slade, influencing a whole generation of British artists, including Walter Sickert, Augustus John and Stanley Spencer. During the First World War he assisted Harold Gillies in his pioneering facial reconstructions, completing a series of graphic studies of the wounded before and after their operations, images that occupy a powerfully ambiguous

position between medical record and art. Throughout his career Tonks was an outspoken critic of another OC, Roger Fry, openly mocking Fry's theories and formalist agenda. But whereas Tonks had influenced a generation of Slade students, Fry changed British taste.

The scion of a wealthy Quaker dynasty, Fry (1866–1934) went into School House in 1881. Virginia Woolf records in later life his violent antipathy to the public school system, but letters home suggest a degree of compliance with the principles of the new school. Following a scientific path – experiments are described in great detail, even his unsuccessful invention for making omelettes – Fry's artistic ambitions seem to have progressed no further than decorating 'a sweet little terra-cotta plate' with flowers. But despite this cultural aridity, Clifton did provide one lasting friendship, that of the Hegelian philosopher John Ellis McTaggart (WiH, 1882–84), who went up to Cambridge with him in 1884.

Above: *Duncan Grant,* Still Life with Bowl of Fruit and Goblets, *1920. Oil on Canvas. Cecil Taylor Bequest, Clifton College.*

Top left: *Vanessa Bell,* Mauve and Red Tulips, *Oil on Canvas. Cecil Taylor Bequest, Clifton College.*

After Cambridge Fry trained as a painter in London and Paris, becoming a vocal and respected art critic. In 1903 he was closely involved with the foundation of the Art Fund with another OC, the founder of the Courtauld Institute's great picture library, Sir Robert Witt (WiH, 1885–90). But Fry is most famous for the series of exhibitions he organized at the Grafton galleries, which introduced Post-Impressionism and the critical apparatus for its discussion to Britain. Fry not only promoted Cézanne, Van Gogh and Gauguin but also contemporary French painting, exhibiting and praising works by Picasso and Matisse. In *Vision and Design* (1920) Fry enthused: 'They do not seek to imitate form, but to create form; not to imitate life, but to find an equivalent for life.' Fry encouraged a younger generation of British artists inspired by the continental avant-garde, including Wyndham Lewis, Duncan Grant and Vanessa Bell. He financially aided the Bloomsbury Group by helping to organize the Omega Workshops from 1913 and sustained them critically, writing with an increasingly formalist aesthetic derived from Clive Bell's concept of 'significant form'.

Although Fry had followed a scientific path at Clifton, he later met and was influenced by one of Percival's earliest and more unusual appointments, John Addington Symonds (1840–93). Symonds, a cultural historian and champion of homosexuality, delivered a series of lectures on Greek art at Clifton in 1869, before publishing his influential *Studies of the Greek Poets* (1873–76). His work on the Italian Renaissance and an encounter with Fry in Italy in the 1890s had an impact on the latter's first book, *Giovanni Bellini* (1899).

By the beginning of the 20th century Clifton had a dedicated art department, and in 1907 Cuthbert Hamilton (1884–1958), a Vorticist collaborator of Wyndham Lewis, was appointed to teach painting. After leaving Clifton, Hamilton was included by Fry in the second Post-Impressionist exhibition of 1912, and the following year became a founder member of the Omega Workshops.

Far right: *Roger Fry at work and, (insert) first edition work by Fry, held in the Percival Library.*

The most celebrated of Clifton's artistic masters was Cecil Taylor, Housemaster of School House from 1926 until 1938. He had been an associate of members of the fledgling Bloomsbury set at Cambridge and bequeathed a modest group of 20th-century British paintings to the School in 1955. Taylor went up to Cambridge in 1906, where he met and embarked upon a relationship with another classicist, John Tresidder Sheppard. It was with Sheppard that Taylor met members of the Bloomsbury set, including Maynard Keynes, James and Lytton Strachey and their cousin Duncan Grant. Grant began a portrait of Taylor in 1909, completing it while Taylor and Sheppard were staying with Keynes at Burford in Oxfordshire. James Strachey wrote to his brother that Sheppard was furious with Grant for flirting with Taylor, so much so that Grant stopped talking to the unfortunate Taylor, even when the pair cycled to Blenheim Palace together. Despite these difficulties, the portrait, now at Clifton, is one of Grant's finest early pictures.

Taylor is shown seated in profile, the diagonal thrust of his body balanced by a Japanese woodcut on the wall. This, combined with the muted palette, makes it is clear that Grant is paying homage to Whistler, while the bold and colourful geometry of the carpet suggests something of his later designs.

Taylor collected Grant's work throughout his career, purchasing the early tribute to Matisse, *Still Life with an Omega Vase* (see p.90), in 1914 and an interior painted at the height of Grant's success in 1927. Taylor also bought from the Omega Workshops, including still-lifes by John Banting, who designed covers for the Hogarth Press, and the South African painter Edward Wolfe. In 1919 Taylor commissioned Wolfe to paint his portrait. During the 1920s he bought from the London Group exhibitions, purchasing a still-life by Vanessa Bell, Virginia Woolf's sister and Grant's closest collaborator, and works by Edward Morland Lewis and Roland Vivian Pitchforth. His interest in contemporary art continued into the 1930s, buying a watercolour study by Paul Nash for the 1935 *Shell Guide to Dorset* and an early Cornish work, *Boswednack*, by Sir Cedric Morris.

Taylor taught Peter Lanyon (1918–64) who, after leaving Clifton, became one of the most prominent St Ives artists of the postwar period. After returning to his native Cornwall, Lanyon was encouraged by Ben Nicholson to follow abstraction, and eventually inspired by Naum Gabo he developed a bold, fluid approach to landscape. After the war Lanyon, ignored by British critics, found success in America, where he encountered Abstract Expressionism and befriended Rothko and Motherwell.

There could be few more extraordinary visual juxtapositions than the pastiche, neo-Gothic of Clifton's main buildings and the vast near-abstract landscapes of Lanyon, but then the spirit does nourish from within.

J.A. Yarker
Pre, WaH, 1996–2004

The Art School

In my day the Art School occupied the top floor of Muir House, a Victorian building in College Road next to Brown's.

Bill Leadbetter graduated from Edinburgh School of Art when the Post-Impressionists, particularly Cézanne and his followers, represented all that was best in modern painting. Roger Fry and Clive Bell were the torchbearers for the movement in Britain. The Art department carried a range of reproductions: Cézanne (of course), Degas, Gauguin, Van Gogh, Picasso, Matisse, Marquet, Braque, Bonnard, Derain, Dufy, Utrillo, Peploe, Duncan Grant, the Nashes, Spencer, Kit Wood, Hitchens and the like, which were to be studied or borrowed by us boys. Many of the classes

Above: *Duncan Grant, Portrait of Cecil Taylor, 1919. Oil on Canvas. Cecil Taylor Bequest, Clifton College.*

were lectures given by Bill with illustrations projected on to the screen by an old epidiascope, which regularly overheated, not to Bill's amusement.

There was some painting in the normal classes, but the really enthusiastic could have extra art sessions twice weekly in the late afternoon. This was where you got the most intensive training. Bill was a stocky figure with a leonine head, steely blue eyes, a strong Scottish accent and a commanding presence. In his youth he had been an outstanding scrum half who would certainly have played for Scotland had he not been badly 'crocked' in a trial match. He was as passionate about rugby, helping to coach the School side, as he was about art, and he brought his fiery temperament to the service of both. Woe betide you if you painted 'fleas' – that is, fiddly details detracting from the whole. That was no way to 'fill the picture space'. The aim was to compose and work boldly. We had no small brushes, only coarse 'hogs', and poster colours ladled from jars (though, when older, we were allowed the use of oils in extra art).

Bill's taste leaned more towards figuration than abstract art, and towards subtle rather than pure colour

The House Art Competition

The competitive nature of boys – especially Cliftonians – was well expressed through the House Art Competition. Though a rather restricted affair when I arrived in 1972, it grew and grew like a proverbial beanstalk as art flourished and we added new media to the available range. Giant paintings jostled for space with pottery and sculpture in a frenzied effort to outdo other Houses. Those with strong talents worked hard to get their show up to scratch and often lights could be seen burning late into the night before adjudication day. The advent of girls added to the fun, the show itself escalating until it finally spawned flamboyant and highly popular fashion shows in the Pre hall, which attracted a great deal of attention from all, including the College Council.

J.F. BAINES
STAFF, 1970–94

Right: *Prize-winning painting by student, Isabel Sandeman (OH), 2007.*

(definitely no Reckitt's blue skies). Each term he would set subjects for painting, usually involving people, such as a café, a market, harvesters and so on, the culmination of the year being the House Art Competition, judged by visiting artists such as Patrick Heron, Julian Trevelyan or Stephen Bone, with the Roger Fry Prize for the best individual. Less prestigious was the MacPherson Prize for Animal Drawing, which occasioned a visit to the Zoo and was awarded by Bill himself at another time. Those of us sitting O and A levels practised life drawing on each other and studied a wider history of art and architecture.

Speaking to other OCs, I gather that Bill terrified some of the 'rabbits', but during my era at least he got a majority of the school painting vigorously, including many of the rugby XV. For the ones who were keen, he was a most inspiring teacher, better than any I had subsequently.

His own painting was, given his character, surprisingly quiet. I think he personally enjoyed woodwork most, and I remember admiring a finely crafted chest of drawers he had made when I visited him and Margaret at their home in Crieff in the 1970s – it was a truly professional job.

B.A. Senior
PH, 1948–53

Worshipping

7

Opposite: *The rose window at the west end of the Chapel.*

Below: *The Chapel before the major structural changes (completed in 1911), which created the hexagonal lantern.*

THE CHAPEL

This is the Chapel: here my son,
Your father thought the thoughts of youth,
And heard the words that one by one
The touch of Life has turned to truth.

Newbolt's words, written in 1897, were steeped in a cultural and social context that seems far away from the hopes and expectations of present pupils at Clifton College. Our understanding of 'truth' may be radically

different, but in a way these words resonate with a continued relevance in a building used almost daily; a building that is appreciated more often by pupils after they leave the School. The soft red and honey-coloured local stone gives a hint of the beauty within. Inside, the unexpected size has powerful presence, and few are untouched by its power.

The Building

When Newbolt wrote his poem the Chapel looked very different from the magnificent building we see today. The original building was designed by Charles Hansom in 1866 and financed by Caroline Guthrie, widow of Canon John Guthrie, the first chairman of the College Council. In the early 1900s the Chapel had become too small for a school that was growing in numbers, and a major reconstruction was proposed that would be in time for the golden jubilee in 1912. The building was imaginatively enlarged to designs by Sir Charles Nicholson. The centre of the long, narrow building was removed and replaced with a central hexagonal 'bulge' crowned by a magnificent lantern. This produced a Chapel that was unexpectedly versatile for the worship of future generations.

The structure of the remodelled Chapel remains much as we see it today, but each generation has focused care on the building with decoration and lighting, notably the ambitious redecoration by Sebastian Comper to mark the centenary of the Chapel's building. He achieved his ambition of transforming 'something rather dull into something radiant and exceptional', employing behind the high altar his

The Memorial Windows

The five memorial windows at the east end of the Chapel were designed by Hugh Easton and dedicated by the Dean of Bristol on 19 March 1939. In vibrant colours they graphically depict apocalyptic scenes from the Revelation of St John the Divine and imagery of the ultimate triumph of good over evil. The three most easterly windows, which were given by Mrs de Gex in memory of R.O. de Gex, depict the Risen Christ appearing to St John on the island of Patmos (Revelation 1:9), a woman clothed with the sun and the moon under her feet (Revelation 12:1–6) and St Michael and his angels fighting the evil dragon (Revelation 12:7–17). The disturbing and haunting figures of the four horsemen of the Apocalypse appear in the latter two windows.

The northernmost window was a gift from Lady Whitehead in memory of her husband, Sir George Whitehead, and her sons, J.H.E. Whitehead and G.W.E. Whitehead. It depicts seven angels sounding seven trumpets (Revelation 8:1), and the hail, fire and blood of God's judgment are hurled down upon the earth. The southernmost window was given by the school in memory of the reign of King George V, and the window shows the Holy City, the New Jerusalem (Revelation 21:2), descending upon Clifton College, where a game of cricket is being played on The Close. What could be more representative of 'heaven on earth' than cricket on The Close of Clifton College?

REV. K. TAPLIN
CHAPLAIN, 2001–

particular trademark – a stunning Comper pink reredos picked out with gold.

Sitting magnificently above are Hugh Easton's vibrant windows. They depict scenes from the Book of Revelation. In the centre St George fights the dragon, and on the far right and dedicated to the memory of George V, the New Jerusalem descends on a cricket match on the Close.

Less easily noticed, but just as arresting, near the entrance is the centenary window by Patrick Reyntiens. The powerful imagery depicts the gifts of the Holy Spirit in abstract representation. Above the organ the rose window casts dappled light with the evening sun and at night shines like jewels to the outside world when lit from within.

Hidden away in the Lady Chapel, which is dedicated as a memorial to Norman Whatley, is Holman Hunt's mosaic *Christ amongst the Doctors*, with a rather feminine-looking boy Christ, but nevertheless a beautiful example of Pre-Raphaelite art (see opposite).

From there, passing a memorial to Newbolt with a hand-written copy of his poem 'Clifton Chapel', the steps lead to the Chapel's secret, for in the crypt is the plain, severe, marble tomb of John Percival, the first Headmaster who, in later years, when he was Bishop of Hereford and chairman of the Council of Clifton, made known his wishes to be buried below the high altar. On 6 December 1918 his wishes were honoured.

The People

Students and staff of all sections of the School have spent many hours in the Chapel, and every quarter hour is punctuated by the tones of the Chapel clock above the main door.

In the early days there were three morning services a week and two compulsory services on Sundays. In more recent times assemblies are held on four days a week, and these allow a fascinating mixture of experiment and tradition presented by Houses and visiting speakers. In the early 1970s many Sunday services became voluntary, and this pattern, a radical move for a public school at the time, encouraged an informal and committed appreciation of worship. Threaded through the regular school pattern were the Thursday evening services of Compline (which continue), allowing both quiet reflection and deep silence. These numinous occasions can be greatly appreciated, as expressed by one young man a year

The Reredos

Commissioned by Canon Wilson for the reredos of the Chapel, the panel *Christ amongst the Doctors* was designed by the Pre-Raphaelite painter William Holman Hunt and executed in mosaic by J. Powell & Sons. The preparatory watercolour (now in Leicester City Museum) was shown in 'the place of honour' at the Royal Watercolour Society in 1887. On its installation in 1890 Wilson commissioned Holman Hunt to write an explanatory essay, published in the *Contemporary Review*. The artist clearly explains his unusually sympathetic rendering of the rabbis, noting that the figure on the far left exhibits the 'frankness and kindliness of the race'. This makes the altarpiece an early testament of tolerance between Clifton College's two religious communities.

J.A. YARKER
PRE, WAH, 1996–2004

after leaving school: 'I only survived the Sixth Form by going to Compline.'

Whatever the occasion, there are always reminders of the people who have sat in those seats and sung those hymns. The history of Clifton is evident in brass plates placed on the back of staff stalls on which are marked the names of those who have become legends of the school. High on the walls are memorials to pupils of another age who died by accident or disease serving the empire.

In the two side chapels hang the banners of Earl Haig and Sir Charles Bonham-Carter, a reminder of the School's strong military connections.

On large School occasions the powerful organ underpins the singing, which is enhanced by the acoustic of the building, and few can fail to be moved by the playing of Widor's *Toccata and Fugue* as they leave the building after their last Chapel.

The Events

The Chapel is the focus of regular memorable events: harvest festivals, carol services, Remembrance Sunday, Commemoration.

A Christmas Day service was introduced in 1979, and the congregation was so unexpectedly large that the School House wine cellar had to be raided to extract some fine claret for use as communion wine. Some years later a Crib and Christingle service was introduced on Christmas Eve. Both continue to flourish, emphasizing the 'parish church' atmosphere of the Chapel.

The potential of the building as a place for experimental drama was spectacularly demonstrated in 1973 by *Apocalypse*, a music-drama that created a sensation talked about at Clifton for many years. After Clifton the production went on to Westminster Cathedral, where it attracted large audiences and received enthusiastic reviews.

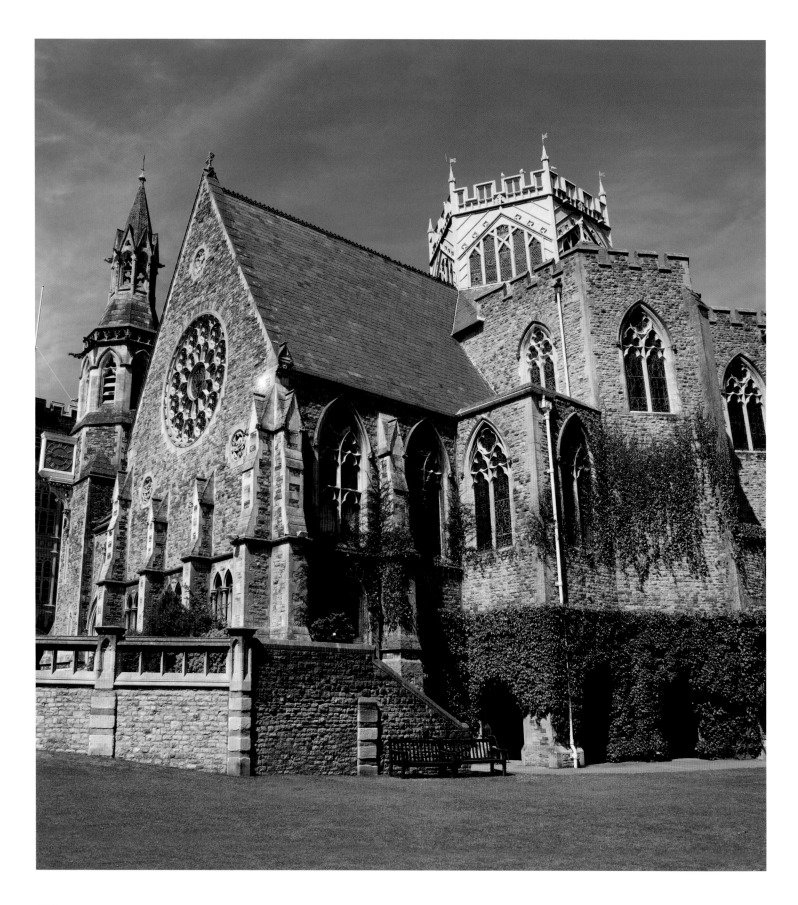

In 1978 an early Easter meant that Holy Week and Easter itself were in term time. This gave a wonderful opportunity for celebrating the greatest Christian festival at school. It became a kind of religious Edinburgh Festival, with main services interspersed with imaginative dramatic and musical contributions – Bach's *St Matthew Passion*, interviews with personalities from the Passion narratives, Fauré's *Requiem*, a crypt presentation on the theme of life–suffering–death–rebirth. Perhaps the most memorable incident was during the all-night vigil. Boys were invited to come to the Chapel at half-hourly intervals throughout the night, and at 3.00 am on Good Friday morning four Dakyns' boys were stopped by a police car as they returned from the Chapel to the House. To the question 'What are you up to at this time of night?', the reply came, 'We've been praying.' The response of the policeman is unprintable.

This occasion was the inspiration for a promenade Passion play a few years later, including a Palm Sunday procession from Brown's House yard, which was led by the Salvation Army band. Boys in the Pre were encouraged to bring large branches to wave. They responded magnificently and formed a travelling forest. A Passover meal in the crypt gave the opportunity for Polackians to teach us Hebrew songs. The interval took the form of a medieval market-place, including Israeli dancing in the South Quad, followed by the trial scene with Pontius Pilate flanked by Roman soldiers on the parapet of the Percival Library. The climax came with a moving Crucifixion in silhouette in front of the flood-lit Comper reredos.

Over several years Franciscan friars visited for mission weeks, asking uncomfortable questions and stirring the soul.

So over the decades the Chapel has been the setting for thoughtful reflection, lusty singing, powerful silence, imaginative presentations, beautiful music, provocative drama, moving memorial services and powerful sermons. Here, as Kim Taplin, the present Chaplain, suggests, is a place of 'corporate belonging', a space that has the power to help us discover ourselves and begin the personal journey that 'the touch of life' turns to truth.

Rev. S.B. Taylor
Chaplain, 1976–88

Apocalypse

The *Apocalypse* began as a post-Oxbridge *divertissement* for boys between their Oxbridge exams and their interviews in 1974. It became a vast affair and had a cast of over 120, including a chorus of virgins (from the High School) and Brian Worthington, as the Devil, in scarlet tights. I wrote the highly schematic music with batteries of bells and gongs and we took it and played it in Westminster Cathedral for three nights afterwards. It was huge fun, an administrative nightmare and filled the Chapel with a three-decker universe in bright aluminium scaffolding.

Rt Rev. Dr D.S. Stancliffe, The Bishop of Salisbury
Chaplain, 1970–77

The Chapel Today

Clifton's Chapel belongs to all three Schools, providing a sacred space at the heart of the community and a still point in the midst of the busy-ness of school days. It continues to be the focus for the joy and discipline of daily worship and reflection on a wide range of religious, spiritual, moral, social and cultural themes. Chapel is a place of corporate belonging but also of rich diversity. There is no room for sectarianism or easy fundamentalist certainties. The approach is inclusive and not judgmental. Open hearts and inquisitive minds are encouraged. The truth is out there to be explored and discovered.

Highlights of each year include the joyful vibrancy of Butcombe's harvest, nativity and spring celebrations, the powerful drama of the Preparatory School's carol service candlelight procession, and the moving

solemnity of the Upper School Remembrance Day service. Smaller groups of pupils and staff gather regularly for the Eucharist, the peaceful and prayerful night services of Compline and the holy simplicity of Celtic and Franciscan liturgies.

Weddings, baptisms, funerals and memorial services of Old Cliftonians, staff and former staff are powerful and moving reminders of the rhythm of life and of the gloriously expansive nature of the Clifton community. The Chapel provides the focus for corporate celebration, thanksgiving or grief. For many, attendance at such occasions evokes tangible feelings of 'homecoming', a return to the most formative place of spiritual nurture, where strength may be found to continue the journey.

In future, schools like Clifton will face significant challenges and opportunities regarding faith and spirituality. Growing secularism in our society means that present generations of students have little foundation in

Christian values, 'church culture' and biblical narratives. The challenge is to be vital and relevant, combining the best of approaches, both traditional and contemporary. The irony is that at a time of decline in institutional Christianity in the West, there is a huge interest in spirituality. The chaplaincy must endeavour to nurture the spiritual quest in an authentic and Christian way.

The Clifton community increasingly reflects the multi-faith and pluralistic cultures of contemporary British society. The challenge is to celebrate diversity, encourage inclusivity and to foster belonging while at the same time encouraging students to explore and grow in their own religious traditions. In a busy, target-obsessed and bureaucratic world, there is little time 'to stand and stare'. Chapel must always provide a place, space and time to reflect and to make the 'journey inwards'. We must always 'value the immeasurable'.

Rev. K. Taplin
Chaplain, 2001–

Above: *The Chapel in use today.*

Right: *Decorative details in the Chapel.*

POLACK'S HOUSE, 1878–2005

By the 1870s an extensive network of rich and influential Anglo-Jewish families was ready to assimilate more fully into English life, including education. However, many prestigious schools were long-established Anglican foundations, which did not at that time admit Jews. After Lionel Cohen had persuaded the Clifton authorities to open a House for Jewish boys in 1878 under Bernard Heymann, an experienced teacher of German and Hebrew who originated from Hamburg, he encouraged his friends and relatives in the Anglo-Jewish community to support it. One of the first four boys was a Sebag-Montefiore, the grandson of the legendary Sir Moses Montefiore and a nephew of Lionel's, and within a few years five Cohens, all relatives of Lionel, were pupils in the House. At first, Heymann took his boys to worship at the Park Row Synagogue, but after a short time he decided that the services were, according to Albert Jessel, one of the original four boys, 'not suitable for us, or at any rate the younger members of the House'. So Heymann conducted services himself in the House and gave religious instruction to his boys as well as teaching them Hebrew. Jessel also put it on record that he never experienced anti-Semitism at Clifton.

Under Heymann the House remained a going concern, although the numbers were small (about ten) and its future was far from assured. Lionel Cohen had also been influential in the opening of a Jewish house at Harrow (1881–1903) and another opened at Cheltenham and lasted from 1892 to 1923. A further boarding house was opened at the Perse School in Cambridge in 1911, and it lasted until 1948. So there were alternatives to Clifton, and the school was lucky to find the Rev. Joseph Polack to succeed Heymann when he left in 1890. Polack had a degree in German from London University and had been minister of the Princes Road Synagogue in Liverpool for a decade. He was 34 years old when he came to Clifton, and he was married to Sophie, with one child and one on the way.

The Polacks were an immediate success, and the Jewish community looked with favour on their attractive appearance and dignified bearing, while valuing highly Joseph's scholarly nature and his experience as a synagogue minister, which recommended him to the more Orthodox Jews, even though the House remained firmly attached to the liberal Jewish tradition. Under Joseph the role of future Housemasters of Polack's was clearly established: he

Above: Three generations of Polack's Housemasters. Standing, from left to right, Philip, Joseph's nephew (1949–64), Albert, Joesph's son (1923–49), and Joseph's grandson, Ernest (1964–79).

was a mainstream classroom teacher in the school at large and in addition he was responsible for the general welfare of his boys, the provision of suitable food, the conduct of religious services in the House, religious instruction and the teaching of Hebrew. It was also accepted that Polack's boys would not take part in any school activities on Saturdays. Jewish houses at other schools were short-lived because it was difficult to find men with the right qualifications and experience to be Housemaster. Luckily, Clifton found the Polack family.

Demand for places rose steadily, and extensions were built in 1896 and 1898 so that the House could accommodate 30 boys. In 1901 the adjoining semi-detached villa was bought so that in 1906 a dramatic transformation took place, as interior walls were knocked through and the House was almost doubled in size. The brochure that was sent to parents emphasized that in the new design 'a room, properly equipped, will be reserved for divine service', and at the opening of the reconfigured House on 27 May 1906 the centrepiece was a religious service in the new House synagogue, preceded in the morning by the ceremony of completing the Scroll of Law. According to one boy, 'this ceremony and the subsequent service were marked by the utmost reverence on the part of the House'.

With numbers now in the forties Polack's could compete on more even terms with other Houses at Clifton, and the rugby XV was admitted to the school 'premier league' in 1910, and the cricket XI in 1912. This, more perhaps than anything else, signalled the fact that Polack's had 'arrived' as a school force to be reckoned with. Joseph was succeeded as Housemaster in 1923 by his surviving son, Albert (two other sons had been killed in action in 1916), who married Betty Cohen, a granddaughter of Lionel. He and Betty took 39 Polack's boys to Bude during the evacuation of 1941–45, living in cramped conditions in a small hotel, the St Hilary. Albert held synagogue services on Friday nights and Saturdays in Flexbury church hall, but during the week his boys joined the whole school for prayers 'based on the consideration of the common religious background of Judaism and Christianity'. Here Albert's own views as a liberal Jew chimed well with those of the Headmaster, Bertrand Hallward, a humanist Christian. Before Bude, Jewish boys had been provided with kosher food in the House, but in Cornwall they dined centrally in the former Headland Café and had the same food as everyone else. After the return to Clifton central feeding was established in Big School, although Polack's boys were provided with kosher food.

Albert retired in 1949, and his successor was his first cousin, Philip Polack, aged 37, an experienced modern languages teacher. He inherited a House of 50 boys, which had risen to 76 when he left 15 years later, and he encouraged the House's interest in all things cultural and intellectual, particularly the production of plays for the School drama competitions. In 1956 the House, which up to that date had not been owned by the School, was bought for it by the children of Sir Robert Waley-Cohen, one of its most distinguished former pupils, and the synagogue was extended and redecorated.

Under Ernest Polack, Albert's son, who took over in 1964, the House reached a record number of 84 boys in 1966. After this, numbers vacillated and actually fell to

Right: *The Synagogue, Polack's House.*

66 in his last year, 1979. Religion came under pressure from sceptics in the House during the late 1960s and the 1970s, just as it did in the School at large, but a new and impressive synagogue, lit by some fine modern stained glass windows, was consecrated in 1974. During the 1980s boy boarding numbers at most schools dropped significantly, and the British Jewish community contracted, especially in Liverpool, Birmingham and Cardiff. Numbers at Polack's declined steadily until 1997, when the closure of Carmel College, a Jewish boarding school which had opened in 1948, brought several Carmel boys and girls to Clifton for a few years. However, numbers were down to 25 again by 2005, the year in which the Polack's House Educational Trust, which had bought the House from the School in 1993 to stave off closure, finally decided that the House could not continue. The Trust sold the House, but its chairman, Nick Tarsh, current president of the College, told the *Jewish Chronicle* in 2004 that it would ensure that at Clifton 'there will be continued opportunities for Jewish worship and Jewish education, addressing what it means to be a Jew'.

D.O. Winterbottom
Staff, 1967–94

Jewish Worship Today

For 127 years Polack's was a House characterized by *Gemeinschaft* relations – that is, it was a community that was homogeneous, based on kinship and organic ties, and with a moral cohesion founded on a common religious sentiment. This is what made the place so special and why it had an effect on the ethos of the whole School way beyond its position as one of many Houses at Clifton. And this sense of community was nurtured by the remarkable Polack family. The dispersal of Jewish pupils to a variety of Houses across the campus therefore created a considerable challenge.

The most important objective was to identify and furnish a suitable venue for the new Polack Centre at the heart of the School. This was achieved by moving the House memorabilia and the Ark, including the Czech scroll on loan from the Westminster synagogue, into the old senior common room, above the current porters' lodge. This means that Jewish boys and girls at Clifton can meet daily to pray and can also congregate on a Friday evening for supper. It provides an opportunity for affirming those ties that bind them together, helps to develop their Jewish identities and consequently enables their Jewishness to impact on the life of the School.

Above: *The Chaplain (Kim Taplin) and pupils.*

Below left: *The Polack Centre, 2008.*

By the 1950s the Meeting, as it was then known, had become an established part of the School. The archive has a memorandum written in March 1954 by the Headmaster to Housemasters suggesting that Peter Brook should 'keep a closer eye on it than hitherto', though the organization continued to remain in the hands of the boys.

The archive lists all the meetings (one each week during term time) for about six years until 1964, and it also contains a register. The average attendance in those days was about 18 boys, with ten or so regulars, and in the early 1960s these regulars included the four Wenham brothers. Regular speakers in the 1960s included staff member G.A.G. Bennet, but most speakers came from outside and included Rev. E.J. Nash (or Bash, as he was always known), who started the Christian holiday camps for public school boys at Iwerne Minster, Dorset, which many Cliftonians attended. For many in those days, Iwerne (as it has always been known) gave them an introduction to the Christian faith and, for those who made a commitment the camps, together with the CF, kept them going in their faith. Rev. David Fletcher took over the camps from Bash, and his first recorded visit was in February 1963, although he remembers speaking at Clifton well before that date. David continues to come to Clifton to give talks at the Christian Forum, which means that his personal association goes back almost 50 years. Many Cliftonians still attend Iwerne holidays, which have now moved to the Norfolk coast.

Although no records exist of CF meetings between 1964 and 1972, I know that they must have continued because when I arrived at Clifton and took over the running of the meeting from Tony Ward (who went from Clifton to train for the Church of England ministry), it was a going concern. Since then, and right up to the present day, the Forum has continued in much the same way. Many things have changed at Clifton since the CF started over 60 years ago, but the essential message of the Christian gospel has, of course, remained the same and has continued to be the focus of the meetings – that is, concerning the good news of God's love and care for us and how anyone can experience His forgiveness through the cross of Christ and live a fulfilled life in His service and in His strength!

C.R.P. Kinsey
Staff, 1972–2006

Kosher food in Big School, Shabbat and festival services at Park Row, links with various student groups and a dash of Jewish studies' teaching combine to provide an infrastructure that enables the Polackian spirit to flourish still at Clifton – and, with the scholarships and bursaries provided by the Polack's House Educational Trust, it remains accessible to the next generation of Anglo and European Jewry. Clifton is a school that has always cherished diversity, and the Jewish contingent is determined to continue to play its part in that noble tradition.

J.H.G. Greenbury
Staff, 1989–

The Christian Forum

The earliest Christian Forum (CF) archive dates from 1959, but it existed well before this. In his autobiography, *Adventure of Faith*, Michael Green tells how, soon after the school had returned from Bude in 1945, he was invited to a 'secret meeting' in the cricket pavilion where some 40 boys listened to a talk about Jesus Christ. The weekly gatherings were led by Richard Gorrie, then head of School, and Richard was instrumental in helping Michael to become a Christian and encouraging him in the early days of his devotional life. It was not long before Michael, along with Julian Charley and Alan Fairhurst, were a Christian triumvirate at the top of the School. All three were later ordained, as was Richard Gorrie.

Playing

PLAYING THE GAME?

There is no doubt that sport has played a major part in the life of the School. The Close has been witness to many a heroic tale in the major games of cricket and rugby, but the story would not be complete without the recollection of physical pursuits played out elsewhere – for example, at Beggar's Bush or on the range, the river and the athletics track, or on a variety of courts.

It all began with Percival's belief that when they were not in the classroom or the library his boys were best occupied in physical activities to prevent them from 'loafing'. In the early years it was cricket that helped to make a name for the School nationally.

Other sports that rose to prominence in Percival's time were rugby football, athletics, rugby fives and cross-country running. The importance of games was evident not only in the fact that before the First World War the head of School was, by default, captain of rugby, but also in the early building programme, which saw the construction of the gymnasium in 1867, a pavilion and the swimming baths in 1869, the fives courts in 1871 and the rackets court in 1872. It is perhaps worth recording that the captains of rugby, cricket and rowing at Oxford in 1881 were all Old Cliftonians from the same House (Oakeley's): R.L. Knight, A.H. Evans and R.S. Kindersley.

'Breathless Hush'

Writing in *The Illustrated Sporting and Dramatic News* in 1934, E.W. Swanton said: 'None of the many Victorian schools leapt more rapidly, and withal more surely, into prominence and favour than Clifton.' On the cricket pitch the Tylecotes were the great players of the earliest days. E.F.S. scored the first two centuries ever scored on The Close, and his score of 404 not out in the Classical versus Modern match stood as an individual world record until A.C. MacLaren scored 424 against Somerset and that, in turn, was superseded by the remarkable feat of the 13-year-old Cliftonian A.E.J. Collins (Pre, NT, 1897–1902), who scored 628 not out in a junior House match between Clarke's and North Town in 1899 on what is now known as Collins' Piece on the lower slope of The Close. The innings was spread over five days and occupied 6 hours and 50 minutes. It was undoubtedly a loss to first-class cricket that Collins went into the army and, until his death on the Western Front in France in November 1914, played a little cricket in India but hardly any in England.

The new century saw the arrival of two players who forged a strong connection with Clifton as both came back to teach at the school. A.D. Imlay (ST, 1897–1904) went on to play for the Gentlemen and Cambridge University before returning to Clifton, where he masterminded the acquisition and development of the Beggar's Bush playing fields. The other, R.P. Keigwin (WaH, 1897–1902), was the most versatile of performers. Keigwin was an English academic and also, surely, one of Clifton's earliest sporting 'superstars'. He played first-class cricket for Cambridge University, the MCC, Essex and Gloucestershire. While at Clifton, Keigwin partnered A.E.J. Collins in the School rackets pair (he was also the rackets captain), and he captained the cricket XI for 1902–3, when Collins also played. He also represented Cambridge University at cricket, rackets, football and hockey and played hockey for Essex and England, and cricket and tennis for Gloucestershire.

Clifton features prominently in the story of the legendary W.G. Grace who lived in Bristol and sent his sons, W.G. and C.B., to the School. W.G. senior played many a great inning on The Close and notched up 13 of his 126 centuries there (as many as he scored in the rest of Gloucestershire put together), including the middle one of the three immortal innings that brought him his 839 runs in eight days in August 1876. W.G. the younger (ST, 1887–1903) achieved a Cambridge blue but suffered the indignity of a 'pair' in his second year at Lord's, much to his father's chagrin.

The Need for New Land
Under Canon Wilson's headship the New Field behind College Fields was purchased when rising pupil numbers meant that pressure on The Close became too intense, and under Rev. A.A. David in 1908, when school games could no longer carry on satisfactorily on the Clifton site, more playing fields were bought on the other side of the Avon Gorge at Beggar's Bush. The 48-acre site was bought by the Old Cliftonian Society for £250 an acre as a memorial for the School's jubilee in 1912. The grounds were not fully fit for play until 1931, having needed considerable clearing and levelling and having also been somewhat affected by the trench digging, mortar practice and potato cultivation that took place there in the war years. The

Above: *Hockey match at Beggar's Bush with the Imlay Pavilion in the background.*

task of transforming the site into level and attractive playing fields fell largely to Imlay, by then a Housemaster at his old school. He was so devoted to his task that he often used to sleep there in a tent after a hard day's work. The Imlay pavilion still stands proud in 'Sunny Corner' (formerly the Yearlings cricket pitches and now the site of the AstroTurf hockey pitches and tennis courts).

BB (as it has become known) soon ceased to be regarded as a white elephant because its acquisition ultimately transformed games at Clifton, and the regular journey out over the Suspension Bridge has been a feature of Clifton life ever since.

The BB Buses
Originally taken in old Albion army trucks, which, when fully laden, were too heavy for the bridge, boys were transported standing up but had to disembark and walk over the bridge itself. The arrival of buses stopped this practice for a while, but new safety regulations meant that the old 'biscuit tin' buses that were still in use in the early 1980s were also then decreed too heavy, and boys were required to cross on foot once again. According to *The Cliftonian* of 1950, no fewer than 9,000 boys were transported a total distance of some 3,000 miles during the winter term.

Of all the games played at BB it was hockey that benefited most, and it became a 'respectable' alternative to rugby, as indeed did soccer to a lesser extent. Then as now, however, transport issues tended to prevail over sporting ones. In the same issue of *The Cliftonian,* for example, a letter to the editor reads:

Beggar's Bush Buses, 1946–50

'You're not on this one, this is A2 – knowing you're rugby, you'll be on C3 – so wait another 40 minutes,' said my North Town tutor, 'Jet' Thompson, in his delicate manner.

The A, B and C buses left from the Memorial Arch at 2.00, 2.40 and 3.20, respectively, and Clifton's three Thorneycrofts had gold numbers 1, 2 and 3 by the entrances. The two teams playing each other were allocated one bus, so that the XVs and the ref were allowed, just, over the Suspension Bridge. Each of these 1927 vehicles did the round trip to Beggar's Bush playing fields three times. So 30 Will Carlings and I were 'bussed' by way of Clifton High School and Christ Church, over the bridge, always being ignored by the staff there, and into the playing fields. We returned by way of the Mansion House and back to the Archway.

These wonderful vehicles were registered in Bristol, HU7244 to 7246, and the special basic lightweight bodies were made by a company called Challands Ross, officially to seat 20. They were in maroon livery with cream bands and a logo of two intertwined Cs on both sides. The seating was arranged around the perimeter.

Thornycroft fitted a 4-cylinder petrol engine of 22.5 horsepower on a chassis with a 14 feet 6 inch (4.42m) wheelbase. The groundsmen at Beggar's Bush, under Geoff Trevelyan, drove them, crashing the gears, but not often. One vehicle had a huge wooden block beside the accelerator pedal for this particular driver's heel as (he said) he had one leg shorter than the other.

Great excitement was generated in 1948 when a Bedford was seen in the queue, delivered in the same colours, but sadly no CC on the sides. So the faithful slow Thorneycrofts were put out to grass, and two had gone by 1949. The third lasted until 1958 as a spare, and everyone wanted to ride on her and not the new ones. These later buses had lightweight bodies by a company called Mulliner, and they lasted until 1978 and 1981.

So, having lost the match, back I came on C3, enjoying the ride more than the game and very envious of the driver, whilst tackling Ma Tom's bread, marg and brown sugar.

P.G. DAVEY

NT, 1946–50 *(previously published in the OC Centenary Edition, 1997)*

Above: *One of the Beggar's Bush buses.*

The present system of running House cricket leagues, by approximately equal times for innings, sometimes leads to acrimonious disagreement. Would it not be better for sides to have innings of, say, eighteen overs each, thus obviating all possibility of injustice to one or the other?

To which the editor replied: '*This suggestion has advantages, but the bus timetable is liable to be disorganized by the uncertain length of games.*'

Athletics

The early days of competitive athletics provided one of the more controversial incidents in the School's history when Clifton beat Harrow and Charterhouse in a fixture in London to the disapproval of the Headmaster (King), who claimed to have been unaware of their participation. He wrote to *The Times*, regretting 'the revival since the war of the tendency to promote public championship competitions amongst schools and generally to exploit school activities for the entertainment of the public'. How times have changed. Today's school marketers would leap at the PR opportunity.

Rugby Football

Meanwhile, rugby football on The Close was thriving and an impressive fixture list developed, including Marlborough, Wellington, Cheltenham and Sherborne. The Clifton versus Marlborough match of 1864 was the first ever fixture between schools, and, according to one of the XV, that game 'had more the appearance of a hostile encounter than a friendly football match'. No doubt those who still annually contest the Governor's Cup between the two schools would recognize the description.

Then as now the School was judged not only on its academic performance but on its results on the games field, so when in 1935 the rugby XV was undefeated there was considerable celebration. At that time Rodney Gee was 'i/c football' and the captain was Francis Alan Way, who played for Cambridge and was subsequently killed in action at Dunkirk.

Clifton now plays on a very tough circuit, so unbeaten seasons are indeed to be applauded and the achievement of Hugh Perry's 1970 side, coached by Jon Gabitass, Tom Gover and Charlie Hannaford, was of particular merit, given the number of games played. No mention of this team would be complete without

recalling Martin Lockyer's last-minute goals from 40 yards against both Downside and Durham. There followed a few years of poor results, but rugby under former England international Peter Knight in the 1980s flourished with his influence culminating in a fine 1986 side, coached by Charlie Colquhoun and Nick Denman, winning eight matches and losing only one.

The appointment in 1986 as head of PE of Kevin Bowring (a former captain of London Welsh who, while at Clifton, coached Wales U21 and Wales A teams before ultimately leaving Clifton to coach the Welsh

national team) led to another successful period of School rugby in the late 1980s and early 1990s. The fear that co-education would herald the demise of rugby was proved unfounded, though the demi-god status of members of the XV proved harder to protect when the girls arrived in 1987. Notwithstanding this seismic shift in the School's social pecking order, the girls were frequent, loyal and vociferous supporters of 1st XV games on The Close. It spoke volumes for Kevin Bowring's approach to School sport and co-education that in November that year, when the girls' hockey team

Above: *Nicholas Treadwell (Pre, WiH, 1945–54) wins a lineout on The Close in 1954. 'I was passionate about rugby. We trained three afternoons a week and played games or matches on the other three afternoons. It wouldn't matter if you had just come out of the Sanatorium, having had a serious bout of bronchitis, or your ear was covered with a nasty dose of the very contagious impetigo, you were thrust out there for the matches.'*

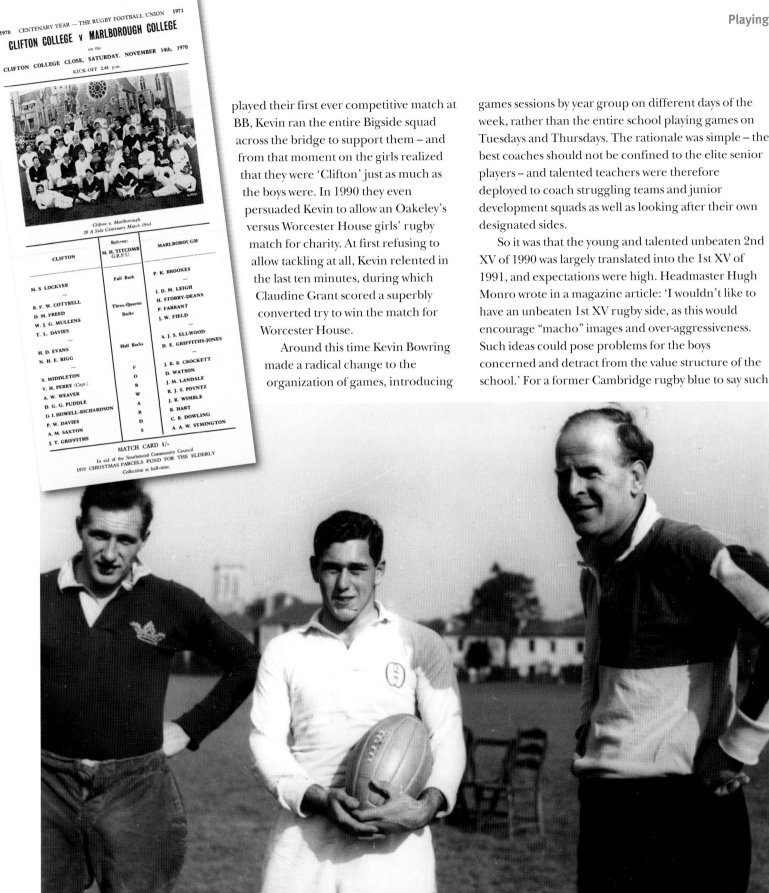

played their first ever competitive match at BB, Kevin ran the entire Bigside squad across the bridge to support them – and from that moment on the girls realized that they were 'Clifton' just as much as the boys were. In 1990 they even persuaded Kevin to allow an Oakeley's versus Worcester House girls' rugby match for charity. At first refusing to allow tackling at all, Kevin relented in the last ten minutes, during which Claudine Grant scored a superbly converted try to win the match for Worcester House.

Around this time Kevin Bowring made a radical change to the organization of games, introducing games sessions by year group on different days of the week, rather than the entire school playing games on Tuesdays and Thursdays. The rationale was simple – the best coaches should not be confined to the elite senior players – and talented teachers were therefore deployed to coach struggling teams and junior development squads as well as looking after their own designated sides.

So it was that the young and talented unbeaten 2nd XV of 1990 was largely translated into the 1st XV of 1991, and expectations were high. Headmaster Hugh Monro wrote in a magazine article: 'I wouldn't like to have an unbeaten 1st XV rugby side, as this would encourage "macho" images and over-aggressiveness. Such ideas could pose problems for the boys concerned and detract from the value structure of the school.' For a former Cambridge rugby blue to say such

Above: Nick Tarsh, now President of Clifton, with his rugby coaches, John Kendall-Carpenter (left) and Peter Brook (right), both former England internationals.

a thing of his rugby team was, indeed, a historic quotation from a public school headmaster, but when the moment arrived that the team was just one game away from an unbeaten season he sent a note wishing them the very best of luck and saying the score in the final game didn't really matter because they had already achieved so much. They won the game, and the Headmaster was, of course, the first to congratulate them. Led by Richard Moffat, the team included several boys who had the potential to go on to greater things. Ed Pearce, who played as a Fifth Former that

season, went on to play professional rugby and represented England A. Tom Morgan's career was cut short by injury, but he went on to play for England Schools and Bridgend. Nick Lloyd played for England U19s after Clifton but was tragically killed in a car accident before he could fulfil his huge potential. Matt Windows, outstanding at any sport he turned his hand to, could have had a professional career in rugby as scrum half but chose cricket instead. Kevin Bowring recalls the glowing post-match tribute to Windows and Lloyd from the Brecon scrum half, a Welsh Schools player, who found himself pummelled by the ruthless determination of the Clifton duo at every scrum.

The example and values set by Hugh Monro and Kevin Bowring in this era are ones that some may argue are missing from competitive sport today. The team of 1991 showed qualities of team spirit, cooperation, determination, honest endeavour, discipline and skill. They did not gloat about their success, and they were modest in accepting the recognition of their achievements. As Kevin Bowring ('The Silver Fox') wrote at the time: 'The purpose of the game is to be a better rugby player, but perhaps it is also to be a better person.'

The most recent unbeaten XV was the side of 2001, coached by Ian Williams and Alan O'Sullivan. Their season started not with the usual two days of pre-season training but with a tour of South Africa, which included tickets to the New Zealand versus South Africa game courtesy of Nigel Drury OC. An exciting draw against Sherborne meant half-term was reached with an unbeaten record intact, and this was maintained until the final match – a new fixture away against RGS Worcester, very much an unknown quantity. Travel difficulties meant the team arrived late and had little or no time to prepare, but as Ian Williams commented: 'From the start we played outstanding rugby. The passing

Cross-country Running

Cross-country running was one of the original sports at Clifton, but it has always tried to preserve the tradition of social pack running alongside the competitive annual Penpole races, know as the Pens.

All the Bigside runs before the First World War were organized as 'hare and hounds', with the hares normally sent out in advance across the Downs towards the Henbury and Shirehampton area – all open fields in those days. A trail of paper was laid, which is why the captain of cross-country still enjoys the splendid title of the Holder of the Bigside Bags, a term copied from Rugby School. The hares laid 'scent', and the hounds strayed across the fields in search of the trail, occasionally whipped in by the Huntsman, which is still the title of the Holder's right-hand man. The hounds were normally out for five hours or more, and the accounts of these runs in *The Cliftonian* are well worth reading, written in a highly precocious style and containing much social comment on the relationships with 'yokels'.

Stories inevitably tend to revolve around the Pens, and one pupil in the late 1920s, Jerry Cornes, went on to Olympic success having first become interested in running at Clifton.

The Long Pen was originally run from Penpole Point in Shirehampton back to school, the finish being in Guthrie Road. More recently it was run from Portbury to Beggar's Bush, and many former pupils will have fond memories of the slog up to St Bartholomew's in Failand. Access rights and tetchy landowners have necessitated further amendments to the course, and it now both starts and finishes in the Ashton Court Estate. Among the many fine runners the School has produced is Justin Chaston (SH), who holds the record for the old Failand course. He went on to be a successful international, reaching the final of the Olympic steeplechase in Barcelona (1992) and Atlanta (1996).

Cross-country has, in the words of a previous Holder of the Bigside Bags, been held in 'a more amateur light' at Clifton than perhaps it is in other schools, and it is unique in that at its heart is the opportunity for boys, girls and teachers of all ages and abilities to run together socially two or three times a week.

I. Scott
Staff, 1971–2003

Arthur Noble writes: 'We found the exact spot in College Road where a photograph of me was taken during the Short Pen in 1955, and we took another picture there. The changes can be seen by comparing the two photographs.

and interlinking between forwards and backs was the best I have seen from a schoolboy team. We ran away with the game, which crowned an outstanding season.'

As Tom Gover has written of unbeaten Clifton XVs: 'It is fruitless to speculate over which was the best team and no doubt this would be galling for other outstanding teams, such as Ian Barlow's 1953 "seven", which was cruelly beaten 5–3 by Sherborne in the final at Rosslyn Park. Peter Brook and John Kendall-Carpenter both coached sides of great ability, which lost the odd match, and I recall the arrogance that can breed in so-called "successful" teams which makes one wary of blowing trumpets.'

Minor Sports

The appointment of Nick Hammond as Headmaster in 1954 did much to revitalize the role of the 'minor' sports, such as rowing, fencing and boxing. In Bill Bailey the school had a real character – he coached fencing, was a PE instructor and masseur. Clifton's fencers, more recently coached by Stuart Scorgie, were (and, by and large, still are) invincible at school level.

The history of boxing at Clifton is essentially the story of one man, Gordon Hazell. Appointed in 1955, he coached boxing for 33 years until it was abolished on his retirement, because Stuart Andrews was fully aware that he would not find a replacement to maintain the standards of skill and safety. Indeed, boxing only lasted as long as it did at Clifton because of Gordon,

Shooting

The early triumphs of the School shooting team have been hard to equal but the sport still thrives, and in the early years of the 21st century, coached by the school marshal, Ron Cross, several Cliftonians had success at Ashburton and Bisley, and national representation was achieved by Kiyah Buck (GB U19, 2001) and (*below*) Olivia Newhouse (GB U19, 2004).

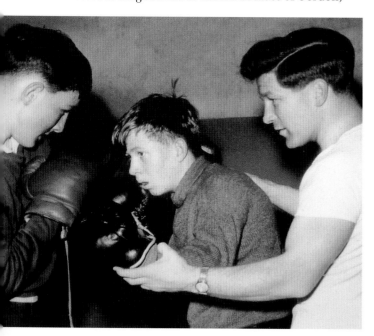

and the national press coverage generated for the House Boxing Competition of 1987 was because it was the last ever such competition at a British public school. But Gordon was much more than a boxing coach to the boys, and his name is still remembered at Clifton through the awarding of the Gordon Hazell Trophy to the boy or girl who has, in the judgement of the Headmaster, epitomized the spirit and values of the School. Tom Gover summed him up as 'a man of simplicity, honesty and integrity with an intuitive and astute wisdom … and an understanding and knowledge of boys that was unparalleled'.

Racket sports, though considered to be minor games at Clifton, have nevertheless produced many success stories. The foundations of rackets as a sport at Clifton were laid by 'Bertie' Barnes, the rackets pro from 1900 to 1950. His immediate successors inherited a group of talented boys whose influence kept Clifton

Left: Gordon Hazell coaching the boys.

in the national eye for many years. J.P. Willcocks won the public schools Incledon-Webber Cup at Queen's in 1968, and with D.G. Parsons he won the public schools colts doubles the following year. More recently, under Terry Whatley's coaching, Matthew Windows (who went on to follow in the footsteps of his father, Tony, in playing professional cricket for Gloucestershire) won the public schools singles at Queen's in 1989 and 1990. In 2005 Clifton hosted the finals of the world championships for the first time.

Though fewer trophies have been won in rugby fives and squash, these games continue to be popular and the current Headmaster, Mark Moore, is a former national champion at Eton fives. In the mid-1990s two prominent Old Cliftonians, John Bretten and Michael Jones, set about a mission to bring real tennis to Clifton. They successfully acquired funding from the National Lottery, and a splendid court was built at BB (on the site of the old garages) and opened by HRH Prince Edward.

Soccer

Although soccer had been played at Clifton recreationally at BB, it was not until 1957 that it gained respectability, when John Cleese's constant badgering of the Headmaster finally succeeded in the establishment of a fixture list. Cleese allegedly enjoyed 'opposition baiting' by indulging in intricate passing moves with a couple of team mates while not really going anywhere. *The Cliftonian* of 1958 reports:

Cleese, the self-styled schemer, has fiddled the ball, himself, his opponents and his fellow forwards into a state of neurotic frenzy! However it is evident that he has the ability to beat two or three defenders in a short space and pinpoint his passes into gaps which would not otherwise have been evident.

It should be remembered that Cleese was also a fine 1st XI cricketer and once famously dismissed Dennis Compton on The Close.

The Rackets Court

School conjures up the images of text books, work and exams. Clifton dispelled any fears that I had as regards education by providing me with a playground of sporting activities that allowed me to embrace the School's motto *Spiritus Intus Alit* (The spirit nourishes within). Clifton never suppressed the spirit of desire to fulfil my ambitions as a sportsman, be it on the rugby or cricket field, but it was on the rackets court that I found my greatest freedom of expression.

Clifton had gone largely unnoticed for many years within the rackets fraternity, with Eton, Harrow and Tonbridge dominating. The public schools championship, held at Queen's Club, provided the prestigious environment for Clifton to demonstrate its force. With myself and partner Justin Crane having won all age group titles, this was our final schoolboy championship. We wanted to retain our title and prove that Clifton ranked amongst the best.

The final saw us drawn against our arch-rivals Eton, which culminated in some fierce hitting, intense rallies and an outcome that saw Clifton victorious (4–2). Two times doubles schoolboy champions was a result for the history books, an accolade achieved by only a handful of partnerships and schools.

While I have been fortunate to continue with my sport and fulfil one of my schoolboy ambitions to play professional cricket, my fondest memories of school are those from the rackets court.

M.G.N. WINDOWS
PRE, WiH, 1980–91

(Matt Windows also twice won the public schools singles. Ed.)

Above: *From left, Justin Crane, Shannon Hazell and Matt Windows.*

Left: The Pool, *1912.*
W.H.Y. Titcomb, pastel.

A World Record?

Sports Day has undoubtedly produced many amusing moments in the School's history, and even the Headmaster Desmond Lee (who was 'not given to raucous mirth') was forced to smile when Tim Mathias 'broke' the world shot putt record in 1954. Knowing he had to pull something special out of the bag to beat K.J.H. Mallett, he stripped off his tracksuit top, emblazoned with GB and a Union Jack, and went through an elaborate performance of chalking the shot, his hands and neck, then launched a world record breaking throw … with the ballcock from the Wiseman's House basement lavatory.

The Modern Era and Girls' Games

The 1978 appeal laid the foundations for the modern era of sport, and in June 1982 the new Sports Centre was opened, incorporating an indoor swimming pool on the site of the old outdoor pool. As well as providing first-class indoor facilities for the School, this development heralded the introduction of commercial activity under the organization of Clifton College Services Limited, at first overseen by the rackets professional Terry Whatley and more recently by Mike Innes. Over the years the considerable and growing profits made from the use of the School's pool, courts, pitches and fitness suites have enabled the School to invest in further improvements both on the main campus and at BB. The AstroTurf hockey pitches, the inflatable 'dome' (an indoor tennis and netball centre) and the 3G artificial soccer/rugby pitch have all done much to improve the standard of sport at Clifton, not least for the girls whose achievements in netball and, in particular, hockey now rival anything the boys can do.

Twice the girls' 1st XI has reached the finals of the National Schools Tournament, being runners-up on both occasions (2005 and 2008), but to be second in the country is an outstanding achievement. Both girls' and boys' teams have gone one better and won the national finals at U13 level. At all age groups Clifton now dominates the county and regional honours, and a large number of girls and boys have represented the School in county (Avon or Gloucestershire) and regional (West of England) squads. International hockey honours have been won by Simon Hazlitt (GB), Fiona Leatt (England U18), Annabel Hockey-Smith (England U16 and U18) and Emily Atkinson (England U16, U18 and U21).

In the modern era there is an unprecedented choice of sports available to boys and girls and many opportunities for them to represent the School. In response to the question from prospective pupils and parents, 'Is Clifton a very sporty school?' I often answer that for the 'sporty' child it is paradise, but point out that that description of the School applies also to those whose interests lie in academic research, music, art and drama. A former Housemaster has written about how games have always been regarded as an essential part of the education here, and how pursuits both inside and outside the classroom have complemented each other, with no artificial divisions. He wrote these sentiments nearly 100 years ago, but they could equally have been written yesterday!

P.C. Hallworth
Staff, 1982–

Old Pool

The old pool was one of the earliest in the country. It was opened in 1867 shortly after the creation of the Bristol Waterworks Company, which ensured a clean water supply in reasonable volume. Michael Brooks (NT, 1944–51) remembers this 'outdoor swimming pool with no heating and little sunshine where we had to swim at least twice a week until the end of November each year. In order to avoid this purgatory a group of us emptied the small indoor pool of rubbish and timber, the residue of American occupation and German bombing, and endeavoured to renovate the pool. It was marginally warmer than outside but the heating system was beyond repair.' This arrangement did not last, and T.J. Mort (SH, 1963–8) recalls: 'When I was in the swimming team it was an outdoor unheated pool, and we started training in 55° and stayed in because it was too cold to dive in.' Although transformed in the 1980s, the indoor pool is still the same hole in the ground. Today activities in the pool include scuba diving, water polo, canoeing, life saving and aerobics.

Upon this ground
A.E.J. COLLINS
in a junior House Match
in June 1899 scored
628 NOT OUT
THIS INNINGS IS THE HIGHEST
RECORDED IN THE HISTORY
OF CRICKET

CRICKET SINCE THE 1960s

It is widely known that in 1899 the 13-year-old A.E.J. Collins hit the world record score of 628 not out, a record that remains intact to this day. Less well known is that the 404 by E.F.S. Tylecote for a splendid game, Classical versus Modern, was a previous world record score, though between the two there were a few others.

Clifton has thus been at the forefront of the game since Victorian times. Until 1968 there were ten schools in the country that played at Lord's: Eton v. Harrow (which continues), Cheltenham v. Haileybury, Rugby v. Marlborough, Clifton v. Tonbridge, and Beaumont v. Oratory. By 1968 there were problems with the Lord's square, and it was decided to dig it up over two years. All fixtures deemed non-essential were asked to move elsewhere, and Clifton v. Tonbridge was one of these (it is scheduled to be played at Lord's in 2012). Instead, the master in charge at Eastbourne, John Lush, who had been at school with Clifton's then master in charge, Tony Record, suggested that the Clifton v. Tonbridge game should be played at his school, and he invited Felsted to form a quartet and have an end-of-season festival. This was the first of many festivals that sprang up round the country after that time, intended to counter the negative effects of the then recent adjustment of the examination and hence school calendar. Hitherto, school term had finished at the end of July, but now it was nearer the beginning of that month, and this continues to cause huge problems for all schools.

After a couple of years Winchester was invited to join, and the festival – the only one with five schools rather than four – flourished for many years. For the first decade or more it was regularly held at Eastbourne, which has the distinction of having two grounds of top

quality. From 1980 the festival started to rotate round the five schools involved, and it was never quite the same. Eventually it began to fold, with assorted problems emerging, not least that of differing term dates and the difficulty of schools to produce their best players. Most other festivals have since gone the same way.

A key figure for just over 30 years was Jim Andrew, who took over as cricket professional from the legendary Reg Sinfield, who retired at Clifton in 1965 and then plied the same trade at Colston's for a further 22 years. Jim had played for Gloucestershire CCC for 13 years from 1952, though his first team appearances were limited, mainly because he was eclipsed by several famous spinners (David Allen, John Mortimore, Sam Cook), for whom the pitches seemed to be prepared.

Top right: *James Kirtley.*

Below right: *Jim Andrew with Douglas Henderson in Barbados, 1995. The Clifton side were competing in the Garfield Sobers International Schools tournament, where they reached the semi-finals for the fourth time.*

Because of his great height he was persuaded to bowl medium-quick (he once took five for eight against Kent), but in my view he was an outstanding spin bowler, able to turn the ball prodigiously and accurately either as a leg-

spinner or, more extraordinarily, as an off-spinner. He tragically died of a heart attack, aged 59, in Barbados in 1996, helping to organize the Sir Garfield Sobers International Schools tournament, a tournament that he himself had been influential in founding.

He was succeeded by Paul Romaines, the outstanding opening batsman for Gloucestershire (and previously Northants and Durham), who has the same knack as Jim Andrew of not merely being a superb coach but also relating to the pupils in ways that can be difficult for other teaching staff. Since 2003 he has worked with John Bobby, the head of boys' games and master in charge of cricket.

The only England player since the war has been James Kirtley (BH, 1988–93). Though wrongly criticized for his action (he has been endlessly filmed without his knowledge, and it has always been shown that it is perfectly legitimate), he was always a player for the big occasion. The more it matters, the better he bowls. He did not arrive at Clifton as a star. Indeed, he was a very modest player until the age of 15. In 1991 we had an outstanding batting side, but absolutely no bowlers. Three of us, Charles Colquhoun (then master i/c), Jim Andrew and myself, did a tour of the nets for younger players, and it struck us all that James had the potential to be a really quick bowler. Jim took him to a grass net and urged him to bowl as quickly as he could. The XI captain had to be vigorously persuaded to play him, but in his first match he took five for ten, and Cheltenham (with three future county players) were dismissed for 62.

Other players have made county appearances, the best known being Matt Windows, who represented Gloucesterhsire CCC from 1992 to 2006. He also played for England A. Although slight of build, he was a pugnacious batsman and outstanding fielder. His father, Tony, was a formidable player, a Cambridge blue in the 1960s and a fine all-rounder for the county before becoming a solicitor. John Meadows was a victim of the county's inability to recognize huge talent, but remains an outstanding cricketer. In Barbados, in the inaugural Sobers tournament of 1987, the main newspaper, the *Barbados Advocate*, picked out three equally gifted players who would assuredly represent their country in the future. John was one. The others were Chris Adams (Sussex and England) and Brian Lara.

In 1987 both John Meadows and Matthew Bailey (son of Bob Bailey, a teacher at Clifton) had the distinction of representing England U19. John played a little for Gloucestershire, and Matthew for Leicestershire. James Williams and Gareth Rees played professionally for Glamorgan. The only blue from this period, indeed since Tony Windows and Mike Ridley in the 1960s, was Adrian Moylan, a stylish and fluent opening batsman, in the mid-1970s.

Others who have donned Gloucestershire colours in recent years are Nic Stovold, Will Rudge, James Pearson and Jamie Whitby-Coles. Outstanding players from the early 1970s without playing first-class cricket were John Cameron-Hayes, Jonathan Willcocks, Marcus Wyburn-Mason, Tim Rees, Huw Evans and David Gladwin. Probably the most brilliant school cricketer of all, however, was Chris Trembath. He arrived at Clifton aged 14 and we immediately batted him at number three. We told him that he would play there for the season, regardless of how well he did. He didn't do well that year, but went on to record a double century two years later. He also became an extremely quick and accurate opening bowler and captained HMC Schools. He also played briefly for Gloucestershire.

These outstanding players, plus many others, such as Bill Lawry, Ashley Fine, Jeremy Brooks, Mark

Eldridge, Richard Holdsworth and Simon Hazlitt, led to increasing success in the prestigious Cricketer Cup for the top 32 Old Boys' teams. From nearly the bottom of the table in the early years of the competition, Clifton won the trophy in 1993 and were runners-up in 1994. Probably the highlight, apart from the two finals, was successfully chasing the 330 scored by Harrow Wanderers on The Close. It was one of several records set by Clifton in the history of the competition.

D.C. Henderson
Staff, 1968–2003

John Cleese and Cricket
In my youth I had the enjoyment of playing cricket with John Cleese. A strange cricketer, at 6 foot 4 inches (1.93m) he towered, stick-like, over us. He was a bowler, well a sort of a bowler. He had a long run-up, which resembled an Arab horse in slow motion, but when he got to the wicket he delivered a slow, loping off-break, bowled off the wrong foot.

Was John funny? Yes he was, but he hid it so well. The 1st XI arrived one day at Cheltenham for a two-day game, and fresh from the bus we were skittled out for next to nothing, with Cheltenham going on to make a good first innings score. Arriving at the crease in the second innings, John decided we had to save the game and batted for almost an hour without scoring, using his long stride to block any attempt by the Cheltenham bowlers to get the ball past him. He refused several obvious runs in his attempt to get into the *Guinness Book of Records*, then a ball swerved off his bat to third man. The frustrated batsman at the other end rushed up the wicket, and John, finding himself occupying the same crease as his partner, reluctantly loped down the wicket with the look of a very sad man.

Left: *John Cleese in the 1st XI.*

My greatest memory of John must be at Lord's in the annual match against Tonbridge. The home of cricket was always a rather pompous place with a crowd of Colonel Blimps thickly clustered in front of the pavilion. I was batting at the time, and when a wicket fell at the other end John was due in next. It is not considered good manners to cross on the pitch, but John lost his way from the changing room and eventually appeared to the disapproving mutters of the MCC ties. When he walked, John always looked as if he was a stork striding through treacle, and he also had the habit of holding his bat underneath his arm as a soldier might hold a baton. It was all taking a very long time, but at last he got to the wicket and took guard, another complicated event. Then he finally settled, and the game seemed about to start. Now I never really knew whether John did things on purpose or in some deliberately twisted way or if that was just how he was. Anyway, he now decided that the sight-screen needed to be moved. More delay and more mutterings from the ties in the pavilion, then we all settled again. The bowler bowled, John stepped forward and nicked the ball straight to slip – out first ball.

John walked off even more slowly than he had arrived. The crowd in front of the pavilion almost hissed as he passed them on his way to the Long Room. As he reached the door to the changing room he turned to two MCC stewards and, as he disappeared from their sight, said, 'Nice little ground you have here.'

J.L. Freeman
DH, 1954–9

ROWING

Although the first issue of *The Cliftonian* in 1867 included a letter asking for a Boat Club to be founded, and although John Percival seems to have taken boys out in a tub four on the Avon at Hanham (rowing himself at stroke, of course), nothing further happened until a young Oxford blue called Reginald Owen joined the staff in 1910 and began to take boys to Saltford to row informally there. Mrs King, the Headmaster's wife, thoughtfully baked a cake each time for their tea. Owen left in 1912 and subsequently became Headmaster of Uppingham and Bishop of Wellington, in New Zealand.

There was no rowing during the war, but in 1919 Charles Payne (a brilliant maths teacher) received formal permission from the School authorities to

Ariel Rowing Club

'The first IV on the River Avon at the Ariel Rowing Club, that CC Boat Club shared when I was at school. The IV were the remaining members of the 1972 VIII coached by Derek Winterbottom. The crew – Andrew Deverson (cox), Chris Iles (stroke and captain), John Sanderson, James Arkle and Phil Hoyland (bow) – were coached by Richard Bland. We travelled down in the old buses, with tea urn and tea – cakes in the winter and squash and biscuits in the summer.'

C.G.A. ILES PRE.ST 1963–73

establish a Boat Club on the Avon at St Anne's Park, the home of Bristol Ariel Rowing Club, to which the School became affiliated. Before long about 50 boys were involved, rowing in fours, and crews were entered for Saltford Regatta, and private races were arranged with Cheltenham and Tonbridge. In the late 1920s the club was run by William McKie, the youthful director of music, who was later knighted for his part in the coronation of Elizabeth II when he was organist of Westminster Abbey. By the 1930s the public schools fours at Marlow Regatta had become the main event for schools with small boat clubs, and Clifton won the trophy there in 1932 and reached the final in 1934, which greatly boosted the popularity and prestige of the sport in the school. Norman Whatley (ex-Radley) generously gave the club a sculling-boat in 1935, at which time about 100 boys were rowing.

There was no suitable water to row on at Bude, but the Boat Club celebrated its return to Bristol by winning

at Marlow for the second time in 1947. Under John McKeown during the 1950s, Clifton moved from fours to competition in eights, and his successor, Brian Mawer, a former Oxford stroke, produced eights during the 1960s that won events at Marlow, Saltford and Bedford and made Clifton's first appearance at Henley. Between 1969 and 1972, with the help of David Tanner, then a Bristol University student and later director of British International Rowing, Clifton crews won 14 regatta trophies. Between 1980 and 1984 ambitious plans were drawn up for building a School boathouse on the Bristol docks, but financial stringencies eventually prevented this. In the 1980s the club rowed chiefly in fours and was often difficult to beat at regattas, winning a total of 54 trophies between 1981 and 1994.

In 1983 five boys were chosen to row in a junior international event in France, and in 1988 a Clifton eight made a second appearance at Henley. Also in this year girls joined the club and won their first regatta event. Ruth Jenkins (OH, 1994–6), although not rowing at Clifton, went on to row at Cambridge and won a Commonwealth medal for Wales.

In 2001 the decision was taken to leave St Anne's and row on the docks, but in 2007 the rowers returned to St Anne's and are once again based at Ariel Rowing Club, where they continue to flourish. Clifton has never set out to be a major rowing school, but since 1919 it has provided great enjoyment on the water for thousands of pupils, and the Boat Club looks forward to the celebration of its centenary in 2019.

D.O. Winterbottom
Staff, 1967–94

Memories and the Making of a Man

It was 15 September 1945, a few days after my eighth birthday. Mother and I were standing on platform one at Paddington Station. The train for Bristol Temple Meads had already arrived, but I wasn't quite ready to cut those apron strings and board it. Mother was talking soothingly about the fun and camaraderie of a boys' boarding school, but having already felt the looks of natural disdain for a new boy of the dozen or so already confident Clifton boys returning to school on the same train, I was not convinced. One of the boys, who I remember only in public school formal family name terms as Boxall, had kindly told my mother that he would make sure I got on the Clifton College bus, which would be waiting at Temple Meads Station,

although once our mothers had left his attitude to me took on what he felt to be an appropriate coolness.

Father had had some leave at the end of the war in Europe and had been shocked to note that his seven-year-old son had been affected by the subversive feminine influences of the four powerful females, my older sister, my mother as well as her two sisters, my aunts Kate and Gladys, who lived with us throughout his five-year absence. He was horrified to hear I was top of the boys' sewing class at my school, and when asked, in his presence, by an uncle what I wanted to be when I grew up, I said I wanted to make dresses like my mother. Very much a man's man himself, he immediately made arrangements for me to be sent off to Clifton, where he expected me to be made a man. He appealed to the sympathy of the School authorities, explaining that he was expecting to be posted to the Far East to fight the war that, at the time, we were still waging with the Japanese. He was consequently able to persuade them to accept me without my having to take the Common Entrance exam, which, considering I was not too academically bright, was just as well. On that last evening before I left home, he stood at the door of the bedroom I shared with my sister, Judy, having had a couple of his customary whiskies, and while unsteadily demonstrating a dubious boxing stance, explained the necessity of learning to box.

Boxing was compulsory at that time at Clifton, and the twice-weekly hour of boxing training taken by the frighteningly disciplined Sergeant Major Hiscock and his assistant (whose name escapes me) when we were paired off, often quite one-sidedly, was, during those first few terms, a horrid ordeal for me. However, I was keen to please my father, and I tried hard. Father's means of encouragement included taking me to various seedy South London boxing halls during the holidays, where we would watch what I later understood to be a rather low standard of British post-war professional boxing. The momentum took hold, and I slowly began to have a taste for this often brutal 'noble art of self-defence'.

I made special friends with Mike Hyde, who arrived at Clifton a few years after me, and we both had a developing interest in the sport. I started subscribing to *Boxing News* and would occasionally buy the American *Ring* magazine, when I had the money, and we both started boxing scrapbooks of great boxing pictures. Mike's mother and father had died in a Japanese prisoner-of-war camp, and he lived with a maiden aunt

Above: *Route to the Bigside pitch from School House lawn, with a view of the pavilion.*

in the respectable seaside town of Clevedon. When my sister died in 1948 and my parents wanted me to invite school friends home in the holidays, I often invited Mike. We discussed boxing interminably, and when we were not talking about it (or girls, of course), we would use one glove each of my only pair of boxing gloves and spar enthusiastically on the lawn of our Bexley home.

During the mid-1950s Clifton was going through a great phase as a boxing school, winning against most of the West Country public schools with which we were regularly matched. By 1954, my last year at Clifton, I had become passionate about boxing and was pretty good, although nowhere near as talented as Mike. I was heavy, however – 14 stone when I was 16 – which meant that I was a heavyweight. During the Easter term of 1954, the term of our inter-school boxing matches, I was chosen to represent the school against the Royal Naval College, Dartmouth. I was fighting their 19-year-old team captain, a certain B.N. Wilson. Despite a pre-fight pep talk from J.D.P. Cooke, our team captain, himself a classic boxer of calculating cool, I lost my fight, although we beat the Royal Naval College by five bouts to four.

I was furious with myself, quietly joining a local boxing club in the holidays in preparation for the inter-House boxing championships in the following Christmas term. When the time came, Mike Hyde and I were fighting in the heavyweight final, both of us having won our halves of the draw. I knew everyone was convinced I would lose, and I did, although it was a terrific fight. It was a December afternoon, close to the end of term, and the gym was packed. We were both well-known School characters, and the boys were aware of our close friendship, as well as there being some special factors to our particular match. Cheering was not allowed during the rounds of these inter-House bouts, but Hillary Crawfurd, my Wiseman's House tutor and the referee, was unable to stop it, finally giving up trying. I felt I deserved a draw, but there was no doubt that the more talented boxer won. That was my last term at Clifton. Mike would be coming back as School boxing captain in the Easter term, when Clifton's new boxing trainer would be Gordon Hazell, a one-time British middleweight champion.

Mike Hyde went on to fight as a heavyweight for Cambridge, as well as captaining their team. He was, pound for pound, almost certainly Clifton's best ever boxer and a great example of the School's fine boxing tradition.

Of course, over-protective political correctness combined with exaggerated parental fears of brain damage have overtaken the concept of compulsory school boxing. I should add that the defensive boxing skills I learned at Clifton have stood me in good stead, helping me to avert certain brain damage during a number of street brawls that have been thrust upon me during my life (particularly since, for theatrical–promotional–fashionable reasons, dyeing my hair flamingo pink).

Mike E. Hyde (Pre, SH, 1948–56) was killed by a ricocheting bullet in a rifle range accident during his National Service, while officer in charge of the butts.

N.J. Treadwell
Pre, WiH, 1945–54

House Rivalry

When I was at Clifton in the 1950s inter-House sporting competitions provided, for many of us, the highlights of our non-academic activities. Becoming Cock House in whichever sport was the ultimate aim, and Wiseman's House, under the great Peter Brook and with the likes of David Perry, Chris Pickwoad and any number of Mathiases on our side, seemed to achieve this goal fairly frequently. Contests were hard-fought, try lines were defended almost to the death, and ingenious methods were invented to overcome the enemy. On one occasion Peter Brook (PWPB) took the entire Wiseman's 1st XV out to Beggar's Bush during a foggy lunch hour for some surreptitious practice before a vital House match – which we won, of course.

I personally added to Wiseman's Cock House tally in 1956 when I was captain of the cricket XI, but in controversial fashion even by the standards of those days. In the final match of the competition we only needed to draw against School House to become Cock House for the first time for many years. Inclement weather had forced a change to the declaration rules (no Duckworth–Lewis system in place then), and a creative interpretation of these seemed the only way to ensure success. I therefore declared our innings closed on the second day of play, leaving School House one meagre hour to score 145. They were, justifiably, furious at my ploy, attacked with all bats blazing from the start and lost nine wickets for 74 in the hour. The match was drawn, Wiseman's was Cock House, and I was booed into Big School at supper that evening. It is a memory that remains vivid to this day, and even after 50 years I apologize to School House for my unsportsmanlike behaviour. However, I remain sure that I did what I had to according to the ethos of the time. Later PWPB gave me a silver ashtray as a leaving present – for services to the House? How times have changed.

M.F. King
WiH, 1952–7

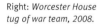

Right: *Worcester House tug of war team, 2008.*

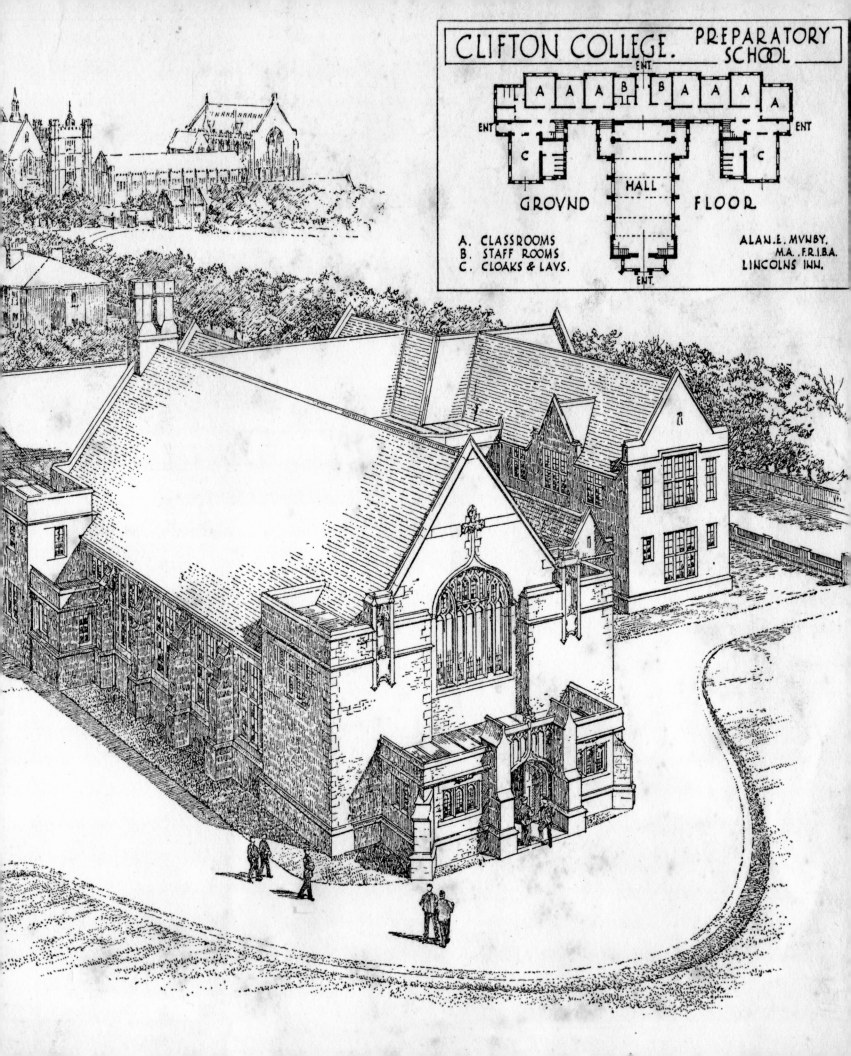

CLIFTON COLLEGE. PREPARATORY SCHOOL

A A A B B B A A A A
ENT.
ENT.
ENT.
C
HALL
C
GROVND
FLOOR

A. CLASSROOMS
B. STAFF ROOMS
C. CLOAKS & LAVS.

ALAN.E. MVNBY.
M.A .F.R.I.B.A.
LINCOLNS INN.

Growing

9

Opposite: *Drawing of the new Clifton College Preparatory School by architect A.E. Mumby with a view of the Pre Hall and the Chapel and Big School in the distance, 1931.*

Below: *Nos. 14, 15 and 16 The Avenue during demolition to make way for the new Preparatory School.*

THE PRE

Consider the unmistakable image of the Pre today: an imposing, 1933-vintage fortress, straddling the stretch from the zoo to The Avenue and dominating an entire Clifton 'block' of ten additional Houses and academic buildings. Its invisible boundaries extend further still, through the shared use of Upper School dining, Chapel and sporting facilities. It's a far cry from the school that first greeted E.G. Sharp on his arrival as Headmaster in 1928, and some imagination is needed to appreciate the phenomenal growth that has taken place over the years, with changes that would amaze and dazzle those of an earlier era.

The 1930s and the War

The Pre that welcomed Mr Sharp was actually only the Lower Pre of today, consisting of 50 boys, aged 7 to 11, including 18 boarders. All its activity took place under the roof of No. 12 The Avenue, known as Matthews' House in honour of that distinguished educator, Harry Norton Matthews, head of Clifton College Preparatory, which had been established in 1908. Dormitories, dining and school rooms were self-contained in 1928, and the 'zoo-end' half of the house had yet to be added as an extension in 1930. It was a small, thriving establishment, but, given the detached location of an Upper Pre (the Junior School for 11- to 13-year-olds, located in Pembroke Road), its fragmented and logistically awkward situation required a remedy.

Imagine the neighbourhood. In the absence of the present main school building, a stroll up The Avenue towards the Downs offered an entirely different view, especially when passing the long-gone Victorian dwellings of Nos. 14, 16 and 18, all as grandly proportioned as their neighbours farther down the road. Finally, one would see the highly reputable Durdham Hall Hotel, standing on what would later become Whatley pitch. The entrance gates (seemingly to nowhere) still remain. One half of what is now the Coach House would later be demolished, which explains the existing stark concrete slab of an outside wall, handy for bashing balls against from the playground.

In a courageous and visionary project, the College Council purchased the acreage north of No. 12 The Avenue, then demolished substantial buildings to prepare the way for a magnificent modern school for

Nos 14, 16 & 18. The Avenue, Clifton, during demolition. 20.XI.31.

Right: *The Duchess of Atholl, recently a Junior Minister at the Board of Education, pictured speaking in the Pre Hall, on 6 May 1933, when she officially opened the new school.*

Far right: *Pre boys raising their boaters and cheering the Duchess of Atholl and guests.*

8- to 13-year-olds. Projected enrolment was never expected to exceed the existing 200 pupils. Academic standards were already high: 'CCPS was then a remarkable school, the French syllabus being controlled, both for the youngest Pre boys as well as the most advanced Oxbridge candidate, by one man.'

Extra-curricular activity in the Pre would raise a present-day eyebrow, as one old boy remembers: 'I particularly hated boxing, which was compulsory. I caused much derision by saying "sorry" every time I hit my opponent.' Boy treble voices were desperately needed to balance the College chapel choir and continued to be well into the 1960s.

Post-economic-depression blues stifled any real growth in the School as numbers seldom exceeded the predicted 200, hardly helped during the Second World War as the Pre boarders were evacuated to the village of Butcombe, 10 miles distant, while the day boys were taught in Matthews' House. In the boarders' absence, the US Army took over the Pre building, using the present upstairs library as a bar and pressing the Hall into service for top-brass dining and briefing sessions.

Expansion under 'Hank'

E.G. Sharp's departure as Headmaster to become the bursar in 1946 opened the door for the dynamic and urbane L.H.A. ('Mark') Hankey, precipitating a major chapter of growth during the latter's reign of 21 years. Starting from a school of 218, rising numbers generated another Upper Pre house known as Butcombe, next to Poole's on Guthrie Road. House rivalry was fierce: 'I once heard the OC parent of a boy in Poole's who confirmed that the House XV were all caned in 1936 for winning the Cock House match by no more than 6–0.'

Such rivalry would continue to be intense over games, especially in rugby: 'In 1951, Hartnell's and Butcombe were then Upper Pre Houses run by two famous Housemasters, "Austin" Read and "Uncle" Jones. On one dark winter's afternoon a titanic struggle was taking place on NF. At the height of battle, the HH tutor who was refereeing came over to Austin and said, "I'm afraid our

scrum half has broken his arm." "Hmm. Right, he'd better go to full back," was the considered response. We can only assume he was not entirely serious.'

Butcombe ultimately outgrew itself as an Upper Pre House, and in 1955 it moved next door to larger accommodation at the corner of Guthrie Road and The Avenue, to be known from then on as Sharp's House. Its previous premises retained the Butcombe name and provided room for 40 Pre-Prep boys. House swapping and name changing would become a regular feature of the Pre throughout the coming decades.

Accelerating numbers meant a tightening squeeze on all facilities. With a head count of 337 in 1959, the post-war dining arrangements in deteriorating Nissen huts on Whatley was enough to deplete anyone's appetite, and when a 'for sale' sign appeared on the Avenue Hotel, directly opposite the Pre's side entrance, the dining huts' days were numbered, and they soon vanished from the green fields of Whatley. Cambridge and Downend Houses gradually shed their resident staff tenants to make way for Tait's, Wollaston's and new classrooms, releasing the north end of the campus for breathing space and activity. The former Avenue Hotel was injected with new life, offering a separate dining room for each House, and it was cheerfully christened Merry House in honour of the popular bursar, Ian Merry.

The growth of the Pre meant that shared Chapel services with the Upper School were no longer possible, especially as the assumption that everyone would show up every Sunday was generally accurate. Separate services now eased the strain of a packed Chapel and also provided Hankey with a forum for his own choral creations.

Bigger and Better

Hankey's growing involvement with the Incorporated Association of Preparatory Schools (IAPS) led to his appointment as full-time secretary of that organization and a distinguished departure from the Pre. His successor, Jim Hornby, arrived as Headmaster from Bramcote School, Scarborough, in 1967. Derek Winterbottom summed him up: 'Hornby was a superb exponent of the art of personal relations … When he spoke to you, he made it seem as though it was the high point of his day.'

When Hornby arrived, the Pre had 325 pupils, a healthy gathering by any account, but with the Upper School numbers in slight decline, the push was on for even more Pre pupils to be enlisted. Two years later, in 1969, with 100 extra boys in the ranks and the existing Houses bulging, the new Upper Pre Hankey's House was opened on the far side of the Zoo. A desperate squeeze in the main School building was eased in 1971 by the twin extensions at the back of the building, adjacent to the Hall, creating the blue computer suite, the language classrooms, the conference room and the staff common room of today. The advance continued with even more newcomers crossing the threshold, making 491 on board by 1975, filling five boys' boarding houses, two of them alone with Lower Pre boys.

By now some of the fabric was becoming frayed. The renaissance of science teaching was gaining momentum, so sharing labs in the Upper School led to a more impressive gear-change with the 1976 addition of Wethered House, adjacent to Merry House, where updated facilities filled the upper two floors. Crucial to any school is a fine library, even if spread across different locations, as the Pre's was during the 1970s. A fiction selection in Cambridge House coupled rather disjointedly with the reference section lurking in room 5, prompting an obvious consolidation of all tomes upstairs in the spacious room 8, with its marvellous backdrop of the Zoo's camels peering over a nearby wall.

The high profile of competitive games has found plenty of scope on Lower Slopes, Collins, Whatley, NF, The Close and Beggar's Bush, and it was often the bus trips to BB where the fun began. Before the appearance of Turner's Coachways' mass transit system, the only way to BB was in the celebrated 'biscuit tin' buses, each shifting about 30 boys.

Indoor sport faced some challenging limitations, since the only large indoor area was the present-day

gymnasium. The swimming pool has always been in its present location, completely open to the elements and generally – but not always – used in the warmer months, as one lad remembers: 'We were obliged to swim in all

Above: *Doc Clay (in the distance) supervising a class working on their 'donkeys'.*

The Zoo Remembered

Rosemary Raymond, E.G. Sharp's daughter, moved to 12 The Avenue with her family in 1928. She recalls the closeness of the Zoo 'and the roaring lions a constant reminder. I had a recurring anxiety that one of the animals had escaped and was coming up the stairs near my bedroom.'

A Conker Record

In 1983 Johnny Morris visited the Pre to congratulate the boys of Matthews' House for making the longest conker chain and so entering the *Guinness Book of Records*.

weathers, once the temperature reached 58°F [about 15°C], and were clad, as Virgil advised, for ploughing and sowing – nude.'

Music's early days revolved around piano lessons taught in the Hall, with a smattering of orchestral instruments sprouting from obscure classrooms. It remained for Gwilym Isaac to establish a fully fledged Music School during the 1960s and 1970s, gradually infiltrating and expanding throughout much of Cambridge House during his 25-year reign as the first director of music in the Pre and as choirmaster. The choral commitment appealed to select aspiring souls, but everyone was conscripted into the annual House singing event. This was rigorously competitive, strictly formal and adjudicated by an outside professional; trophies were awarded, and musical and House reputations were completely on the line. Nowadays the event follows an outlandishly relaxed format, and any

'judging' is left to the applause decibels. The splendid grand piano, a generous Verkade bequest, remains the focus for countless concerts, and the Hall organ, personally financed and designed in 1986 by a versatile schoolmaster of long standing, David Moorhouse, dominates assemblies and hymn singing.

The late 1970s was an idyllically innocent time for Pre boys. The nine- and ten-year-olds regularly made their way on foot to Dawson's toy shop on Whiteladies Road, unsupervised, walking in pairs as the main safety precaution. Careful road use was simply assumed and expected when dealing with the lighter traffic of those days, and the same was true for excursions (in threes) to the Zoo after school hours.

Clare Hornby's welcoming Matthews' kitchen was always the main attraction for many younger boarders, as much for the steady stream of boys passing through as for the Hornby family themselves, not to mention the surprising array of invited guests, visiting heads, even members of the government. Prior to one Commemoration, the Archbishop of Canterbury just happened to wander in before preaching in the Chapel the following day.

Sunday outings certainly stretched the limits, relying on reasonable common sense rather than any notion of the rigorous health and safety regulations of today. Rock faces in the Avon Gorge invited some adventurous manoeuvring, but the ultimate thrill of the climb was, in the words of one survivor, finally 'sitting on the edge of a 200-foot drop, thence, along a two-foot ledge along the Gorge and thus into Leigh Woods. Does this happen today? Has some of the fun and adventure disappeared?' Among less testing activities, the obsessive schoolboy diversion of conker chains reached manic proportions when an entire drawing room in Matthews' House was carpeted with linked chestnuts, gaining an entry in the *Guinness Book of Records* during the early 1980s.

Onwards … to co-education

Numbers in the Pre had swelled the enrolment (from the age of six upwards) to a whopping 554 at the time of Jim Hornby's departure in 1982, but he knew that changing attitudes to boarding might soon lead to a decline from the then level of 190. The subsequent interregnum was sagely handled under the seasoned and avuncular wisdom of Paul Hutchinson, one of a succession of second masters who have added an indispensable dimension to the proceedings of the school.

The next incumbent, from 1983, was Roger Trafford, previously Headmaster at Pyrland Hall in Taunton. Trafford inherited a large ship and a tall order for maintaining traditions but also the necessity for essential changes. For a start, art, pottery and design were scattered across the campus. The pottery kiln could be found in the basement of Wollaston's – convenient, but isolated. The woodworking shop lay on the far side of The Close in the Worcester House basement, though at that time it was the School San. Meanwhile, the painting studio was in the upper corner of the school in room 17, under the firm hand of P.R. Clay: 'Scenery for school plays was always PRC's province, often done during teaching time (when he wasn't telling ghost stories) and invariably achieving striking effects. As the curtain went back, he was always the first to clap!' These three strands of creativity were ingeniously united when the old Terriers' Hut made way for the Hornby Arts and Technology Centre, begun in 1984 and a welcome improvement in space and facility.

The first Preamble crept on to the spring calendar in 1984. This now traditional biennial walk-in-the-woods fundraiser has generated over £200,000 for various charities over its 25 years. Instigated and launched by Roger Trafford as the Helen House Walk for the benefit of that hospice, this all-day event involves pupils, staff, parents and friends of the Pre on a pleasantly exacting six-mile countryside loop devised by Hamish Bergin. Multiple circuits, barbecues and picnics fill the hours, now under the able organization of Roger Mills.

The Pre fired the co-education gun in January 1987 with the arrival of the first two pioneers, Zillah Bowes and Rachel Ellis, later joined by Misses Whatley, Waymouth and Baker in the summer term, all as Matthews' day girls, making it the only co-ed House in

Clifton's history to date. There was a discernible ripple in the football, cricket, athletics and swimming ranks, and a few boys tried that much harder in Sports Day events that year. Meanwhile, Poole's was refurbished for the official September intake, and for the first Housemistress, Sarah Meunier, and her family. She was soon succeeded by Anne Turnbull, who would remain for 15 years. Another major redevelopment took place in 1990, with the creation of the library resources centre along the upper corridor, giving the Pre a world-class facility among prep schools.

The transition year of 1992–93 saw the close of another Headmastership, as Roger and Cheryl Trafford departed for the Dragon School, Oxford, after a decade that had seen considerable change at the Pre, but not before the launch of an enlarged Butcombe Pre-Prep, now for three- to eight-year-olds. This establishment would commandeer Sharp's House on the corner of The Avenue and Guthrie Road. The resulting space on Guthrie Road was filled, in turn, by Hankey's House under Ian Nuttall, as it moved from its original Cecil Road home of 23 years and became next-door neighbour to Poole's, for a few years at least.

Into the 21st Century

And so the baton was passed to Bob and Jill Acheson from St Andrew's School, Pangbourne, eager to make their mark with new school uniforms, fully carpeted

Above: *Sister Frances Dominica in 1984 receiving a donation towards the cost of building Helen House, Oxford, the first children's hospice. Some energetic boys are pictured having done four laps of the circuit. With them are Hamish Bergin, left, and Roger Trafford, Pre Headmaster.*

Far left: *New Library/ Resource centre.*

Above right: *Girls' dormitory in Poole's House, 2009.*

Below right: *John Milne, Pre Headmaster 2008– .*

hallways and classrooms, and elaborately choreographed plays. Larger projects loomed, the grandest being the 1995 conversion of the Merry House dining rooms to an impressive layered enterprise with a lofty Music School on the entire top floor and an updated Science School in the middle of the sandwich. South Town (home to girls since 1992) and North Town moved their premises from Nos. 6 and 11 on The Avenue to become a linked House on the lower floors. The knock-on effect freed No. 6 to accommodate the expanding Butcombe Pre-Prep and an upper level Sharp's House for younger boarders. Hartnell's House migrated from Percival Road closer to campus in 1996, taking over the Matthews' House building, as it had been known for some 80 years.

Tait's and Wollaston's also underwent a refreshing facelift in claiming additional upgraded floor space for a heady expansion of day boys in the new millennium. Gone now were the original 'cloakrooms' at both ends of the main school, no longer needed for TT and WT, and replaced in succession by the drama studio, the Headmaster's study, the red computer suite and a dance studio.

Utilizing every inch of available space, the fives courts were removed to make way for the John Bretten Memorial Hall, offering Butcombe dining space and a multi-purpose room and gymnasium for all. At the same time as laying a new soft surface on the Pre playground, its boundaries were also extended to provide tennis and netball courts, while just around the corner the newly renovated Coach House was established as a special needs unit and EFL centre.

More changes and improvements were to follow in 2005 as Hankey's House experienced its third incarnation farther along Guthrie Road, vacating its premises (the original Butcombe) for Guthrie House, now for younger boarding and day boys. Meanwhile, a

slightly forgotten and somewhat neglected original Pre edifice received a massive make-over, as No. 8 Northcote Road became an administrative hub, accommodating the Headmaster's study and senior management offices.

In 2007 Bob and Jill Acheson announced their plans to leave, and they left in the following year after 15 years in command, a tenure that underlined the established permanency of Pre Headmasters ever since the time of E.G. Sharp. Only five heads had held the reins over the intervening 80 years, with each of them since Sharp also serving as chairman of the IAPS, a remarkable leadership record for any school.

The Achesons' farewell was preceded by a final fanfare when the upper floor library witnessed a magnificent expansion into the attic. This was unknown territory except to those who could recall the indoor shooting range running the length of the school's eaves. At a stroke, this extra space doubled the resources of the library (further enhanced by high-tech skylights) and provided another computer suite.

The Preparatory School that John Milne inherited as Headmaster in 2008 came with a solid foundation and tradition, which had been nurtured by his predecessors into a vital part of Clifton College. Today's 400-pupil Pre, together with its separate Pre-Prep of 200, is a striking contrast with 1928's compact crowd, but a strong sense of continuity between the two ensures that this thriving community remains firmly linked to its origins. John and Helen Milne are securely poised to keep the ship positively and happily on course.

J.F. Hatton
Staff, 1975–

All unattributed quotations in this chapter are reproduced from an article by Tom Jenkins, 'The Pre as we knew it', in *The Old Cliftonian*, centenary edition, 1997.

THE NISSEN HUTS AND MERRY HOUSE

Although the Second World War ended in 1945 the period following was one of austerity. The Pre had their meals in a pair of Nissen huts on what is now referred to as Whatley. I suspect that these temporary buildings may have been erected by the US army during its occupation of the School. They were the rather bleak dining rooms that greeted me when I first arrived at Clifton in the summer of 1945.

We sat at long tables, and at the head of each was a member of staff. I remember little about our food, but these were frugal times. Rationing remained in place for some while, and the fare we were served would not have taken many prizes in gourmet competitions. However I do remember that the fried bread went down very well. Two or three puddings spring to mind: frogs' spawn (tapioca), Avon mud and rhubarb jelly, again, I believe, with tapioca. Less palatable were tripe and onions, which I still find hard to eat.

These comments apart, the meals themselves made no lasting impression. Few of the staff were young – the younger men had gone off to war – and there were women teaching in the lower classes, although female staff were very much in the minority in those times. I do remember one master, Archie Maclaren, whose party trick was to stand on his chair and pour tea into his cup from a great height. I suspect this same man was behind the thunder-flash that was ignited just outside the Nissen huts as we ate tea one November evening. For the uninitiated, thunder-flashes are like very loud fireworks and were sometimes used in army exercises. They make a terrifying noise, and this particular one went off without warning so that the effect on us boys aged 8 to 13 was spectacular.

Eventually, in the early 1960s, the Pre took over the Avenue Hotel and Pre dining moved to that building. Subsequently the Nissen huts were razed to the ground. It is hard to believe now that the area outside Tait's and Wollaston's and behind the Pre was where school ate. The buildings that are now Tait's and Wollaston's were originally flats rented by members of the staff.

Living as it does cheek by jowl with the Zoo, it is perhaps not surprising that sometimes animals impinged on the lives of people involved with the School. As a special concession school boys were allowed into the Zoo for 1d (an old penny). They did have to identify themselves by wearing their caps, which were natty little numbers that perched on the back of their heads and,

Above: Pre dorm, 1970s.

incidentally, did service as pen wipers in the classroom. (Fountain pens were a rarity and biros did not exist, so most pupils used pens that were dipped into ink wells, and some of us had difficulty controlling the ink!)

I remember one small boy, probably no more than seven or eight years old, being terrified by the roaring of the lions. He came from Kenya and was certain that there was a lion roaming the streets. It took all the diplomatic skills of the Headmaster's wife at the time, Mrs Hankey, to persuade the little chap that the lion was safely locked up in a cage.

Another incident that made quite an impression some time before the war was when some practical jokers put a ladder into the monkey temple. The monkeys, I believe, swarmed out and scattered. One of them found its way to Cambridge/Downend House and gave the occupants of one of the flats a very nasty surprise when she drew back the curtains.

There have, of course, been many changes in the last 50 years. When I was there Poole's was a boys' House. All of us were in just two large dormitories, and from our dormitory window we could see the polar bears just below us. They have now gone, but more intrusive were the peacocks, which during the mating season make an unbelievable noise, especially in the early morning.

Immediately following the war the San was where Worcester House is now. It was a lovely, airy building and in 1945 still had a small operating theatre. It was there that I underwent a small operation, which was

carried out by a well-known Bristol ENT Surgeon, Mr Angel James. The building, which is today the Sanatorium but was then called the Old San, was in those days used as an overflow. One glorious spring we had a chicken pox epidemic following close on a measles outbreak. As soon as our temperatures were down we were shipped off to the Old San to convalesce. Normally, if a boy spent any time in the San he was automatically put 'off games' by Dr Craig for a week, but during the time we were recovering, some of us from chicken pox and measles, we played football and other improvised games on the Lower Slope all day long in the glorious sunshine, and the authorities didn't seem to notice.

C.R.J. Millar
Pre, WiH, 1945–52; Staff, 1963–94

DRIVE THOSE ARMS

I was 8¼ when I arrived at Sharp's House in the autumn of 1972. Armed with a huge tuck box and a large blue trunk, I quickly settled in to boarding school life, comforting other homesick boys. My abiding memories were of queuing up for our daily tuck allowance just after supper and matron allowing us either three sweets or a half a bar of chocolate. Food and tuck seemed to be the most important commodity at prep school. I once was so desperately hungry I swapped my watch for four ounces of lemon bon-bons.

Bob Frampton was our indomitable Housemaster, and Hamish Bergin was our House tutor. They somehow saw some potential in me as an athlete and drilled me in the skills to jump over seven flights of hurdles when I was ten years old. I will never forget the words 'drive those arms' resonating as Mr Frampton urged me to athletic greatness, drilling me day after day in the freezing cold. I discovered to my surprise that I liked the event and realized that I actually had some potential and talent over the sticks.

The following year, 1975, I was entered into the new event, the 75 metres hurdles for under-12s. In front of my parents, sister, and a

Right: Also known as Ben – nicknamed so by Bergin in Sharp's. 'This was because there were three Jewish boys in a house of 45 boys and I was the youngest one of them. Out of these three boys there were two Anthonys, and he thought that may be confusing, so he nicknamed me Ben (Benjamin being the youngest son of Jacob). This stuck with me throughout my schooldays and indeed I am still called Ben.'

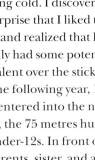

packed Sports Day crowd I jiggled nervously at the start line, lining up against my fiercest rivals, including Joe Lalonde, who everyone knew was the fastest runner in the School. Take your marks, get set, and on the 'B' of bang I catapulted out of my starting blocks and sprinted over the first six flights of hurdles. Everything went completely silent and still, and I approached the last flight in the lead, Lalonde hot on my heels. I broke the tape as a winner. It was the first time I had experienced that magnificent feeling of accomplishment, and I'll never forget that day. My parents were delighted for me and that inspired me to hurdle for Avon in 1978 and the Middlesex counties in 1983. Of course, if it wasn't for Bob Frampton and his famous words I might never have discovered the joys of competing and, better still, winning.

At the age of 13 I entered Polack's House and became Head of House in the summer of 1981.

Those early athletic experiences equipped me to become a boxing promoter, and in 1998 I staged the first ever boxing shown live on Front Row and Bravo TV featuring Cornelius Carr, the then WBF middleweight champion of the world versus Dingan Thobela (the Rose of Soweto), one of South Africa's greatest boxers.

My son Samuel is now four and is also showing tremendous jumping ability. Maybe, just maybe, he may go on to athletic prowess. Who knows?

A.H. Stone
Pre, PH, 1972–81

A Bit about Old Staff

'Write a bit about old staff' was the request. 'You know the ones I mean. The characters. The legends.' Ah yes, I thought … them.

I actually do recall, despite the passing of oh so many years, the very first time I walked into the Pre common room. It was, to say the least, a curious menagerie. In the corner, coalescing into a rather battered leather armchair, was an equally battered old man whose nose and eyes positively glowed with the long-term effects of the sherry glass he, even now, clutched in his hand. Uncle Jones was, I later realized, in every sense a fixture. A large man with a huge barrelled chest, a small moustache and a booming voice, which caused even adults to shudder at their unspoken guilt, held court in the other corner. This was, I was eventually told, Lewin, the one and only Lewin.

And then there was Peter Clay, the slightly manic head of art and the even more manic proselytizing Catholic, whose stated aim for the next few years would be to try and drive me back into the ways from which I had long since departed. He held sway with a sawn-off cricket bat and a mischievous charm, which he invariably lavished on anything in a skirt. And 'Frampo', the ex-bomber pilot whose moustache would bristle with indignation, but whose heart was of gold and whose talents seemed never ending. Then there was Bob Overton, my guide in those moments of uncertainty, a man straight out of a Noël Coward play, whose every languid move spoke of a different era.

Yes, it was definitely a most curious menagerie, but it was, I was horrified to see, staring at me with a somewhat slack-jawed expression on its collective face. For a moment I thought it must be someone else, but then I realized that, with hair down below my shoulders and beard nearly as long, the curiosity was, as far as they were concerned, standing at the door.

Over the years that followed there were to be many other characters. Nick Spruytenburg, Sprout of Mastermind and 'sproutmen' fame, Eliot Watkins with his deliciously camp humour and breakfast clubs, Jim Barker, the whispering ghost that was Ian Gillett, 'Wooders', a man of quality whose stated aim was sadly to become a couch potato, Millington of the locks and Moorhouse of the clocks.

But there were three who stick in the mind, sadly all now dead. There was Jimbo, who, despite my Oxfam suit, appointed me! The pipe-smoking Jim Hornby, a true liberal in every sense of that much misused word, whose occasional and unexpected irritations simply served to emphasize his bigness of heart. Then there was Basil, whom I first encountered in a flurry of dust and profanities, cleaning out the English store cupboard. Another great liberal, another eccentric, another heart of gold. And finally there was Bergin. 'Hairy' to the

Far Left: *Jim and Claire Hornby with their youngest son, Andy.*

Right: *Nigel Siddall.*

children and a man who had Clifton in his every drop of blood. By his own admission a rascal when a child in the Pre, he had been a praepostor in the Upper School and then, after spells as a trainee doctor and policeman, had returned to his roots as a teacher. And what a teacher! Probably the most natural one I ever saw.

And yet, as I think about it now, there were so many more. Men and women who flickered in the light and then were gone, some too early, some in the fullness of time. But that was the Pre, and that I suppose was one of the reasons why I stayed … and, mad fool, continue to stay.

N.E. Siddall
Staff, 1976–

Adventuring

Because I was away from home for the very first time, the Pre was so much more than a school, and the academic side of life was much secondary to the wealth of other activities available. However, for those of us lucky enough to have it, double art on Saturday mornings was the holy grail of the Pre timetable. Peter 'Doc' Clay's ghost stories were the highlight of any school week. Nothing else quite had the emphasis of

his 'persuader', as he brought it crashing down onto a bench to punctuate his terrifying tales. 'The Beast with Five Fingers' still haunts me today.

So many reminiscences of the Pre begin with a frantic dash up the steps from the Matthews' basement, gathering a streak of saltpetre on my jacket from the limestone wall, then bursting on to the great expanse of the playground, the site of many feats of heroism during hard-fought games of 'catchers and escapers' after prep. The various trenches and wells around the buildings provided us with an adventure playground par excellence.

Adventuring was a major part of life in the Pre. One early-morning adventure took place in June 1983. Planning for a mass break-out by the members of Euston had occupied part of letter-writing time the previous Sunday. We intended to get to New Field just before dawn to watch foxes. Unfortunately no one was up then, but there were stirrings by about 5.00 am. A group of us in dressing gowns duly stepped into the early morning sunshine. Hugging walls and making the best use of available dead ground, we skirted the fives courts and clambered through the wire gate on to Northcote Road. From there we wandered along the pavements. All would have been fine had we not encountered the milkman, making his delivery to Hankey's. Unsure who was more surprised at seeing whom, the herd of dressing-gown-clad ten-year-olds rushed all the way back to the Matthews' and never saw if there were foxes on New Field.

The Pre excelled in putting on plays, both boys' and staff productions. Who could ever forget Mr Lewin in *Any Number Can Die*? Two landmark productions from my time were the co-production of *Bugsy Malone* with Clifton High School and the world premiere stage production of William Golding's *Lord of the Flies* (adapted by Poole's House tutor, Eliot Watkins, over five years before the London staging). This production left many parents horrified, watching aghast as their cherubs donned war paint, stuck a real pig's head on a spike and hunted down Ralph, with Orff's *O, Fortuna* blaring about the School Hall. I shall never forget the pallid faces looking up at us when the spell was broken by the arrival of Mr Denman in his navy whites.

Despite school matters sometimes getting in the way of our fun, my overriding memories of the Pre are of being extremely happy, secure and very, very lucky.

D. Witherow
Pre, SH, 1981–91

FIRST GIRLS

Zillah Bowes and I were 11 years old when we started in January 1987 at the Pre, the only girls in the whole School. Our base was Matthews' House sick bay, next to Mr and Mrs Trafford's living quarters. Luckily the boys were rarely ill.

We were best friends at our old school, but the full enormity of the situation came home when we entered the assembly hall. The boys were all animatedly catching up from their holidays, but quickly the tones dulled down to whispers, and we knew all eyes were upon us. Being in year two we had to sit on the floor, so we found the biggest space we could. Zillah and I nervously talked and giggled and the ring of space around us reluctantly became smaller as the hall filled up, but the gap was still pretty noticeable.

Initially, we had mixed reactions from the boys. Most just stared at us and kept to their groups; others were inquisitive and asked lots of questions; a few showed off. However, we soon got used to each other. I suppose we were all about the age of starting to be attracted to the opposite sex, although it wasn't cool to admit it, so it made life interesting. I particularly remember watching the boys playing table tennis for a while, but they soon invited us to join in. The boys were competitive and didn't want to be beaten by girls, but as neither of us had played before there wasn't any danger of that happening. There were no separate sports for us, so we joined in with the football, taught by our Housemaster, Mr Hatton. There were no expectations, so we just enjoyed ourselves and got muddy like the boys. I also tried the cross-country but got lost on the route.

By the end of the first term the gap in assembly had almost vanished, and we felt that the boys had accepted us. We all performed in a French evening and sang 'Thank Heavens for Little Girls' in French. It was quite a bonding experience, as we were working together and were equally nervous. Zillah and I dressed up with a wrap and handbag each, and at one point had to bash the boys with the bags, which I have to admit was great fun.

The following September Clifton became fully co-educational, and we became part of Poole's. We had more space to ourselves, more female friends, and we started to compete in our own games and the House competitions. I have very fond memories of those first two terms and especially the many people who helped make it such a positive success.

R. Arthur (née Ellis)
Pre, WoH, 1987–92

Left: *South Town (Pre) girls, 2009.*

PREP SCHOOL SEVENS

In 1986 the Pre 1st VII won the national prep schools' sevens at Rosslyn Park for the first time, and this was followed by a second success in 1989, the only ones in the history of the School to have achieved this.

Although the ultimate accolade was the same for both teams and there were many similarities in their qualities, there were also notable differences. The 1986 team was expected to do well. Five of the players had the experience of playing the previous year, and they had already won two tournaments. The 1989 squad had enjoyed no such success. What both teams did, however, was to beat in the final at Rosslyn Park teams that had defeated them in earlier tournaments and to show a strong team spirit and a fierce determination to win.

The 1986 team were 'thoroughbreds', including six backs and only one genuine forward, with an emphasis on a running game and solid defence. Three years later the team had strength and speed across the whole team. They scored 198 points (41 tries against one), showing their skill and teamwork. This even surpassed the 1986 tally of 146 points (31 tries).

Both teams beat the favourites in their respective finals. In 1986 Prior Park was considered one of the strongest teams in the tournament and had defeated us

immediately before the nationals. However, having overcome Millfield in a tight and exciting quarter-final, we were not daunted by the prospect of facing Prior Park again. Outstanding defence blunted any attacks, and we were always in command, eventually winning 12–0. A neutral spectator was heard to comment that we played 'the best sevens seen in the prep schools' tournament for a long time'.

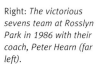

Right: *The victorious sevens team at Rosslyn Park in 1986 with their coach, Peter Hearn (far left).*

In 1989 Papplewick had a team that had contested the final the previous year. However, we were playing with growing confidence and belief. The final proved to be our toughest game, and it is fitting that one piece of brilliance was the pivotal moment in that final. When we were leading 4–0, their 'flyer', who had wreaked havoc in previous tournaments, was caught from behind. This seemed to deflate the opposition, and soon after we scored again to secure victory 8–0.

Both victorious teams produced an outstanding and consistent level of rugby. The running, handling and defence were of the highest order, mistakes were few and teamwork was paramount. It was Clifton rugby at its best.

P.M. Hearn
Staff, 1984–97

BUTCOMBE

As Clifton moved into the 1990s one of the most important changes to the shape and structure of the organization took place: the establishment of Butcombe as a pre-preparatory department catering for pupils three to eight years of age.

For many years the Pre had accepted boys – and from 1988 girls – from the age of seven. In the 1980s these seven-year-olds were in the Lower School in the building next to Poole's, later called Hankey's and now Guthrie's. Sharp's House, on the corner, had been an independent prep school, called Colchester House, until 1933, but the building was named Butcombe, after the village to which most of the Pre were evacuated during the war. There were a number of reasons to extend downwards the Clifton age group, and the idea to establish a pre-prep was the brainchild of the then Headmaster of the Pre, Roger Trafford.

Pre Children

Pre children are much as any other children. They delight, they infuriate, they can move you to tears, and they can move you to laughter – all at the flick of a switch. Well, perhaps that is not quite true. One of the features that characterizes them as a group is a lack of arrogance. Confident? Yes. But not arrogant. There are many reasons for this. The Pre – and the College, for that matter – has its feet pretty firmly on the ground and therefore tends to attract the kind of parent and the kind of staff who share that ethos. But it goes deeper than this. There is a spiritual depth to Clifton, and this goes back to its foundation. Visitors, including inspectors, comment regularly on the children's openness, tolerance, firm sense of what is right and what is wrong and good humour, courtesy and compassion for others.

DR R.J. ACHESON
HEADMASTER, THE PRE, 1993–2008

After much thought and planning, Butcombe was opened in 1992 as Clifton's pre-preparatory department, with Mrs Ansell Landen as Headmistress. A total of 57 children turned up on the first day in their royal blue sweatshirts and grey tunics or trousers, proudly carrying their kit bags, which contained their tracksuits with 'Clifton' emblazoned on the back. Butcombe, with its team of early years' teachers, had begun.

Dr Bob Acheson arrived as Headmaster of the Pre in 1993 following Roger Trafford, and he also recognized the potential of the pre-prep, not only as a way of generating income and securing numbers but also as the best way of preparing young children for a school career at Clifton through the establishment of the best early-years education. In 1995 I was appointed head of Butcombe, and Clifton moved into the era in which Clifton College was characterized by the phrase 'three schools, one college', emphasizing the

Left: Butcombe, 2009.

Right: *Butcombe playground.*

uniqueness and individuality of the three schools, yet ensuring there was just one alma mater.

I inherited a school with 91 pupils on my first day. With a massive injection of funds from the College Council to buy new furniture and fittings and up-to-date resources, and to develop the outdoor play space, Butcombe soon took on the look of a state-of-the-art pre-prep, with bright primary colour decor in each classroom, beech-framed notice boards throughout and two networked computers in each classroom. The curriculum was completely overhauled, establishing a topic-based approach to humanities as well as specialist teaching in core and other foundation subjects. In addition, a great emphasis was placed on extending the range of extra-curricular activities on offer and on increasing the number of special events that the pupils and their families could take part in. One year later the new academic year started with 129 pupils, and over the next ten years the steady increase in pupil numbers continued until it reached a peak (an uncomfortable one) of 265 in 2004.

As numbers increased, so it became necessary to increase the amount of teaching space, and first the lower two floors and then the whole of the next building in The Avenue (then Sharp's but for many years North Town Pre) were taken over. A multi-purpose hall, known as the Bretten Memorial Hall, was built in 2001 to provide a venue for pre-prep lunch, indoor sports facilities, assemblies and parents' meetings.

The year 2009 sees Butcombe as a well-established, integral part of the College. Staff work very closely with colleagues in the Pre to make sure that pupils are prepared appropriately for their future school careers, yet the overall provision is very much determined by the needs of younger pupils and their families. The latest development in the Butcombe curriculum is the inclusion of the Forest School programme, which regularly takes pupils of all ages out of the classroom to extend their learning within the woodland classroom settings that have been created at Beggar's Bush.

Butcombe pupils have an identity with Clifton and are extremely proud to belong to such a special community. All concerned with Butcombe, young and old, feel proud to help make Clifton College 'the best school of all'.

Dr W.E. Bowring
Headmistress, Butcombe, 1995–

Changing

10

GIRLS

On Valentine's Day 1986 Clifton announced the admission of girls. Unusually for Clifton, this came as a great surprise to nearly everybody. Council had recently set up the Anson Committee to look into the possibility of a co-ed Sixth Form, and other options included the creation of a campus college of both the College and Clifton High School, one of several attempts over the years to join the two schools together. The Merrison Committee, after a year's work, demonstrated that a joint Sixth Form was practicable, as long as the will existed. On 22 October 1985, at a meeting of the staff of both Upper and Preparatory Schools, the merger with the High School at Sixth-Form level was easily defeated. However, a proposal for which there had been no preliminary papers nor any debate – that we should grow our own girls from within – was carried overwhelmingly. Few there expected it to happen.

Council agreed that Oakeley's should become a girls' House. A steering committee was set up, which, greatly helped by Richard Bland, the Housemaster of Oakeley's, moved rapidly but in complete secrecy. Stuart Andrews, using military precision and detailed planning as an academic historian and strategist, orchestrated the sequence of announcements about co-education. The then Housemasters still recall with astonishment their normal leisurely monthly evening meeting around the dining table at Auburn House on 13 February. They rattled through the agenda in 30 minutes and then proceeded rapidly to any other business, when, to a silent audience, the Headmaster announced the move. The news was greeted with

approval by almost all, particularly the decision to take girls at every age level from the Preparatory School upwards, not just the Sixth Form as so many other HMC schools had decided. If Clifton was going to do 'it', it was to be done properly!

The move to co-education was positively received in every corner, apart from the concern felt by some Old Cliftonians and by those boys who were to be uprooted from their beloved Oakeley's. Matters of practical detail followed. How would the female staff and pupils be addressed? What would be the uniform? Would there be sufficient girls to play fixtures? Lacrosse or hockey? A committee considered, debated and resolved these issues, while Fiona Hallworth, the Housemistress designate, toured girls' accommodation in HMC schools across the country, generally deciding what not to do. The OC reaction was mixed but generally supportive. Not surprisingly, some of the founding girls

Opposite: Clifton doors reflecting many changes.

Right: Oakeley's House drawing room, 1880s. Original photo donated by the Oakeley family in 1987.

were daughters and sisters of current OCs. One of the first, Ella Duval, abandoned by the closure of her school mid-A level, arrived as a member of the upper sixth and became the first girl blue tie. Peter Brook, an ex-England rugby player, had retired from teaching but was still regularly dining in the masters' refectory, and consuming coffee and biscuits in his own chair in the upper common room. He was very much in favour of admitting girls. Although traditionally praepostors are awarded their ties by the Headmaster, Peter asked if he could personally present Ella with her tie – he had after all been her father's Housemaster in South Town.

Which House?

It was soon agreed that Oakeley's needed more than a lick of paint to accommodate girls. The talented Glaswegian architect Ron Wilkinson, who had already linked two classroom blocks to form the Coulson Centre, was given the task of refurbishing and re-modelling Oakeley's. Wilkinson was linked to Clifton's beginnings. Watkins, who worked for the original builders of the College, later set up his own company, training Cyril Woodgate (a Clifton governor), whose own firm employed Ron in the redesign of Big School for central feeding. Apart

Above: *Big School cafeteria.*

Opposite top: *Girls having supper in Oakeley's.*

162

from Oakeley's, Ron Wilkinson went on to redesign Poole's, Worcester House and West Town. His experience of designing a Nigerian prison and the *Daily Telegraph* building proved very useful and was based on the sometimes neglected belief that buildings should be designed to meet the needs of the people using them. So many aspects of the design impressed local HMI, Neville Grenyer, that he incorporated Ron's ideas into the standards for boarding accommodation by which all boarding facilities in Britain were later to be measured and judged under the rules of The Children Act.

A New Start

The Oakeley's girls arrived two days before the start of the September 1987 term for an intensive briefing on the mysteries of Clifton, because there was no existing hierarchy in the House to hand down wisdom. The first House meeting fell into silence, stunned by the Housemistress announcing that 'there are no rules because you are the first, so you are going to make the rules'. The girls, having outgrown the restrictions of their former schools, grasped this concept with enthusiasm and in the same breath introduced their 'traditions' drawn from schools across the world. These traditions remain today, and some, such as secret buddies and T-shirts, have spread to other Houses. Sadly, the full-volume singing on every sports bus journey has died out with the personal music player.

Meanwhile, two girls had quietly arrived in The Preparatory School in the January before co-education was formally launched (see Chapter 9). With the three who joined in April, they helped make Matthews' the only co-ed House in Clifton's history – so far.

The first day was puzzling, challenging and confusing in a number of areas. In Chapel the inward-facing pews made the girls a potential spectacle, but they were all seated before the boys arrived, which led to re-seating for most Houses. Girls reported feeling faint from the overpowering use of aftershave and were shocked by the volume of male voices singing the first hymn, as they

Oakeley's House

LENT '89 NEWSLETTER

would later be jolted by the robust bellow of 'jolly days' in the School Song.

In Big School would the staple diet of chips meet the needs of the girls? Portions remained the same, and the girls needed the busy school routine to offset the chocolate cake and jam doughnuts for afternoon tea, a feature of School life that would disappear and reappear at the whim of finances and healthy-eating campaigns. The erosion of 'tea' was bemoaned more for the loss of the social camaraderie than the loss of calories. In fact, the gradual change to salads and yogurts was generally welcomed by all. Finding a seat in Big School was not so easy because, despite self-service, most Houses sat where they had 'always' been when food had been delivered to tables.

Changing Emphasis

Co-education was not without its challenges, and it had a significant impact on many aspects of School life. First, the shape and structure of the College was altered. Admitting girls inevitably meant a bigger Sixth Form, and this was to become a permanent feature. Girls left their single-sex schools at 16 for the greater breadth of education offered at Clifton and to experience boarding before moving on to university. This meant that the Clifton curriculum had to become wider. Girls gained their share of scholarships and contributed significantly every year to Clifton's considerable Oxbridge success.

Second, there were shifts in the sporting ethos. New games appeared on the agenda, and girls joined in every existing sport. Dance later became part of the curriculum, but boxing disappeared as the girls arrived, although this was due to the retirement of a much respected instructor. The girls at the same time discovered the delights of inter-House water polo against the boys and, at Commemoration, the fun of tug of war introduced by the marshal, Ron Cross. In their desire to compete against the boys they devised hockey, netball and touch-rugby matches to raise money for charity, but they also much enjoyed the fun and games involved in the training sessions beforehand. The remarkable successes of Clifton girls today may have had their beginnings when Kevin Bowring, well known in international rugby circles, and his deputy director of PE (Susan Kerr from Cheltenham Ladies' College) made the 1st XV join the girls' aerobic sessions.

Girls also brought more breadth to the arts. The inter-House drama competition was changed when Oakeley's entered their whole House. The competition became a spectacular highlight of the College calendar, with costumes, lighting and musical accompaniment. Most plays are written for both sexes, and even Shakespeare would have enjoyed his girls' parts being played by Clifton girls!

One of the biggest debates was over the way girls and members of staff would address one another. In the 1980s boys in the Sixth Form were addressed by their first name, and younger boys by their surname. But in 1987, almost overnight, all pupils were called by their first name,

and staff generally by their formal title, though 'sir' has, of course, survived. When the boys didn't speak to the girls, ESU scholar Nina-Marie Gardiner, now a prize-winning author, suggested that girls ask to borrow pencils from the boys. This seemed to do the trick.

One of the first blue ties, Clare Perkins (daughter and niece of Old Cliftonians) reports that the Black Watch tartan kilt (a masterly choice by Marie Andrews, the Headmaster's wife who set Clifton's standards and manners in Debrett-like fashion), required the additional reinforcement of running shorts, so that girls could decently get to the toaster before the boy praepostors used their hockey sticks to reveal the hoped-for stocking tops.

In a very short time, the introduction of girls seemed a completely natural part of Clifton life, and even the bachelor staff were converted. This was not just because girls brought their own particular style of studiousness but because the girls enlivened debate in class and tempered behaviour among the more high-spirited boys. Clare Perkins's reports from her history teacher John Barratt, and her Housemistress, Fiona Hallworth, show just what girls had brought so quickly to Clifton.

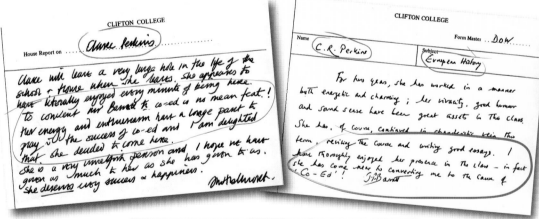

Left: *Oakeley's win the House Music with Vicky Dicker.*

Far left: *Oakeley's first girls playing cricket.*

Far right: Programme for girls' rugby match, 1990.

There is no doubt that in a period when long hair and scruffiness were prevalent the boys began to look a lot smarter, while comments about the quantities of make-up worn by the girls received criticism in the early days. But soon the effort of it all became too much. Common sense in the long run prevailed, although some boys longed for earrings and challenged the system, wishing to have pony tails like the girls, and testing to the full the equal opportunities legislation of the 1970s.

Girls pushed the rules, boys just broke them is a generalization with an element of truth.

Growing Numbers

Within a year 55 girls had grown to 86, and the building opposite Oakeley's (once the Headmaster's house, but later occupied by a succession of bursars and members of staff) became the overflow for 16 of the Upper sixth. As the popularity and demand for places for girls grew, another building, the New San, which had been donated by the Wills family in the 1920s, became Worcester House. The Sanatorium and its medical staff thus went back to the original building, the Old San, the present health centre, which for some time had provided accommodation for teaching and administrative staff

and for a Sixth Form common room, in addition to serving as a refuge for those characters who had 'grown out' of school.

Before Worcester House was finished the Oakeley's overflow building was reshaped into West Town, a House for day girls. Within four years the School was 30 per cent girls. In 2004 a further girls' House, Hallward's (named after the former Headmaster), was opened, bringing numbers close to the target of 40 per cent girls. This was a new style of Clifton House, reflecting changes yet again in the boarding market, and consisting predominantly of day pupils in the first three years and boarders in the Sixth Form. Improved financial circumstances have enabled the standard of all the boarding accommodation to be raised to meet the expectations of 21st century parents when the benefits of boarding, perhaps encouraged by Harry Potter, have led to increased demand, especially in the Sixth Form.

The fact that Clifton was the first major boarding school to embrace full co-education led to a stream of Headmasters' Conference schools visiting Clifton to see how our successful all-through pattern worked. Meanwhile, the first Housemistress was invited to talk to other schools. In retaining the House structure of Victorian times while turning the school co-educational, Clifton was trying something new. We think John Percival would have approved.

F.J.W. Hallworth
Staff, 1986–

Below: Fashion Show 2008, compered by Will Hanson and Zoë Black. The event raised £3,000 for Opportunity International.

MEMORIES

Nightmare! Last night I had a nightmare. The setting was Clifton College. In fact, a great many of my most unpleasant dreams are set at Clifton. I used to be embarrassed that I remained, in my thirties, so deeply affected by my time in high school that my subconscious mind kept it as the locus for all my anxieties and fears. But Clifton was a part of my life long before I ever attended the School, so it is only fitting that it should remain a part of me long after I have left.

I represent the third generation of Moselys to attend Clifton College. My father, John Mosely, was the second naughtiest boy ever to attend the School. No one can quite remember the exploits of the first, but my father's pranks are legendary. Growing up in America, with a portrait of Clifton on my living-room wall, I heard the stories about my father's time there. It seemed to me that both England and Clifton were wonderful places, and I longed to go there. When I finally took my place at Clifton College in 1987 as one of the first girls ever to attend, people were still talking about John Mosely. On my first day I heard he 'made quite an impression on Polack's', referring to the portrait of Ernest Polack that my father etched in acid in the study window. 'Quite good at signalling,' mused

Editorial, *The Cliftonian*, 1987

1987 sees a change at Clifton, a change now proven popular even among the most sceptical.

Although the proposal was not made regardless of the school's budget, it promises to create an improvement throughout our community, not only in the system but in the individual ... The aim is to create a more wholesome product, and a pupil better prepared for life as a result of the experience gained at school ... I describe, of course, the introduction of the new healthier diet at Clifton, implemented by our catering manager Mr Simpson.

The introduction of girls to the school in September will be easy by comparison, as in the past we have never really managed without them. We have enticed them on to the premises to take part in plays, parties and sport.

Our own girls will, of course, be welcomed into the classroom too and with a female monarch and prime minister as examples, perhaps the Headmaster should be the one to feel uneasy.

another master, remembering the time my father broke into the PA system and answered the minister's prayer as the voice of God Himself.

Thus, coming to Clifton was strange and new, and yet familiar, a homecoming of sorts. At the same time, Clifton was embarking on its own adventure, admitting girls for the first time in its 125-year history. My father was keen that I should follow in his footsteps, but I didn't have his talent for good-natured mischief. Nonetheless, I was to cause my own kind of trouble at Clifton. The truth is that neither Clifton nor I was quite prepared for the other. The traditions of the School both inspired and infuriated me. The slow conversion to a mixed-sex school and the kinks not quite worked out prompted the odd act of rebellion. I'd wander into the restricted areas and stand under the signs that proclaimed 'No boys allowed'. I refused to copy lines from the rule book in which sentences began 'Boys must not ...', reasoning that they surely did not apply to me. The books and signs were reprinted soon after. I

fastened my kilt with decorative pins, wore the wrong kind of laces in my shoes, challenged authority and generally made a nuisance of myself.

I struggled hard to find my place at Clifton, and I was broken and hurt in ways that still affect me to this day. I know now that nearly all the first girls were. Yet, Clifton made me incredibly strong; we challenged each other, Clifton and I. The academic standards were excellent and enabled me to attend the university of my choice, and in addition to my studies, Clifton taught me discipline, independence, courage and determination. It taught me a way to temper my strong-willed individualism with a respect for tradition and taught me what it means to be a part of history. I like to think that the School learned a thing or two from me as well.

My time at Clifton was a paradox. I moved thousands of miles from my father in order to know him better. I had to push against the boundaries of others, and be pushed back in turn, in order to know myself. Clifton College is a part of me as it was a part of my father. I am no longer ashamed that I dream of Clifton. Nightmares are just as often about confronting and overcoming obstacles as they are about falling before them. Clifton was a proving ground for me, and, as I learned at a recent reunion, for almost all of us who made up that first class of girls. My four years there have embedded themselves so firmly in my consciousness that 20 years later, my time there shapes me in ways I am still struggling to understand. The portrait of Clifton still sits on the wall of my childhood home, and now there is a picture of us, the first girls, here in the home of my own.

A. Mosely
OH, 1987–92

MANNERS

Co-ed is very important for development later on in life. Friends of mine who went to all-girls schools always tell me that their first year at university was terribly difficult because they had to interact with chaps. My mother went to an all-girls school (St Mary's, Wantage) and found the same, and so she stipulated that the three of us (Ros, Alex and I) would go to a co-ed.

Unfortunately, in the City women in high positions are few and far between, so any opportunity you have to start off being able to negotiate your way from an early age with both sexes will be an enormous bonus. Clifton, therefore, stood me in good stead because working on the trading floor is rather like walking along the

parapet (though I'm sure the boy–girl ratio has evened itself out now). The fact that there aren't that many women (who aren't secretaries) who are able to interact easily has been a major advantage.

I even told off one senior managing director for barging past me while going through a door. I shrieked after him 'manners maketh man!', and doors were dutifully opened after that.

I do remember when I tried to get out of Chapel one Sunday, saying that because I wore a little jade buddha I was Buddhist and couldn't possibly attend. My Housemistress quickly quipped: 'Shave your head and wear orange clothes, and then I will believe you.' Vanity won, and off I trotted to Chapel.

E. de Sybel
OH, 1989–94

Above: *Oakeley's girls getting ready for the 1990 House photo.*

Right: *House Song competition in Big School, 1991. Bottom right is Martina Topley-Bird, who became a professional singer.*

CLIFTON IN THE 1980s AND 1990s

I think it would be true to say that when I joined the staff Clifton was still largely recognizable as the same School that had re-convened back in Bristol after the Second World War. A number of the traditions and structures that had survived beyond the 1940s had, as a result of the social and educational developments of the time, been dropped by the end of the 1950s, and the winds of socio-political unrest that blew hard through the Western world in the 1960s changed much, including public schools, and Clifton was no exception. Nonetheless, it was, in the early 1980s, in its essentials much as it had always been. Several stout stanchions were still in place maintaining the canopy of tradition: it was still exclusively a boys' school; it was predominantly a boarding school with only three day Houses; many of the most senior masters remained in post until they were 65 years old; the campus was huge and self-contained; and the staff were largely residential. There was an expectation, even a belief, among some of the masters that the School should be traditional even if self-consciously traditional. These feelings of the existing masters were in accord with the values and preferences of the new young masters with their post-modern sensibilities, characterized by Young Fogeyism and the code of the Sloane Rangers.

So Clifton in the 1980s was a boys' school guaranteed to have an almost exclusively male staff, and in 1982 there was only one female member of the full-time teaching staff, a colourfully eccentric English teacher who was an inspiration in the classroom, a gifted cook and a creative dresser, who never failed to cut a dash. But she was only one. Arrayed against her was a very male, grey flannel and tweedy common room.

Boarding school life with no girls meant no in-built social life, and the boys tended to make full use of the activities programme. The workshops and studios of the then broadly based art faculty were absolutely teeming with boys painting, drawing, throwing pots, woodturning and making furniture on any Tuesday and Thursday afternoon. The House art show each year bore witness to the prodigious output from these sessions, and the photographs in *The Cliftonian* of those exhibitions show displays crammed with a range of vigorously creative but high-quality work in a variety of materials and idioms.

The presence of a number of masters still working at Clifton into their sixties provided a real and strong link with the past. Men who had joined the staff in the

1950s still held senior management posts or were heads of department in the 1980s, and their confidence and vast experience provided a real steadying ballast to the common room. For some of them retirement did not mean the end of their time at Clifton, and several legendary figures who had been instrumental in shaping the school and directing its recovery in the postwar years were to be found regularly throughout the 1980s taking tea and engaging in animated conversations in the common room at morning break.

Above: *Staff posing on the parapet for a caption competition.*

Below: *Staff cricket team XI c.1985.*

Spurr to Success

The greatest change at Clifton in the last 50 years was the introduction of co-education throughout the School in 1987. Stuart Andrews retired in 1990, having planned and executed the transition meticulously, and his successor, Hugh Monro, came with plenty of experience of girls' education, having run a girls' boarding house at Loretto. While numbers declined in the recession of 1989–92, they rose throughout the 1990s, along with academic results. Stephen Spurr (below), who became Headmaster in 2000, was a distinguished classicist and a careful planner. Under him, academic achievements increased still further, and substantial cash surpluses were realized, allowing major improvements to be made to the School's fabric. Stephen Spurr moved on to Westminster School, but the Clifton he left behind was a strong school ready to chart its own course and establish a strong brand.

It was still a collegiate campus school with a resident staff. The boys lived in College, and so did most of the masters and their families. The campus itself was enormous, its corners marked on the western fringe by Polack's and Auburn House on Canynge Road, all the way over to Radnor Lodge on Pembroke Road and up to Merry House at the top of The Avenue. Much of what was contained within that vast square of land, bounded to the north by the Downs Road and to the south by Worcester Road, was either the Zoo or the College, and the College was our home. With such a large community living on campus the social life was busy but structured and inclusive. The boarding Housemasters and the Headmaster would take it in turns to host large parties. At Christmas Dakyns' (and later Wiseman's) would host a huge children's party for all the staff children, at which Father Christmas would make an appearance with a gift for every child, and there would be a traditional and effective Punch and Judy show, which was put on, to the surprise of many adults and unknown to the children, by the Headmaster. Sundays that were not whole-school services saw the Chapel used in the office of a parish church by the staff community with a service known as the Family Service, which included a Sunday school for the children.

There also existed the idea of tradition for tradition's sake. The 1980s were a time when imaginations and sensibilities were informed by the television version of *Brideshead Revisited* and by *The Sloane Rangers' Handbook*, *The Tatler* and *The Spectator*. Twenty-something schoolmasters newly out of art school or down from Cambridge might not have had enough money to be a fully fledged Sloane, but they could adopt the knowing, intellectually elitist (but cheap) pose of a Young Fogey. Thus it was that we styled ourselves after those earlier young-old men of the 1950s, such as Gerard Hoffnung and Evelyn Waugh, and spent our time picnicking in white flannels and blazers, working in real Harris Tweeds (with leather elbow patches) and Tricker's brogues, playing 78 rpm records on wind-up gramophones, talking about where you could buy really good marmalade or sausages, decrying the horrors of recent architecture and lamenting the loss of the old traditional counties of England. It was all rather silly but great fun, and at that time reactionary chic had become so fashionable among teens that the boys loved it all too. The 1980s at Clifton were the Indian summer of a great Victorian foundation.

Clifton did manage to weather the financial buffeting of the economic crises of the early 1990s but only just and only by making considerable economies. The most obvious of these – and the one that would have the single greatest effect on the character of Clifton as a school and community since the evacuation of 1941 – was the sale of all the staff accommodation. The spirit of the traditional school faded as the buildings and even streets were sold off. By contrast, and as if to counterbalance what was being lost in other ways, the decision to enrol girls into the School in the late 1980s enhanced and improved all that was best about Clifton, and by the mid-1990s, with two girls' boarding Houses and one girls' day House, Clifton team sports, the visual and performing arts and academic achievements were all back at the top, with a tremendous boost from some extraordinarily talented girls.

The nature and type of staff who came to work at Clifton and the route by which they arrived changed in the 1990s. No longer were we largely staffed by what the Headmaster characterized in the 1980s as 'the all-round schoolmaster'. Most new staff in the 1990s would probably have a post-graduate teaching qualification and their first year would be mentored and monitored in a very formal way. They were now teachers rather than schoolmasters, but, to give all of my colleagues their due, their commitment to school life is total, with many hours gladly given to activities beyond the classroom. However, some of the most exciting, uplifting and inspirational individuals who have worked, albeit always briefly, at Clifton during my time have had little or no formal training as teachers but have instead had an energy and a way of interacting with all those they meet and a love of their subject – writing, literature, music, design, mathematics or whatever it may be – that is infectious. They seem to live and experience life more intensely than the rest of us, and their energy seems to beget energy. That is what is so rewarding about working for any length of time at Clifton. Ordinary as I am, I have met – among the staff or their families and among the pupils – some quite extraordinarily special and gifted people, and having witnessed part of their growth and perhaps even having been part of their story has made my time here worthwhile.

M.R. Barnacle
Staff, 1982–

Above: *Various Cliftonians disembarking on to the rough airstrip at Eureka on Ellesmere Island.*

CLIFTON IN THE HIGH ARCTIC, 1990

By the summer of 1989 the hard work of staff and pupils alike had ensured that girls were integrated well into every facet of school life. If there were any lingering doubts about the arrival of girls, they were to be dispelled in compelling fashion after Robin Barton, leader of the Svalbard 1987 expedition, announced his intention to mount another similar expedition in 1990, this time with Ranulph Fiennes as its patron. The make-up of this expedition was to be broadly similar to that of earlier ventures, drawing as it did on the ranks of staff, pupils and OCs alike. The most significant difference this time was the fact that this would be a mixed-sex team.

The destination for the expedition was the far north of the Canadian High Arctic on Axel Heilberg Island, near to the jumping-off point for attempts on the North Pole. Challenging training took place on Skye and in the Brecon Beacons, and under the rigours of outdoor life it soon became clear that the girls would be more than able to match the boys, and the team began to bond well. A member of the teaching staff at Clifton High School joined the expedition to provide pastoral support for the female members.

In due course we departed for the Arctic by way of Montreal, where we slept on the floor of a gym and where the showers became an impromptu auditorium for a stirring rendition of the School Song. As we boarded our charter flight we discovered that a number of our female contingent had made a unilateral decision to leave behind some of their cold-weather gear in Montreal because the weather had been so nice.

From Resolute Bay we flew north to Eureka on Ellesmere Island, and a Twin Otter then lifted us to our base camp. Another camp was established some miles away where the main part of the scientific work was undertaken. Here a small gaggle of young Cliftonians of both sexes, armed with outsized butterfly nets, was soon chasing speedy arctic hares across the landscape. A resident population of wolves put in an appearance in the first few days of the expedition and were chased away without incident. Climbing teams operated as much as three full days' walk from base camp at any time. Ice fields in the middle of the island were the main area of operations for most of these teams. The climbing was technically challenging on exposed

glaciers with extensive crevasse fields. These teams covered an awful lot of ground and returned to base camp exhausted but in high spirits. Camp life required a certain preparedness to be unabashed in various states of undress in the presence of a mixed audience, as demonstrated when a helicopter blew down a modesty panel around the 'personal admin' trench as it landed. That the expedition was a resounding success is testament to the mature attitude displayed by all involved when dealing with matters of this sort.

We arrived back at Clifton having achieved much of what we had set out to do. For some it was a bittersweet homecoming as we were now faced with the reality of job hunting or university and beyond, having put off the inevitable to participate in what had undoubtedly been another ground-breaking adventure. Expeditions of this nature served to demonstrate some of the most important values that Clifton had sought to instil in us: teamwork, self-reliance, self-sacrifice and resilience.

S.J. Heath
Pre, ET, 1979–89

Right: *The leader's hut at Ellesmere Island with Helen Miles (OH) looking on.*

Inset: *Simon Heath at Lake Buchanan on his 19th birthday.*

25

Reaching Out

11

VICTORIAN CLIFTON

Imagine if you can a completely different Clifton and Bristol. Developing along the banks of the River Avon and up the steep slopes leading to Clifton and the Downs, the industrial city was rapidly expanding and engulfing, and by 1835 the village of Clifton became officially absorbed into the City. Although the port in the centre of the city was beginning to silt up, new docks were opened in Avonmouth in 1877. On top of more traditional industries there was a boom in shipbuilding, chocolate production, soap making and tobacco. I.K. Brunel attracted further investment with the creation of the Great Western Railway Company, leading to the establishment of important rail links with

London (1841), Exeter (1844), Plymouth (1848) and beyond. Brunel's aim was to connect New York to London through Bristol using the locally built SS *Great Britain* and the SS *Great Western*. Ambition and travel were in the air.

When the land was purchased for the school its only neighbour to the north was the Bristol, Clifton and West Zoological Society (1836), the world's oldest provincial zoo. To the east was Whiteladies Road, to the south was Cornwallis Crescent, and to the west was the rim of the Avon Gorge. However, this feeling of space did not last for long. Not only did the Zoo spread towards the school, but the suburb grew too. John Betjeman described the 'tall Italianate houses, the Victorian hangover from the Georgian classic tradition of earlier Clifton, encroaching nearer and nearer the College'. Boarding houses, usually built at the Housemasters' expense, quickly followed the building of Big School (1862) and School House (1863). Brown's opened on 15 September 1864, and Cay's (later Dakyns') in 1866, followed by Watson's in 1873 and Wiseman's in 1878. As the School grew rapidly, so too did Clifton. The School brought business to tradesmen and employment in the School and the Houses, and builders were hard at work. There must have been a feeling of excitement and enterprise in the air. The Clifton Suspension Bridge was finally completed in 1864, linking Leigh Woods and bringing many visitors to view this wonderful architectural achievement and to enjoy the new hotels.

The School was very much part of this developing community, particularly as it was welcoming both day boys and boarders. John and Louisa Percival took their

Schools Class No. 927

In the early 1920s the Southern Railway directed its chief mechanical engineer, R.E.L. Maunsell, to design a new 4–4–0 type express passenger locomotive. The first engine in the class, numbered E900, appeared in 1930, and eventually 40 engines were built and named after famous public schools. No. 927, built in 1934 at Eastleigh, was named Clifton. It spent most of its life hauling trains between the south coast resorts and London. During the war it was badly damaged when the engine next to it received a direct hit from a German bomb, but it was repaired and on nationalization renumbered Southern Region 30927. Clifton was eventually withdrawn in January 1962 and cut up shortly afterwards. One of the two surviving nameplates can be seen in the cricket pavilion.

part in the community, entertaining at School House and establishing the Guthrie Commemoration in 1868. Percival was involved in founding other schools in the locality and with the establishment of Bristol University. The strong tradition started by Percival and continued by Wilson of looking out into the community and helping remains important today. Within a generation pupils were travelling from all parts of the empire to study at Clifton, and today the links around the world continue to be maintained. Physically and spiritually Clifton has always reached out.

C. Trafford

THE OLD CLIFTONIAN SOCIETY

Although the Old Cliftonian Society was founded in 1897, there had been a Scottish branch since 1884. Boarding in public schools had flourished as the result of the ever-expanding railway network in Britain since the beginning of Queen Victoria's reign, and the easy rail access to such schools as Rugby and Clifton from

Scotland explains the apparent paradox of our first branch being founded north of the border. The clannish and tribal nature of the Celtic character may also help explain this loyalty to an English school. Before the days of motorways and constant exeat weekends, parents did not think it odd that they would only see their children during four months of the year.

In the first 30 years of Clifton's history OC activities took place on a sporadic and somewhat *ad hoc* basis. Periodic dinners were held in Scotland, South Africa and India. A first triennial dinner was held in London in 1887, with Dr Percival in the chair. Writing in 1925, F. Borwick, the first assistant master to become Housemaster of School House, asserted that these dinners gradually took place on a yearly basis. In 1896 the committee of the triennial dinner proposed the formation of the Old Cliftonian Society, which held its first general meeting in the Hotel Metropole in March 1897 with J.A. Neale (Head of School 1866–8) in the chair. A.W. Paul (first Head of School, 1863–6) was elected president. The Society started with 40 members, the first secretary being R.E. Whitehead, to whose energetic administration the Society's initial success was mainly due. By 1898 there were 400 members, and numbers had grown to 2,500 by 1925. Some 80 years ago the following branches were in existence: Scotland, Bristol, Liverpool, Manchester, Birmingham, Cardiff and South Wales, Yorkshire, Devon and Cornwall, Ireland, New York, Nairobi, Shanghai and Ceylon. At

Below: *OC lunch, 2008.*

the time of writing there are just over 50 branches at home and abroad, although some are, inevitably, more active than others. Regular dinners or lunches take place in: Scotland, Wales, London, Bristol, Birmingham, Oxford, Cambridge, Devon and Cornwall, New York, California and Tokyo. On an occasional basis enjoyable events have been organised in Dublin, Lancashire, Yorkshire, Sussex, the East Midlands, Dorset and Wiltshire, the Isle of Man, Australia (Sydney and Perth), Hong Kong, British Columbia, France, Switzerland, South Africa (Cape Town and Johannesburg) and Gibraltar. In the capable hands of Richard Whiley, secretary of the New South Wales branch, we have had some happy dinners combined with the Old Malvernian Society.

Immense debts are owed to the local secretaries, who have a somewhat thankless task in organizing events and in offering such warm hospitality, not only to guests from the School but to other Cliftonian visitors. Membership of the Society is now 9,741.

The main purpose of the Society is to facilitate good relations between Old Cliftonians and the School and to give financial help with important projects. In recent times grants have been given for the refurbishment of the Percival Library, the Pre playground, the real tennis court, the restoration and cleaning of stonework on the parapet and cloisters, the complete refurbishment of the cricket pavilion and the Music School, and for the replanting of the Whitehead Memorial Garden at Beggar's Bush. In addition, there have been numerous grants to help the Art School, the Rowing Club, rackets and shooting, and towards funding rugger, cricket and hockey tours to South Africa and Australia. Individual current Cliftonians have been helped when seeking to raise money for charity or research. Interest from the

endowment fund can offer grants to help OCs who need assistance with school fees.

The present vibrant state of the Society owes a great deal to the OC secretaries since the 1940s. During the war the scholarly Cecil Taylor spent much of his energy writing to OCs serving in the armed forces abroad, and I know how much comfort and happiness his letters brought to men risking their lives so far from home. Jock Crawfurd, a robust and congenial Scot, had an encyclopedic knowledge of Cliftonians from 1920 to 1960. This bluff and brave old soldier became a legend, not only as Housemaster of Wiseman's, but as the convivial life and soul of all Old Cliftonian gatherings for over 30 years.

Harry Edwards retired from his highly successful headmastership of Queen Elizabeth's Hospital in 1978 and held the reins of the OC Society until 1994. Harry was an exceedingly cultivated man with a deep love of all things artistic and musical. The St George's Music Trust, based in the former St George's Church just off Park Street, makes it possible for the finest instrumentalists to be seen in Bristol, and Harry's dedication and energy did much to ensure its successful foundation. His experience as a staff officer in Intelligence during the war had equipped him with the most acute mind, and under his guidance Watson's became an outstanding House; nobody could have taken more care with individual boys. He brought great style to the OC Society and transformed the annual report into a much more informative and interesting document. He travelled all over the world, from San Francisco to Sydney, to meet up with Old Cliftonians. Colourful and happy reunions did much to cement OC relations abroad, and in particular one recalls his friendship with the late John Mosely (PH, 1946–50). John and his wife hosted a series of unforgettable occasions in their Hollywood home and on the *Queen Mary* in Los Angeles dry dock. Only the irrepressible Mosely could have masterminded the chairman of governors, Admiral Sir James Eberle, and the Headmaster, Hugh Monro, starring in a typical Moselyesque bonanza at Universal Studios.

I succeeded Harry in 1994 and attempted to carry on his success in expanding the Society. In the last five years Charlie Colquhoun, a big man in every sense, has brought his inimitable bonhomie and smile to countless gatherings, but his early and tragic death in September 2008 means that the reins have temporally returned to my hands. Charlie worked wonders with the new format of *The Cliftonian* and inspired great affection wherever he encountered Old Cliftonians. The beautiful restoration of the cricket pavilion owes much to his hard work and can perhaps stand as his memorial.

The OC secretaries have been particularly fortunate in the loyalty, cheerfulness and efficiency of their own secretaries. Joyce Callard, Margaret Kelly and Frances Stretton have done so much to make the Society a happy and going concern.

T.C.W. Gover
Staff, 1960–2001

OLD CLIFTONIAN LODGE, 1909–2009

The OC Lodge is one of the oldest of the public school lodges, and it was one of the five founders of what became the Public Schools Lodges Council, which now includes 33 lodges. It exists to provide a Masonic home in London for Old Cliftonians and Clifton staff, and it combines both Masonic and Cliftonian traditions and spirit.

The lodge was consecrated in January 1909, and the first master was Philip Colville-Smith (SH, 1880), who subsequently became Grand Secretary of the United Grand Lodge of England. He was a barrister and was knighted in 1925 for services to Freemasonry. Two Headmasters of Clifton have been members of the Lodge. Rt Rev. A.A. David, Bishop of Liverpool after his Headmastership, was the first initiate and was master in 1919–20. Dr J.E. King, David's successor as Headmaster and as master of the lodge, presided over the first Public Schools Lodges Festival, which was held at Clifton in spectacular fashion in 1920. Apparently, the procession from Big School to Chapel immensely impressed the waiting boys and also the local newspaper.

At the PSLC Festival in 1920 the bell with which the School was opened in 1862 and which was later used to summon boys out of the swimming pool was presented to the lodge; it is still rung by the master at the appropriate moment when the School song is sung after dinner. Among the other items of regalia in the lodge is a rough ashlar, a piece of the Temple of Ammon at Thebes. This was presented by the Old Pauline Lodge following the visit in 1921 to Egypt of the Grand Secretary, our founding master, and is inscribed with a Greek couplet, which reads (in translation): 'The masons of Paul gave me, who before lay in the foundations of Zeus Ammon, to the masons of Clifton.'

The First World War affected numbers, and five brethren lost their lives, but the lodge progressed well

until the peace was once again shattered by war. In 1943 a letter from Jock Crawfurd was read to one of the regular meetings, giving news of the School's exile to Bude. In 1959 the lodge's jubilee was celebrated, graced by the presence of Lord Evershed, Master of the Rolls and president of Clifton College, together with representatives of 28 sister lodges. Sir Clyde (later Lord) Hewlett was master in 1968 when Clifton next hosted the PSLC Festival, and 345 brethren from other lodges were warmed by his words and by champagne on School House lawn.

The lodge has always enjoyed an excellent relationship with the School. In recent years, with the cooperation of the OC Society, the lodge has been welcomed to tea at Clifton each November before its meeting in the Bristol Masonic Centre. In 2001 the lodge launched a charity appeal, and in February 2003 a first instalment of £8,000 was presented to the School with a further £6,000 two years later. It was agreed that the capital should be invested and the income used at the discretion of the Headmaster to support pupils who wished to participate in activities that would enhance their education and that their parents might otherwise not be able to afford.

The festival returned to Clifton in 1997, and in 2004 the lodge became a founder lodge of the new Metropolitan Grand Lodge of London. Despite the conflicting pressures of modern life, the lodge's spirit remains strong as does the camaraderie among members. Although times change, the lodge's essential values remain the same, and members will ensure that this heritage will be faithfully preserved through its second century.

J.F. King
NT, ET, 1955–9

Left: *'Run Girls Run'* raises £10,000 for charity.

Above: *I.O.D. breakfast attended by Clifton pupils.*

Below right: *Laura Davies working in an Oxfam shop.*

TODAY

The Clifton of the 20th century exemplifies the traditions of it founders. The CCF is still a fundamental part of the School, offering opportunities for pupils to affiliate with the armed services, whose sections aim to instruct and help the cadets achieve their potential as team members, leaders and teachers, thus promoting their confidence, self-respect and integrity.

For many Cliftonians, the alternative opportunity of volunteering for the Clifton in the Community programme is rewarding. The project has many strands, reaching out into the community and giving pupils the chance to gain experience in sport, care, the arts, education and charity work. Nearly 300 Sixth Formers take part and are able to gain a certificate acknowledging 100 hours of community work and to achieve the Millennium Volunteers Award of Excellence when they complete 200 hours. Regular visits are made to the homes and clubs of the elderly, who are welcomed to carol services and concerts in the School. Pupils from the music and art departments perform and work with young children in the community, and those working in the sports leadership programme are each week supporting primary and prep schools on the sports field, in the swimming pool, in the gym and in dance lessons.

Clifton continues to feel strongly that pupils should develop a positive commitment to those who work and live around them. An awareness of others is fostered early: Butcombe children regularly raise money for their adopted school in Sri Lanka, and the annual Preamble, a huge family walk, is at the forefront of the Pre's fundraising for charities near and far. The emphasis on charitable giving continues in the Upper School with organizations as diverse as Opportunity International and Caring at Christmas being among those supported. The Chapel and The Close provide venues for charitable events, such as a carol service for BRACE, concerts for Rotary and functions for the NSPCC, whose connection goes back over 120 years when the first ever Bristol meeting was held in Big School.

Every year a considerable number of Cliftonians work towards every level of the Duke of Edinburgh awards, enabling them to overcome many challenges. The Ten Tors race on Dartmoor annually tests their teamwork and competitiveness. Third Formers have an opportunity to sail Moosk, a century-old sailing ship in Plymouth Sound, as part of their introduction into Upper School life. Dyffryn, the school's cottage in the Brecon Beacons, has only marginally become more civilized over the years and is used for House camps and for leadership and military training. The appointment of an outdoor activities specialist in 2008 underlines Clifton's commitment to exploration and self-reliance.

Expeditions have been enterprising and far-reaching. Svalbard was explored in 1987 and 1990, at the time the most northerly school expeditions in the world. The Mexican exchange, begun by John Gibbs in response to the earthquake of 1985, remains popular with budding Hispanists, and cultural trips are frequently taken to Greece, Paris and Rome. Both the Pre and Upper School have gone on numerous sporting trips, from Barbados to Sri Lanka and from Australia to South Africa.

Clifton has always aimed to provide help for parents who could not otherwise afford to send their children to the School. Apart from the School itself and, for a while, the assisted places scheme, scholarships and bursaries have been funded by, among others, Joseph Cooper, John James, Harry Crook and Trevor Howard, as well as by the OC Masonic Society and the OC Society itself.

Connections with local business and industry remain strong. The School's membership of the CBI enables staff and pupils to be aware of, and take part in, strategic discussions. GWE Business West and the IOD regularly hold working breakfasts at Clifton, which economics and business students are able to attend. A recently launched Clifton lecture series attracts parents, OCs and eminent business people from the city and region to listen to wide-ranging and topical talks. As ever the innovator in education, Clifton became a training institution for science teachers and a base for the Boarding Schools Association to train pastoral staff for schools across the country. There are links with the Royal West Academy, hardly surprising given the artistic roots of Clifton in the Bloomsbury and St Ives groups.

In 1999 Clifton College Services Limited (CCSL) was founded to ensure that the College made full use of its extensive facilities. The decision to add a commercial stream to increase income was an important one, and the School owes much to CCSL. At Beggar's Bush, an earlier agreement with an insurance company provided three AstroTurf pitches and a pavilion and was used as the company's sports club. The facilities were run by the School, which bought out the company and has developed them further. The fields have been levelled, a covered area holds four tennis and netball courts and the latest 3G pitch has been added. Bristol City have used BB as the base for their academy, and during the week over 5,000 people use the facilities, providing a sizeable income for the School. In addition, a Real Tennis court was built, and CCSL manage the Ashton Court golf course. On the main campus CCSL runs a sports club with nearly 5,000 members, Easter revision courses, residential business and other holiday courses and the Manchester United soccer school. Weddings and similar events are catered for, and a flourishing Kids Club adds to income, as does the Prom on The Close, with such stars as José Carreras, Lesley Garratt and Russell Watson.

In the 21st century Clifton remains a school of remarkable diversity, which is demonstrated by the success of OCs across an extraordinary range.

F.J.W. Hallworth
Staff, 1986–

WRITERS REACHING OUT

Clifton's international outreach may be seen in *Sweet Kwai Run Softly* (1995), Stephen Alexander's (SH, 1959–63) vivid recollection of the transition from young recruit to prisoner on the deadly Burma Railway. Tim Mackintosh-Smith's (Pre WiH, 1971–8) accounts of his adopted Yemen in *Travels with a Tangerine* (2001) and *The Hall of a Thousand Columns* (2005) bring to mind a kind of contemporary T.E. Lawrence. Perhaps his Housemaster John Barratt sowed the seed of adventure with *Through Lightest Africa* (1974), an enchanting and now historic picture of that lost world before decolonization.

Below: *Prom on The Close, 2009.*

Right: Tom Gover and Steve Scott (OC) in the Sixth Form room.

The CCF

As the youngest of the third generation of Farrimond family army officers and Old Cliftonians, it is probably no surprise that I joined the army section of the CCF. Monday afternoons were filled with everything from section attacks to drill, and, of course, there was the annual summer camp with a variety of activities. All this was apparently very much the same routine for previous generations. While I was at Clifton the association with the Light Infantry was further cemented with the change from blue to green berets.

During my time with the CCF I was awarded an army scholarship and spent a year as the lord lieutenant's cadet. I particularly enjoyed the visits by serving military units, one of which was to have a lasting effect. It was when the Army Air Corps brought a Gazelle helicopter to take cadets flying. That day in March 1994, which I was 15 years old, I decided that I wanted to fly helicopters in the army. Some 14 years later I am currently on an exchange posting with the Canadian Air Force as a Griffon pilot, having completed operational tours to both Iraq and Afghanistan flying the Lynx, the latter as detachment commander. These are added to a number of tours my father and two brothers served in Northern Ireland, Kosovo and Sierra Leone. I have thoroughly enjoyed my career as an army officer and look back with fond memories to my time in the CCF where it all started.

P.G. FARRIMOND
PRE, NT, 1987–97

Two rather different examples of Clifton abroad are Cyril Rofe's (Pre, 1925–9) *Against the Wind* (1956), a description of his escape to Russia from a German prisoner-of-war camp and, at the age of 85 his first publication, the former Bursar Hank Adlam's graphic recollections of the appalling dangers faced daily by a Fleet Air Arm fighter pilot operating from aircraft carriers, *On and Off the Flight Deck* (2007).

In psychotherapy Adam Phillips (PH, 1967–72) has built an international (if not always orthodox) reputation with such works as *On Kissing, Tickling and Being Bored* (1994), *Darwin's Worms* (2000) and *Going Sane* (2005). A polymath, Phillips has edited the complete Penguin *Freud* and writes extensively on philosophy and literature.

One of the marked features in the School's last 50 years has been the ubiquitous advance of the media. Here Cliftonians are widely successful. In the USA David Royle (DH, 1968–73) is in charge of all film, television and radio projects for the Smithsonian Institution; Melik Kaylan (Pre, WaH, 1967–74) writes elegantly on cultural and international topics for the Wall Street Journal; and Andrew Wilson (Pre, SH, 1969–77) has been Washington correspondent for Sky. Among the first distinguished reporters from China was David Bonavia (OH, 1953–7), and today Adrian Bradshaw (Pre, OH, 1975–82) continues this by his writings and photography. The global reach has ranged from Sir Peter Job (Pre, DH, 1949–59), who before becoming chief executive of Reuters was the managing director for Asia, Australia and New Zealand, to George Arney (Pre, ET, 1965–75), BBC correspondent in Pakistan, and Hugh Schofield (SH, 1974–8) in France. The writings and internet journalism of Jeremy Bradshaw (Pre, OH, 1976–85) embrace the Middle East, as well as home and international politics and economics. Roger Alton (OH, 1961–5) was for ten years

Captain Pete Farrimond inspects the map between missions at Camp Bastion, Afghanistan, April 2008.

a successful and highly regarded editor of the *Observer*, and in April 2008 he became editor of the *Independent*.

In sport John Inverdale's (ET, 1971–5) lively commentaries, written and broadcast, are widely admired, and Steve Scott (Pre, ET, 1969–79) is an established local and national television newsreader. Commenting lucidly and laconically on many aspects of television for four decades is Stephen Pile (ST, 1964–7), perhaps not always aware of how many programmes are the work of Old Cliftonians such as Richard Maher (WiH, 1970–74), David Bartlett (Pre, ET, 1984–91), Gareth Edwards (Pre, ST, 1977–84) and Izzy Pick (OH WoH, 1988–2000).

B. Worthington
Staff, 1970–2000

REFLECTING

Being asked to reflect on my days at Clifton awoke some inexplicably random senses: the sound of peacocks squawking in the zoo, for example, the smell of a damp and bloated leather football, and belting out 'The day thou gavest' during last Chapel while disguising a not-so-cool lump in my throat. The click of a rackets ball, hiding on the floor of a Beggar's Bush bus to avoid walking across the Suspension Bridge, the pit in my stomach explaining away another 'lost' homework, the distinctive aroma of the science labs and the daily ritual of pulling my collar down to pass the marshal's hair-length test.

It's strange how the least significant events seem to have fought their way to the front of my consciousness. I say 'least significant', but maybe that's what Clifton was all about then: a collection of diverse experiences during one long journey, a journey that helped shape who I am today. I certainly wasn't a scholar – I had what must have been an infuriatingly *laissez-faire* attitude to

Head Girl

I think that if you want to take on challenges Clifton helps you to become a leader rather than a follower. Although it can be tough, the end result is rewarding. Whether it is producing a House play or cheering on your team as it competes in a hockey match, it is all about being part of a team. Clifton has taught me to learn from many, to be myself and to lead others.

C. PIERCE
PRE, HH, 1994–2009

studying – and I was difficult to motivate, unless, of course, a ball was involved. Predictably, my approach to exam work is something I regret now, but I believe what Clifton gave me that has undoubtedly helped my career as a journalist was an inquisitive, questioning nature and an inner confidence, which is something you can't put a price on and without which I doubt I would have ever had the chance to travel the world, report from some of the most hostile places on the planet and speak to some of the most incredible people, from presidents and prime ministers to gun-toting rebel soldiers in the heart of Africa.

S.Y.C. Scott
Pre, ET, 1969–79

FRIENDS

Of the many and quite remarkably varied influences during my time at Clifton that helped to shape my interests and ambitions, one of the strongest must have been my friends. Some people leave school and simply drift out into the world with never a backward look. Others, like me, are lucky enough to have forged lifelong friendships, both with boys and girls, from all over the globe and widely diverse cultures. This undoubtedly engendered in me a desire to travel and to encounter and ultimately serve needy people, wherever in the world they might be.

Having missed what some might now think of as the traditional year out between school and university, immediately after graduating I set about earning the money to travel and duly embarked on a round-the-world trip. Twelve months later I returned to England only to pause briefly before setting off on lap two. It was during this journey that I found myself working in an orphanage in Cambodia, dedicated to caring for children who had lost their parents to Aids, and incidentally found my metier.

Returning to England, I completed my MSc at the London School of Tropical Medicine and have, ever since, worked in a wide range of African countries, specializing in therapeutic nutrition.

There can be no doubt whatever that the seeds of my love for, and desire to work with, people from some of the most deprived and not infrequently dangerous parts of the world were sown and successfully germinated at Clifton.

H. Newhouse
Pre, WoH, 1988–94

Commem

outside the College to preach the Commemoration sermon, and the first was the Rev. Dr Jex Blake. Commemoration was also celebrated by cricket matches between several teams of Old Cliftonians and the school and by shooting matches. In 1871 the supper was moved to the gymnasium, and in 1877 to Big School. In 1937 necessity dictated a change in arrangements, for in that year the floor of Big School had to be repaired and the Friday evening ceremony could not take place there. A large marquee was set up on The Close – so large that it could accommodate the entire school with parents and OCs, and it was known as the Loch Ness Monster, which was then much in the news.

Until the early 1990s, members of the wider Clifton community were welcomed by the HM and his wife to a garden party in the marque (see left, in a queue waiting to be received). Undoubtedly less formal today, Commem still remains a highlight in the School's calendar.

C. TRAFFORD

The first Guthrie Commemoration was held on 22 May 1868. It consisted of a dinner at the Clifton Down Hotel with Canon Moseley, president of the Council, in the chair. Several members of the Council, the masters and Old Cliftonians and a few members of the Sixth Form were present – about 50 in all.

The event is a commemoration of the building of the Chapel and of John Guthrie and Caroline his wife, its founders, and all other 'founders and benefactors, by whose benefit this whole school is brought up to Godliness and good learning'. It was the custom to invite someone from

From Head of School's speech, Commem, 2008:

'The beautiful paradox of our Clifton experience is that we have been able to be the individuals that we wanted to be and still be Cliftonians. The more things will change for us, as our lives unfold in the future, the more they will remain the same, because of our shared identity. Clifton has breathed life into us and now we must exclaim *lahaim* (to life).'

G. GREENBURY
PRE, NT, 1993–2008

Moving On

12

Opposite: *Clifton's sail training boat,* Moosk.

Right: *Sam Stokes in 2003 teaching pupils at Clifton's partner school in South Africa.*

VALUES AND PRINCIPLES

T.S. Eliot observed that art never changes though the means for its production change, and much the same is true of education. In many ways Clifton in the 21st century would be easily recognized by Percival, not just in terms of its buildings but in terms of its ethos, its values. What really matters in education has not changed and cannot change, because what really matters is what we want our pupils to be like as young adults and how a school can influence that. With that in mind the founding principles of Clifton stated that Clifton would provide a 'thoroughly good and liberal education' and that remains as true now as then. Liberal has become a discredited word since the 1960s, often confused with licence and permissiveness. But it is worth returning to the original definition as the School's founding fathers knew it. Liberal, as defined by the Oxford English Dictionary means the following: 'Worthy of a free man, generous, open hearted, free in speech and action.' According to that definition, Clifton continues to provide a 'thoroughly good and liberal education'; that is what Clifton stands for, always has, always will. In education we must stick fast to our principles and Clifton's founding principles were the right ones.

In his autobiography Lord Admiral Chatfield lavished praise on his son's school because 'its main aim was to develop character while ensuring an adequate education'. He defined character as 'self-confidence and high principles', terms we aren't now accustomed to hearing in educational debate today which is all about that which can be measured and monitored. As any farmer will tell you, you don't make sheep any

fatter by weighing them. Fundamentally, Lord Chatfield was right; education is about character and the things that build character, things that can't necessarily be measured, such as curiosity, creativity, imagination, risk taking, sensitivity, adaptability, motivation, drive and enthusiasm. That list is not mine by the way; it is what the Graduate Recruitment Agency list as the key criteria employers look for today. In our extensive extra-curricular programme we offer many opportunities for development of precisely these skills through: project management (House music, drama, art – to name but three); risk taking (the Podcast and Vodcast, the student area of the website, Young Enterprise, debating, youth parliament, Chapel addresses, charities projects); cultural sensitivity (there are many different languages spoken at Clifton and pupils from all over the world with

different religious backgrounds and experiences); leadership (the praepostors and heads and deputy heads of House, the CCF, the extensive music groups and sports teams all offer plenty of leadership opportunities). All of these foster good communication skills, adaptability, and team working. A Clifton education has at its heart the same things that it has always had. The modern means of production create an unchanged art, the art of providing a thoroughly good and liberal education, an education of the whole person: the intellect, the body, and the spirit, or 'the humane life' as Percival described it.

PUPILS

Clifton is today a much bigger school than the one Percival began. There are now 1,320 pupils. The Upper School has over 700 pupils divided into eleven Houses, seven for boarders and four town houses for day pupils. When Percival opened the School there were 30 boarders and 30 day pupils: today there are about 350 of each so the proportion remains about the same. But of course the School is now fully co-educational throughout, with a Prep School and Pre-prep too. There are currently around 500 girls and as we move on we expect to see increasing numbers of girls at Clifton.

As the world becomes a global village the population of the school has also changed. In 2008 there are pupils from all over the world studying at Clifton: about 20 per cent of the total number of pupils live overseas. Some of those are UK citizens living abroad, but there are pupils from most European countries, especially, Germany,

France, Switzerland and Poland, as well as Russia, Latvia, Estonia and Ukraine. Further afield there are pupils from Qatar, UAE, Brunei, Singapore, Malaysia, South Korea, Taiwan, Japan, China (mainland and Hong Kong) and the US. The reasons for this are numerous. For many the goal is a place at a top UK university, and this can best be achieved by spending the Sixth-Form years, if not longer, in a UK school. Clifton has a very good record of placing pupils in the best universities. In 2008, 23 Cliftonians won places at Oxford, Cambridge, Imperial and University College London, the four UK universities in the global top ten (by rank, 3, 2, 7, and 6 respectively), the other six all being in the US.

Secondly, many are attracted by the fact that Bristol is a vibrant city with easy access via Bristol Airport, and by road and rail from London. Many parents see the advantage of being at a boarding school in a part of a city with a reputation not only for the grace and beauty of its architecture and its surroundings, but also because it offers everything a young person in today's world could want and need. This increasingly cosmopolitan school population is matched by that of the city itself, a city as commercial and entrepreneurial as it was in the 1860s but with more and more to offer.

The School is fully engaged with the city of Bristol in many ways, increasingly so, and this is a great attraction to pupils of all kinds. So, as we move forward, the School will continue to have four concentric circles of catchment: Greater Bristol for day pupils, and regional, national and international for boarders. Clifton, as always, has an eclectic and diverse mix of pupils and parents: there is no such thing as a typical Cliftonian – as a quick survey of the occupations and whereabouts of Old Cliftonians will reveal. The increasingly diverse range of nationalities and languages at Clifton provides an ideal preparation for life. Of course, Jewish pupils are still very welcome, despite the closure of Polack's, the Jewish boys' boarding House, and the opportunities for Jewish worship remain, though as we move on there are fewer Jewish pupils than there used to be. The Polack's House Educational Trust, together with the School, is able to offer financial assistance to Jewish families and there will continue to be a strong Jewish presence at Clifton.

The School offers a substantial number of scholarships and bursaries to enable pupils to come to Clifton. There are academic scholarships, including those specifically for excellence in art, music and, from 2008, science; scholarships, too, for outstanding sportsmen and women. In addition, there are bursaries for children of Armed Forces Service personnel and for those of the clergy. More significantly in terms of financial assistance, there are means-tested bursaries available up to the value of 100 per cent of the fees, including a specific award for pupils from the city of Bristol, which would have pleased Percival. (This is known as the Governors' Scholarship because recipients will be scholars, but the funding is given in the form of a bursary).

Opposite: *Julia Hwang accompanied by Charles Matthews (OC) entertain guests at the opening of the Joseph Cooper Music School, September 2009.*

Right: *Sir David Willcocks (OC) opening the Joseph Cooper Music School, regaling the audience with his memories of Clifton music.*

SCIENCE AND MUSIC

Percival gave equal weight in the curriculum to science and religion, opening the first physics and chemistry laboratories in 1867. In 2008 the Science School was given a major overhaul and the refurbished building, designed to keep Clifton in the vanguard of science teaching and learning, was officially opened by Lord Winston on 10 November 2008. Maths, sciences and economics candidates comprised 52 per cent of Clifton's A level entries in 2008 (with 112 A grades) and many 2008 leavers went on to study engineering (10) medicine (10), natural sciences (8) and maths(6). The new laboratories are equipped to provide the maximum possible number of practical experiments, a further example of '*plus ça change, plus c'est la même chose*' at Clifton.

In 2009 Sir David Willcocks returned to his alma mater to open a brand new extension to the Music School on Guthrie Road. Replacing the 1960s extension, this new building houses a recording studio, many rehearsal rooms and a concert space. It is partly funded by the generosity of Joseph Cooper, whose bequest enables us to keep music at the heart of a Clifton education.

THE WAY FORWARD

There is no doubt that digital technology has changed the world and, with it, changed education. Where for so many years so much time and effort in the school day was devoted to the acquisition of knowledge: now, with knowledge, and exponentially increasing amounts of it, available in microseconds at the touch of a button, education is more to do with learning how to navigate along the digital highway. Young people have different skills and abilities; as a result the curriculum changes and methods of teaching and learning change and develop with them. But young people have the same needs that they have always had: the need to be cherished, nurtured and allowed to flourish into the adult versions of themselves. Clifton exists to do precisely that, to inspire young people, and whatever further developments are made to Clifton's fine buildings and to its educational provision, the spirit will always nourish from within at the best school of all.

Because Clifton has always welcomed an eclectic mix of pupils, not surprisingly it produces a very eclectic mix of Old Cliftonians. They have one thing in common: that their experience of Clifton is such that they can go anywhere in the world, meet people from all kinds of different backgrounds, diverse in race, creed, colour, financial status, social context and philosophy, and be able to communicate with, work with and feel comfortable with them. Clifton is uniquely able to do this because of its pupil mix and because of its prevailing ethos. As a result Clifton has produced people who have made their mark in just about every walk of life, every profession and on every continent. The images opposite, which complete the book, are just the tip of the iceberg, but they show the variety and richness of experience that Clifton College gives rise to in those who have been through its care.

M.J. Moore
Head of College and Head Master of the Upper School

List of Subscribers

This book has been made possible through the generosity of the following subscribers:

Alexander J. Adams	ST, 1991–2002
Nicholas D. Adams	ST, left 2001
Norman Agran	PH, 1961–66
Sophia Alden	2008–09
Michael J. Allen	NT, 1949–53
A. Keith Amor	OH, 1954–58
Stuart Andrews	Headmaster, 1975–90
Dr Michael J. Apter (Smith)	NT, 1953–57
J.H. Astle-Fletcher	SH, 1936–44
John Atherton	WaH, 1961–72
Peter Atkin	NT, 2002–04
George Pownall Atkinson	WaH, 1925–34
Andrew Bailey	ET, 1983–94
Andrew F.D. Bailey	ST, 2000–07
Mark Bailey	ET, 1970–83
Mrs Andrea Ballance	Staff, 2007–
J.D. Baldwin	SH, 1952–55
David M. Barclay	ST, 1966–71
James D. Barker	1940–46
J.D. Barker	BH, 1935–45
I.M.M. Barlow	WiH, 1948–54
Mr Mark Barnacle	Staff, 1982–
Robert Barnfield	MH, 1997–2005
Professor and Mrs John P. Barron	DH, 1947–52
Dr Marcus R. Barton	ET, 1974–84
Hans Jacob Bassoe	WiH, 2007–08
Charles Roger Bath	SH, 1969–73
M.C.T. Bath	WiH, 1973–75
Jeremy Roland Batte	BH, 1955–64
J.H. Bazley	SH, 1942–47
S.N. Beare	BH, 1950–55
Julian Beauchamp	WiH, 1962–66
Christopher Beauman Jr	MH, 1999–2001
T.J.H. Bennett	ST, 1940–44
D.R. Benson	ST, 1939–43
Neil W. Benson OBE	PH, 1951–55
Dr Charles Beresford	WiH, 1957–62
Alex Berry	ET, 2003–
Derek G. Bevan	WaH, 1952–61
Matthew Biddle	WaH, 1976–87

Julie Blackman	
Gillian Blakeman	Admissions Sec., 1985–93
Professor John Blandy CBE FRCS	DH, 1943–45
J.S. Bonavia	OH, 1951–54
G.R. Bonham-Carter	SH, 1973–78
J. Borek	Staff, 2001–
James Cleland Bowman	1920–24
Amy Bowring	WT, 1994–2005
Ben Bowring	ST, 1994–2002
Kevin Bowring	Staff, 1986–95
Wendy Bowring	Staff, 1995–
Mrs C.R.H. Boyd	
Matthew Boyd	left 1965
Jeremy S. Bradshaw	OH, 1976–85
Quintin Bradshaw	OH, 1974–80
Michael P. Braham	PH, 1962–67
Isabella Brandalise	
R.N. Braybrooke Esq.	1976–81
Richard Braybrooke	SH, 1977–81
Simon Brewer	ET, 1970–81
D.C. Brian	SH, 1944–48
Ajlaan Bridle	NT, 2001–07
Hamzaan Bridle	NT, 2001–08
Manaal Bridle	NT, 2001–06
Peter L. Bright	Staff, 1971–2001
S.H. Brilliant	PH, 1965–69
P.J.W. Broadhurst	1943–48
Nick Edward Bromilow	ET, 1996–2009
Len-Lubbert Brons	WaH, 2007–08
Philipp Brons	WaH, 2006–07
T.N. Brook	DH, 1959–66
Mrs K.F. Brooks	
Simon Brooks	1938–40
Alan Browning	NT, 1962–73
Phyllis Bryant	Staff, 1976–2007
Annie, Yannick and Ella-Rose Budd	WT, NT, 2003–
S.P. Budd	
Sophie Burfitt	HH, 2006–08
Rev. J.M. Burgess	WiH, 1939–49
A.J. Burton	PH, 1931–35

Peter Bush	NT, 1957–59
Mrs Roma Butler	Bursar's Sec., 1969–2004
Michael J. Butterfield	ST, 1955–66
Bruno G.R. Callaghan	SH, 1978–83
Melissa Callum	WoH, 2004–09
Michael Richard Callum (McAneny)	1980–84
Simon Cansdale	ST, 1975–86
Robin A.R. Carr	DH, 1954–64
James Louis Carrier	ST, 1997–2007
Oliver Jacques Carrier	ST, 2001–09
Katharine Chambers	OH, 1989–97
Stephen Chapman	OH, 1956–61
N.P.S. 'Perry' Chesser	WaH, 1963–68
Jeremy Chidson	BH, 1963–67
Patrick John Chiswell	WiH, 1942–48
Canon Thomas Christie	SH, 1944–50
Ali Clark	OH, 2008–
Mr and Mrs Ivan Clark	
Simon Mark Clark	ET, 1972–83
Ben Edward Clatworthy	NT, 2001–
Mrs Rebecca Clear	Pre Librarian, 2006–
Alexander James Clough	WiH, 1996–2003
Graham F.J. Clowes	WiH, 1945–54
David Clymo	WaH, 1972–78
Ashley Coates	NT, 1996–2008
Harvey Coates	Pre, 2003–
John D. Coates	1945–51
Loxley Coates	NT, 1996–
P.D. Coates	WiH, 1950–55
Peter Coë	NT, 1972–77
Mark Coker	NT, 1973–82
James R.B. Cole	SH, 1978–83
Gus' Robert Collins	WiH, 1950–59
John P. Comerford	BH, 1943–50
Charlotte, Sarah and Hannah Cook	WT, 1995–
Karl Cook	ST, 1975–82
Guy Edward Cooper	NT, 1944–52
Richard D.B. Cooper	NT, 1950–61
T.S.B. Cooper	NT, 1947–52
Matthew Cornish	NT, 2004–

Dr John Court Cornwell	NT, 1930–39
Farquharson Cousins	ST, 1931–36
Rodney Craig	SH, 1951–57
J.C.A. Craik	BH, 1956–60
P.C. Crampton	OH, 1934–43
Tom John Crane	WaH, 2004–09
Tony Crook	WiH, 1934–38
Gemma S.E. Crowther	OH, 2004–09
Kathryn Cruse	WoH, 1991–95
Andrew G. Dakyns	DH, 1944–52
Oliver and Jamie Daniels	Pre, But, 2007–
William David Daniels	ST, 2002–08
Emma Jane Davey	OH, 1987–89
Brian David	DH, 1970–74
Jonathan J.L. David	DH, 1975–80
R.M.Davidson	SH, 1951–56
Howell M. Davies	WiH, 1953–58
Lydia Rose Davies	HH, 2008–
Peter G. Davies	SH, 1971–75
Jeremy Simon Gronow Davis	WiH, 1952–57
J.A. Dayer MBE FCA	NT, 1938–48
M.H. de L. Coombs	SH, 1943–45
Hugh W. de Winton	Pre, ET, 1989–96, 1999–2001
Benjamin Dembo	PH, 1972–82
Harriet Dembo	HH, 2007–
Oliver Dembo	ET, 2000–
Marianna D. Demetriou	
Dr Michael Denman	1947–51
Christopher Denny	WiH, 1998–2004
Michelle Denny	OH, 1998–2007
Dr Mark Denyer	SH, 1956–65
Dr Brian J. Dicker	OH, 1948–53
Patrick Dickinson	OH, 1946–51
Duncan Douglas	OH, 1933–43
Elizabeth C.M. Down	WT, 2002–
James M.H. Down	Pre, 2004–
Julien E.F. Down	
C.M. Draper	SH, 1947–57
Tansy Alice Grace Duncan	WoH, 2002–09
Alexandra Dunn	HH, 2004–06
Jason Durbridge	WiH, 2000–07
Jennifer Durbridge	WoH, 2000–09
Peter Dyson	SH, 1968–68
Julian Edgell	ST, 1974–80
Oliver R.T. Edwards	ST, 1979–89
Richard H.C. Edwards	ST, 1977–86
Douglas L. Edwards	WaH, 1947–50
Maten Egry	WaH, 2005–07
Milly Ellard	Pre, 2005–
Toby Ellard	Pre, 2005–
T.B. Elliott	OH, 1945–50
Daniel Ellis	PH, 1984–89
Rachel Ellis	WoH, 1987–92
Hal Elston	NT, 2001–08
John C.L. Emanuel	WaH, 1955–60
Alexander W.H. Enderby	Pre, 2004–
Oliver C.H. Enderby	But, 2006–
Benjamin Engley	ET, 1998–93
Robin Engley	NT, 1991–2000
Anthony R. Ennis	OH, 1961–71

Henry W. Ennis	MH, 1995–2000
Hugo C. Ennis	MH, 1997–2002
Dr Joerg Ertle	
Jonathan Evans	NT, 1964–68
Keith Evans	ST, 1943–49
Martin G. Evans	SH, 1953–58
Nigel L Evans	WaH, 1973–75
Trevor M. Faber	PH, 1960–64
Charles M. Fallon	ST, 1968–80
Andrew J. Farrimond	BH, 1984–93
David R. Farrimond	SH, 1981–91
Peter G. Farrimond	NT, 1987–97
Richard A. Farrimond	WaH, 1961–65
Alexander Douglas Fear	ST, 1927–36
Angus Crawford Fear	ST, 1927–36
Luke Alexander Fear	WaH, 2002–07
R.C.L. Feneley	NT, 1943–52
Jay Ferman	ET, 1994–2000
James Fern	1983–93
Richard W. Fielding	OH, 1947–51
Kenneth K. Fok	WiH, 1963–73
Julian E.L. Foot	ST, 1973–84
Christopher Forbes	
Peter C. Forbes	BH, 1945–47
Bryan H. Foster	BH, 1936–46
R. Hugh Foster	NT, 1931–40
Samuel Edward Abraham Foster	SH, 2007–
Scott J. Foster	PH, 1974–79
Toby Michael Abraham Foster	SH, 2007–09
Charles Robert Fischer Foulkes	BH, 1962–66
Owen Franklin	ET, 1998–2009
Michael As. Freeman	PH, 1948–53
Luke H.G. Fromant	OH, 1979–83
Mr and Mrs R.K. Frost	
Timothy Fry	WiH, 2007–
Ian Daniel Fulton	ET, 1982–89
Herbert Futter	OH, 1936–41
Thomas Marc Futter	OH, 1935–39
Elliot Gallacher	Pre, 2004–
Robin Rowan Gallagher	
Dr Martyn J. Gay	BH, 1947–55
Thomas Gentinetta	Pre, 2008–
Andrew George	BH, 1976–80
Mrs Debbie George	
Rear Admiral J.R.S. Gerard-Pearse	DH, 1938–42
Robin Gerard-Pearse	DH, 1939–45
R.J.S. Gilchrist	ST, 1958–69
Thomas Gilks	ET, 1995–2000
Richard and Rita Gliddon	Staff, 1969–85
Geoff Gollop	ST, 1965–73
Alexander Gordon	ST, 2001–09
Sophia Gordon	WT, 2001–
Philip Gowman	BH, 1975–79
Nasser Gramian	OH, 1958–63
Rob Grant	ST, 1993–98
Nick Gutfreund	ET, 1968–78
Anthony Gwilliam	NT, 1945–48
Ignatius Besthadi Pryoga Hadi	WiH, 2008–
Dr L.K. Hall	
Cheryl Hall-Moore	

Geraint J. Hall-Moore	
Joanne K. Hall-Moore	
John F. Hall-Moore	
Jonathan D. Hall-Moore	
Dr Colin Grenville Hallward	ST, 1945–53
Abi Hallworth	HH, 1995–
Fiona Hallworth	Staff, 1986–
Philip Hallworth	Staff, 1982–
Fox Hambly	SH, 2002–09
Donald W.G. Hamilton	WaH, 1967–73
J.D.L. Hamilton	WiH, 1932–35
Mrs Jessie Hamilton	
Major Tom W. Hancock DL	SH, 1942–46
Mrs S. Hands	
Richard Hann	OH, 1952–61
James Hanson	MH, 1997–
Louise Hanson	Bursar, 2006–
William Hanson	MH, 1996–2008
Richard Harding	MH, 1992–2001
Tessa Harding	WoH, 1994–2001
Tony Harding	NT, 1941–45
David W.G. Hardy	ST, 1945–52
G.V. Hardyman	Staff, 1945–50
Hugh J.W. Harper	WiH, 1984–86
John S. Harper	DH, 1947–50
G.S.H. Harris	ET, 1951–61
Richard Harris	NT, 1954–59
Toby Harris	MH, 1994–99
Robert Harris	BH, 1955–65
Viktoria Haub	WoH, 2009–
Jonathan A. Haward	SH, 1967–76
Dr M.W.A. Haward	SH, 1935–40
M.L. Hawken	NT, 1964–69
Paul Hawkins	OH, 1960–64
Haydon Lyons	WiH, 2006–08
Francis Alexander Burns Hearne	ET, 1972–82
Charlotte Heffernan	OH, 1990–98
Councillor John D.O. Henchley TD	WiH, 1942–52
Alexander I. Hett	DH, 1942–46
Giles Heyring	WiH, 1982–88
Roger Higgins	SH, 1946–51
John Walton Hill-Wilson	OH, 1937–43
Professor Richard Hitchcock	DH, 1951–59
Mike Hobbs	BH, 1967–71
Group Captain M.E. Hobson	WiH, 1940–44
Philip Claude Leslie Hodge	WiH, 1974–76
Nick Hodgson	NT, 1969–80
Mrs S.F.M. Hole	
Jonathan Holl	OH, 1965–70
Julianne Holling	
John Holmes	SH, 1946–56
Piotr M. Holysz	SH, 2001–03
Nicholas Hood CBE	SH, 1944–55
T.J. Hood	SH, 1947–51
Dr Nicholas R.J. Hooper	ST, 1955–65
Maxwell Hope	NT, 1990–98
Frank M. Horwill	OH, 1946–50
Barney Houlford	WaH, 1974–85
Matthew Howard-Cairns	ST, 1991–2002
Sebastian D.L Hoyle	DH, 1980–91

193

J.D. Hulme — ST, 1965–72
William Huntington — Staff, 2005–
Derek J. Hyams — PH, 1938–44
H.G. 'Harry' Hyams — PH, 1936–39
Andrew Imlay — BH, 1972–76
Michiel In der Rieden — WiH, 1986–91
M.S. Ispahani — SH, 1955–59
Tom Davies Jackson — Pre, 2006–
Louis Davies Jackson — But, 2006–
Sophie Elizabeth Jackson — HH, 2007–09
David M. Jacobs — NT, 1938–48
Nick Jaffray — OH, 1967–72
Andrew James
Andrew Jardine — ET, 1969–81
Katherine Ann Jeffery (née Virgo) — WoH, Staff, 1990–94
Major Charles J. Jenkins — NT, 1967–77
Dr Dean James Jenkins — DH, 1970–80
Paul D.T. Johnson — NT, 1942–52
Jean Joice
David M. Jones — BH, 1948–55
Mr Michael E. Jones — ST, 1962–65
Nick R. Jones — ET, 1980–91
Richard C. Jones — ST, 1976–87
Mrs Ruth Jones — Staff, 1975–1983
Dr Stephen G. Jones — ST, 1962–69
Benjamin Joseland — But, 2005–
Thomas 'T.J.' Joseland — Pre, 2005–
A.J. Karter — PH, 1968–73
Raymond Kelly — WiH, 1969–79
Alexander Kilbride — Pre, 2004–
James F. King — ET, 1955–59
Katie King and Cameron King — Pre, HH, 2006–
Martin King — WiH, 1952–57
George Kinsey — MH, 2003–
Benjamin Kirrage — Pre, 2008–
Verena Koelln — WoH, 2007–09
Soeren Krause — MH, 2002–04
Michael Ian Causer Ladd — WaH, 1946–50
Richard Lalonde — DH, 1944–48
Simon and Joe Lalonde — ST, 1968–79
George Lambert — Pre, 2008–
Christopher C. Lane — ET, 1999–2006
Jeremy Lang — DH, 1948–54
Stewart Lang — ST, 1955–66
Charles Langler — DH, 1955–60
Dr Gabriel Laszlo — WaH, 1949–54
Stuart Lawson — ST, 1972–77
Mr N.P. Le Sueur — DH, 1968–77
Robin M.C. Leach — NT, 1959–63
Michael Leek — PH, 1944–49
R.J. Lees — SH, 1955–60
Bernard Lever — PH, 1965–69
Oliver Jack Lewis Levi — PH, 1999–2004
Daniel Thomas Lewis — Pre, 2008–
Edward W. Lewis — ET, 1996–
Georgina R. Lewis — WT, 1998–
Rebecca J. Lewis — Pre, 2001–
Douglas E. Lidgitt — ST, 1993–2005
Duncan D. Lidgitt — ST, 1993–2002
Laura C. Lidgitt (née Baxter) — OH, 2000–2002

Murray J. Lidgitt — WiH, 1995–
Raymund B. Lidiard — WaH, 1945–52
Peter Lidington — Staff, 1988–
Gavin Littaur — PH, 1963–68
Nicholas John Llewellyn — ET, 1962–66
Bruce Lloyd and Family — NT, 1973–84
Michael Longman
P.A.T. Loucas — ET, 1977–85
R.J. Loveridge — BH, 1950–60
Mr A.J. Lowe
R.K.G. MacEwen — 1936–42
Alastair I.F. Mackenzie — BH, 1946–52
David Ch. Mander — WiH, 1952–61
Alan Mann (Kleiner) — PH, 1960–65
R.J. Marjoribanks — WiH, 1941–51
David J. Mark — PH, 1967–72
R. Neil Marshman — DH, 1977–79
Toby F.J. Marshman — WaH, 2007–09
Dr Hugh Mather — DH, 1959–63
R.W. Mathias — SH, 1949–58
Dr Peter C. Matthews — WaH, 1975–84
Roger Mayhew — NT, 1969–80
Oliver McAndrew — NT, 2005–
Victoria McAulay — WoH, 2008–09
Alex McComas — Staff, 1996–2009
Angus and William McEwen Smith — ET, 2002–09
Tom McGeoch and Ben McGeoch — ET, 2003–
Dominic McInerney — ET, 2002–09
D.J.K. McKay — WiH, 1957–67
John R. Melville-Jones — WiH, 1947–52
Tom Mendham — ET, 2002–09
Savvas George Michael — WaH, 2005–
Drew Mitchell — Pre, 2004–
Charlotte Miles — WT, 1998–
John Farrall Miles
Richard Miles — ST, 1983–85
Colin Millar — WiH, Staff, 1945–52, 1963–2000
Michael C. d'E. Miller — WiH, 1942–47
Roger and Pippa Mills — Staff, 1984–
Henry and Philippa Milne — But, 2009–
George Mitchell — WaH, 1965–70
Neill P.G. Mitchell — OH, 1962–71
John Mocatta — PH, 1949–54
P. Mogg
Justin Monsen-Fry — WaH, 1973–78
Alan Montefiore — PH, 1941–45
Dinah A. Moore — Council Member, 2003–
W.H. Moreland — DH, 1935–39
Eric G. Morgan-Fletcher — ST, 1932–35
Patricia Ann Morgan-Fletcher
Alan Morgan — Council Member, 1964–69
Sophie Morgan — WT, 2007–09
Milan S. Morjaria — SH, 1980–85
Mark Morison — NT, 1955–64
Tim Mort — SH, 1963–68
Shannon Mortimore — Pre, 2009–
Jamie Moss — NT, 2003–
Alice, Katherine and Stephen Moul — WT, ET, 2001–
Mr and Mrs A. Moyle
Nick Murphy — ET, 1956–61

M.A.C Murray — DH, 1946–49
John Musson — BH, 1941–45
David J.N. Nabarro — PH, 1961–66
Behzad Nahai — WiH, 1972–76
Rev. Richard Neill MA Oxon — DH, 1980–84
Robert Neill — SH, 1946–51
Neville Nelder — BH, 1951–57
David H.A.W. Newman — ST, 1946–50
R.G. Newman — SH, 1947–52
Bruce Nightingale OBE — OH, 1946–50
A.A.R. Niven — WaH, 1976–85
Jeremy North — BH, 1946–52
Mr I.A. Nuttall — Staff, 1976–
Mr Alan O'Sullivan — Staff, 1991–
Benjamin and Jack O'Sullivan — Pre, 1999–
Mrs Catherine O'Sullivan
Robin Orbell — ET, 1956–65
Alan Ormrod — BH, 1947–51
Guy Osmond — OH, 1969–72
Rachel Gillian Overton — Pre, 2003–
Callum Paine — MH, 2007–09
Marc Palley — PH, 1962–71
Charlotte Eva Palmer — Pre, 2003–
Clive Panto — PH, 1968–72
Madeleine Panto — Pre, 2008–
Philip Panto — PH, 1935–39
J.R.W. Pardey — 1947–54
Lisa Pardo — WoH, 1988–90
James Alexander Parker — MH, 1990–94
Daniel G. Parsons OBE FIBE — NT, 1919–23
Mike Patterson — BH, 1965–68
Harriet Ann Payne — WT, 2002–09
James Pearce — WaH, 2007–09
David S. Penny — BH, 1973–78
David G. Perry — WiH, 1951–56
Sebastian Perry — SH, 2008–
Christopher E. Phelps — WaH, 1940–50
Edward J. Phelps — WaH, 1978–83
William T. Phelps — WaH, 1984–89
Amy V. Pickles — WT, 1995–2000
Benjamin J.J. Pickles — NT, 1995–2006
Briony C. Pickles — WT, 1995–2002
Thomas J. Pickles — NT, 1995–2004
Pidgeon Family, Cardiff
Robert P.N. Pierce — WiH, 1947–51
Graham Pilcher MC TD — OH, 1930–35
John Pittalis — WaH, 1973–78
Julian Platt — WaH, 1955–60
Dr Adrian C. Pont — ST, 1950–59
Nicholas Poole — MH, 1993–2009
Christopher J. Pople — NT, 1966–76
Richard Pople — NT, 1962–72
Reverend Sir Stephen Porter STL KCHS — BH, 1962–67
Elizabeth Powell — Pre, 2006–
Matthew Powell — SH, 2006–
Bruce Preddy — DH, 1987–92
Ian Preddy — MH, 1990–95
John Preston — BH, 1944–49
Zoe Price — WoH, 2003–05
Arthur J.W Probert — NT, 1937–43

Tara Karlin Proske	2008–09
John Puddepha	DH, 1961–66
B.J.M. Pugsley	NT, 1952–60
Annabel Purnell	Staff, 2001–
David J.E. Pye	ST, 1978–89
Patrick-Alexander Rainbird	SH, 1990–97
Canon John Rankin	Staff, 1978–86
Christopher Rayfield	NT, 1991–96
Matthew Reader	Pre, 2002–
Thomas Reader	But, 2004–
W.D. Reardon	WiH, 1944–49
A.C. Record	Staff, 1995–92
Simon Reece	Staff, 1973–
Mr Anthony Reeves	Staff, 2007–
Liddon Richards	Staff, 1955–75
W.J.H. Richardson	DH, 1940–44
Paul Richardson	WiH, 1982–85
Mr Charles Rifkind	PH, 1971–76
Captain John Ritchie	WiH, 1942–46
Tamsin Robertson (née Jervis)	OH, 1994–98
Geoffrey Robinson	SH, 1949–53
William Roff	SH, 1976–80
T.D. Rogers	DH, Staff, 1973–78, 1990–92
C.G.I. Rose	ST, 1945–50
Tamara Rosenberg	
Henry George de Sola Rossiter	Pre, 2007–
Sebastian Piers Bennis Rossiter	But, 2008–
Tobias Raphael Wingate Rossiter	Pre , 2007–
A.L. Rowell	In Memoriam, 1930–33
Jayne Rowley	Staff, 1989–
Ben Royston	Staff, 2001–
Ruoxuan Cai	Pre, 2008–
Mrs Susan Rushworth	
Lee A. Russe	ST, 1979–89
Andrew Rutherford	OH, 1957–66
District Judge Mark Rutherford	WaH, 1951–59
Daniel Sacks	2004–
David H. Sacof	NT, 1941–48
Chris, Jeremy and Joanna Sampson	
Felicity Sampson	WT, 1990–93
Jonathan Sanderson	DH, 1968–73
Hector W.H. Sants	BH, 1966–73
Decho S. Sariputra	DH, 1953–59
Dori Alexander Schmetterling	PH, 1968–69
Harry Scrase	ET, 2001–
Opus Precious Sekibo	SH, 2004–09
Howard P.R. Shelton	WaH, 1977–81
Iain R.S. Shore	ET, 1963–73
J. Christopher Shorrock	DH, 1950–55
Mr Llewelin Siddons	Staff, 2003–
Mr R. Sidwell	ST, 1942–47
Paul Simcox	Marshal, 2008–
Andrew J.O. Sinclair	OH, 1979–86
Colin Sinnett	OH, 1979–88
Maria Skotchko	OH, 2008–
J.A. Slatton-Buell	
Alexander J. Smith	NT, 1997–
C.W. Smith	NT, 1952–61
Michael J.C. Smith	ET, 1967–71
Richard Ashey Smith	WiH, 1982–90

Robin M. Smith	NT, 1989–2000
Nina Sara Solomon	WT, 1997–2000
R. Michael Southcombe	SH, 1946–50
Jonathan Southgate	ET, 1978–87
P.G. Spencer	WiH, 1947–51
Robin F. Spencer-Smith	ET, 1966–76
R.C.F. Squibbs	WiH, 1948–54
John B. Squire	NT, 1930–35
Hamish Stafford	SH, 1998–2008
Izzy Stafford	WoH, HH, 1998–
Hector N. Stamboulieh	Pre, 1971–75
D.A. Peter Stanley	ST, 1963–72
David Livingston Stanley	ST, 1929–37
Thomas John Harvey Stanley	ST, 1932–39
Sebastian Pearce Stoakley	
Angus Stokes	Pre, 2002–
Elysia Stokes	Pre, 2001–
Laura Stokes	HH, 1998–
Anthony Stone	PH, 1972–81
Irving Stone	PH, 1954–58
Jolyon Stonehouse ACA	DH, 1975–85
Harry James Stowey	ST, 2001–05
Jack Joshua Stowey	NT, 2004–07
Martyn James Stowey	ST, 1962–73
Donald G. Stradling	ST, 1940–48
Andrew Strang	WaH, 1961–65
William Stump	Pre, 2003–
Geoffrey Sutton	Staff, 1974–2003
David Swift	PH, 1944–49
Anthony J.P. Sykes	WaH, 1962–67
Richard Symons	PH, 1978–83
Finella Harriet Rachel Tancred-Holmes	HH, 2007–09
Nick Tarsh	PH, 1947–52
Ellie Taylor	HH, 2008–
James Taylor	BH, 1980–84
Michael Bowes Taylor	DH, 1955–60
Stuart Taylor	Chaplain, 1976–88
Tim Taylor	BH, 1968–72
Miss Alexander Tebay	Staff, 1990–
Julian Telling	Wah, 1968–79
N.C. Thomas	BH, 1954–59
Wayne Thomas	OH, 1956–61
Professor Brian J. Thorne	ST, 1948–55
Dr Adrian Tibbitts	BH, 1958–61
H.J. Tilney	OH, 1956–60
Nick Tolchard	ST, 1970–80
Mrs Helen Toogood	
Malcolm Charles Tosh	SH, 1948–51
Philip P.M. Tosh	SH, 1980–84
J.R.E. Trafford	Pre, WiH, 1983–92
G.R.E. Trafford	Pre, ST, 1983–94
Anthony Travis	BH, 1961–65
David Tribe	OH, 1960–64
George M. Tricks	SH, 1945–50
Masafumi Usui	WaH, 1993–98
Colin Van Der Pauw	SH, 1960–69
Florence Van Der Spek	OH, 2008–
Alan Vening	DH, 1947–52
Christian Von Struensee	NT, 1954–59
Charles Richard Vyvyan	DH, 1952–57

Professor Geoffrey Walford	
Alan Walker	DH, 1970–73
Craig Walker	
Jack Walker	Pre, 2007–
Christopher J.C. Ward	WiH, 1980–90
Keith L. Warner	WaH, 1948–52
Michael Warren	WaH, 1948–52
Myles Watkins	WiH, 1979–84
Oliver Watkinson	WaH, 1989–2000
Miles W. Watson	ET, 1981–88
John Watts	Pre, 1998–
Poppy Watts	Pre, 2002–
Andrew N. Way	DH, 1948–52
Abigail Waycott	Pre, 2006–
Tom Waycott	NT, 2003–
Kingsley and Katharine Webb	
Mark Webber	NT, 1970–81
A.J.T. Wells	NT, 1975–81
A.N. Wells	NT, 1975–83
P.N.T. Wells	ST, 1945–54
Peter Wells	Staff, 1959–68
T.P.E. Wells	ST, 1980–88
Michael West	Staff, 1972–
Richard West	ET, 1952–59
Ryan, Megan and Lauren Westley	Pre, WiH, 2007–
A. Westcott-Weaver	DH, 1963–73
Richard K. Whiley	
Damian White	PH, 1979–87
Duncan R. White	PH, 1956–60
Roger Whiteway	DH, 1951–55
Morgan E.W. Whitting	BH, 1938–42
Mr Allan J. Wilkie	Staff, 2004–
Heather Williams	Staff, 2004–
Tim Williams	WiH, 1983–91
A.R. Windows	NT, 1951–61
Ngan Sze Wing	
Dominic Witherow	SH, 1981–91
Mr Rupert M.G. Witherow	SH, 1979–89
Graeme Witts	BH, 1951–56
Nigel Wolters	DH, 1973–83
James William Wood	But, 2008–
Stephen Wood	WaH, 1949–60
Ben Woodford	NT, 1969–80
Mr Thomas A. Woodland	MH, 1998–2002
Simon A. Woodruff	OH, 1975–85
Philip Wookey	DH, 1958–62
Richard Lansdown Woolley	ST, 1932–39
Peter R. Woolf	PH, 1963–67
Henrietta Worthington	WT, 1999–2004
Emily Tao Wright	Pre, 2008–
Matthew Wrigley	SH, 1993–98
Yarker Family	WaH, 1992–2004
Tom Young	OH, 1938–43
Michael A. Ziff	PH, 1966–71
Daniel Shea Zimbler	PH, 1999–2001
Jarad Jon Zimbler	PH, 1997–99
Kelly Samantha Zimbler	OH, 2001–03

Index

Names and page references in red refer to a contributor and their accompanying text; page references in **bold** refer to articles

Acknowledgements

The Editorial Committee: Cheryl Trafford, Fiona Hallworth, Philip Hallworth, Heather Williams and the late Charlie Colquhoun; S.M. Andrews, G. Hardyman, D.C. Henderson and R.S. Trafford for their help with the text; Arc Data Storage; The OC Society; Chris Taplin for his contemporary photographs; *The Public Sculpture of Bristol* by Douglas Meritt and Francis Greenacre; *A History of Clifton College 1862–1934* by O.F. Christie; *Clifton After Percival* by D.O. Winterbottom; *Centenary Essays on Clifton College* edited by N.G.L. Hammond; Clifton College Archives; *The Cliftonian*; *Maltese Cross* (Watson's House magazine); *A Fowey Jig–Saw* compiled by Joan Coombs, bookends of Fowey.

Every effort has been made to contact the copyright holders of all works reproduced in this book. However, if acknowledgements have been omitted, the publishers ask those concerned to contact Third Millennium Publishing.

PHOTOGRAPHS

G.P. Atkinson (from Mr Pavey's album): 29, 42, 43

James Barke: 53, 59, 121, 185

Martin Bennett: 97

Bush & Berry Conservation Studio: 33

The Cavalry and Guards Club, London: 36

City Art Gallery, Bristol: 13

Commission Air: 12

Corbis: 93, 107, 109

David Pratt Photography: 71, 72, 82–3, 98, 102, 118, 122–3, 140, 142, 150, 153, 156, 157, 158, 159, 162–3, 184, 186, 187

P.G. Farrimond: 179

Dudley Fromant: 77

Dez Futak: 178

Getty Images: 19

June Goodenough: 45

Fiona Hallworth: 163, 164, 166–7

S.J. Heath: 170, 171

Douglas Henderson: 137

C.G.A. Iles (from R.A. Iles album): 46, 139

R. Lees: 66, 68, 70

Barbara Lynam: 70

Rosemary Raymond (from E.G. Sharp's album): 146

Peter Smith: 124

A.H. Stone: 153

Christopher Taplin: 1, 7, 8, 13, 14, 17, 22, 23, 26, 27, 28, 40, 41, 52, 69, 75, 76, 86, 87, 90, 99, 100, 101, 106, 108, 110, 112, 113, 114, 115, 116, 119, 125, 136, 136–7, 143, 145, 154, 160, 161, 165, 172, 173, 174, 179

N. Tarsh: 129

A.R. Thornhill: 130

Nicholas Treadwell: 128

Paul Wigginton: 70, 106, 111

Heather Williams: 4, 11, 41, 49, 55, 176, 177, 185

Matthew Wilson: 73, 80, 80, 86, 94

Endpaper etching by Allan Wilkie (BA), produced for the Art Exhibition and Auction in 2012, the College's 150th anniversary.

Vitaï Lampada

By Sir Henry Newbolt

There's a breathless hush in the Close tonight –
Ten to make and the match to win –
A bumping pitch and a blinding light,
An hour to play and the last man in.
And it's not for the sake of a ribboned coat,
Or the selfish hope of a season's fame,
But his Captain's hand on his shoulder smote
'Play up! play up! And play the game!'

The sand of the desert is sodden red, –
Red with the wreck of a square that broke; –
The Gatling's jammed and the colonel dead,
And the regiment blind with dust and smoke.
The river of death has brimmed his banks,
And England's far, and Honour a name,
But the voice of a schoolboy rallies the ranks,
'Play up! play up! and play the game!'

This is the word that year by year
While in her place the School is set
Every one of her sons must hear,
And none that hears it dare forget.
This they all with a joyful mind
Bear through life like a torch in flame,
And falling fling to the host behind –
'Play up! play up! and play the game!'